The Development of International Investment Law

Lessons from the OECD MAI Negotiations and Their Application to a Possible Multilateral Agreement on Investment

Yusuf Caliskan

DISSERTATION.COM

Boca Raton

The Development of International Investment Law: Lessons from the OECD MAI Negotiations and Their Application to a Possible Multilateral Agreement on Investment

Copyright © 2002 Yusuf Caliskan
All rights reserved. No part of this book may be reproduced or transmitted in any form or by any means, electronic or mechanical, including photocopying, recording, or by any information storage and retrieval system, without written permission from the publisher.

Dissertation.com
Boca Raton, Florida
USA • 2008

ISBN-10: 1-59942-670-6
ISBN-13: 978-1-59942-670-9

WASHINGTON UNIVERSITY

SCHOOL OF LAW

THE DEVELOPMENT OF INTERNATIONAL INVESTMENT LAW:
LESSONS FROM THE OECD MAI NEGOTIATIONS AND THEIR APPLICATION TO A POSSIBLE MULTILATERAL AGREEMENT ON INVESTMENT

By

Yusuf Caliskan

A dissertation submitted in partial fulfillment of the requirements for
the degree of Juris Scientiae Doctoris
at Washington University School of Law

August, 2002

St. Louis, Missouri

ACKNOWLEDGEMENT

I would never have been able to complete this dissertation without support, encouragement and help from many people who deserve my sincere thanks.

First of all, I want to express my sincere gratitude and appreciation to my advisor, Professor A. Peter Mutharika, for his invaluable comments, and for his expert and constant guidance, and for his encouragement, patience and support during the entire process of this dissertation. I thank the other members of my dissertation committee, Professor Charles R. Mcmanis, and Professor John Owen Haley for their willingness to serve on the committee, and for reading this dissertation and help.

I gratefully acknowledge the financial support of the Turkish Ministry of Education during the years of my JSD study in the USA.

I would like to thank the staff of the Writing Center, particularly Angelica Michaels, and Ruth Berson without their editing directions and advice, this dissertation could not have been completed. In addition, they were very kind to me for which I am very grateful.

I would also like to thank my mother and siblings, and my aunt Leyla, for all their moral support, and understanding. This dissertation is dedicated to the memory of my father who inspired me to pursue academic career.

Needless to say, that I am grateful to all my friends for their support. I have also been very lucky to have friends like Roz, and Metin in Saint Louis. Their friendship, and support was invaluable.

It is impossible to enumerate everybody's name. So, I simply express my sincere thanks to all.

ABSTRACT OF THE DISSERTATION

THE DEVELOPMENT OF INTERNATIONAL INVESTMENT LAW: LESSONS FROM THE OECD MAI NEGOTIATIONS AND THEIR APPLICATION TO A POSSIBLE MULTILATERAL AGREMENT ON INVESTMENT

By

Yusuf Caliskan

Juris Scientiae Doctoris

Washington University School of Law

Saint Louis, Missouri

2002

Professor A. Peter Mutharika, Chairperson

This dissertation analyses developments in the international regulation of foreign direct investment (FDI). The international legal framework of investment encompasses numerous binding or non-binding legal instruments, including customary international law, bilateral investment treaties, and international organizations' decisions and resolutions. The rules established by the international legal framework become effective and significant when they are able to be adapted by appropriate and compatible domestic law frameworks. Through analyzing the Turkish foreign investment regulations and policies, this study concludes that that there is a successful and complex interaction between international rules and domestic rules on FDI. Like many developing countries, since the 1980s Turkey has revamped its FDI regulations in response to changes and developments in international investment law. This interaction will reach its culmination, if there is a comprehensive multilateral agreement on investment. This dissertation examines failures of the OECD MAI draft treaty since there are lessons to be learned from the MAI negotiations. Thus, it makes some recommendations both in relation to the substance and the procedure for a possible future negotiation of multilateral investment agreement.

TABLE OF CONTENTS

ACKNOWLEDGEMENT … iii

ABSTRACT … iv

CHAPTER ONE. INTRODUCTION … 1

CHAPTER TWO. THE SOURCES OF INTERNATIONAL INVESTMENT LAW

I.	The International Legal Framework for FDI	9
II.	International Conventions	11
III.	Customary International Law	13
	A. General Knowledge	13
	B. Hull Rule and the New Development on FDI	16
	C. Findings on Customary International Investment	20
IV.	General Principles of Law	22
	A. General Knowledge	22
	B. The Principle of Pacta Sunt Servanda	23
	C. The Principle of Rebus Sic Stantibus	24
V.	Judicial Decisions and Publicists	27
	A. Implication of Barcelona Traction Case	28
	B. Implication of ELSI Case	32

CHAPTER THREE. ANALYSIS OF BILATERAL INVESTMENT TREATIES

| I | General Knowledge | 37 |
| II. | The Origin of BITS | 38 |

III.	Analysis of BITs Provisions	40
	A. The Provisions of BITs Pertaining to the Investment Security	41
	1. Substantive Rules	41
	a. Expropriation and Compensation Provision	41
	b. Protection from Strife Provision	42
	c. Non-discrimination Provision	42
	d. Rules on currency transfers	42
	d.1. General knowledge of the transfer of payments	42
	d.2. Exchange rate	43
	2. Procedural Rules (Dispute Settlement Process)	44
	a. Disputes between Contracting Parties	45
	b. Disputes between a Contracting Party and an Investor	46
	B. The Provisions of BITs Pertaining to the Investment Neutrality	48
	C. The Provisions of BITs Pertaining to the Market Facilitation	49
IV.	The Impact of BITS on Customary International Law	50
V.	The Benefit of BITS to The World Community	54

CHAPTER FOUR.

INTERNATIONAL ORGANIZATIONS AND INTERNATIONAL INVESTMENT

I.	The United Nations and International Investment	58
	A. General Knowledge	58
	B. The UN Work on Transnational Corporations	60
	C. The Resolutions and Recommendations of the UN Dealing with FDI	65

		D. UNCTAD and International Investment	67
		1. General Knowledge	67
		2. Hosting Bilateral Investment Treaty Negotiations	68
		3. UNCTAD Works on Possible Multilateral Investment Treaty	69
		E. United Nations Regional Economic Commissions	75
II.	Regional Organizations		80
III.	OECD and International Investment		84
		A. The OECD Codes of Liberalization	85
		1. Capital Movements Code	85
		2. Invisible Code	87
		3. Evaluation of Both Codes	89
		B. The OECD Draft Convention of 1967 on the Protection of Foreign Property	90
		C. Declaration on Foreign Investment and Multinational Enterprises	90
		1. National Treatment Instrument	91
		2. The International Investment Incentives and Disincentives Instrument	94
		3. The OECD Guidelines for Multinational Enterprises	95
		4. The Instrument on Conflicting Requirements	98
		D. OECD Activities on Combating Corruption	99
		E. Evaluation of the OECD Instruments	104
IV.	The Role of International Organizations on the development of International Investment Law		108

CHAPTER. FIVE. ANALYSIS OF THE OECD MULTILATERAL AGREEMENT ON INVESTMENT TREATY

I.	Preliminary Remarks: Multilateral Agreement on Investment (MAI)	110
II.	The Legal Status of Draft Treaties Under the International Law	111
III.	General Provisions	115
IV.	Scope and Application	118
	A. Definitions	118
	B. Geographical Application	122
V.	The Main Substantive Provisions of the MAI	123
	A. Non-Discrimination Principle	123
	B. Transparency of Laws	126
	C. Investment Protection Obligations	127
	1. General Treatment	127
	2. Expropriation and Compensation	129
	a. Ethyl Corp. V. Government of Canada	131
	b. Metalclad Corp. v United Mexican States	134
	3. Protection from strife	140
	4. Transfer of Funds	142
	D. New Elements	144
	1. Key Personnel Provisions	144
	2. Performance Requirements	146
	3. Privatization and Monopolies	150
	4. Investment Incentives	153
VI.	Procedural Provisions (Dispute Settlement)	155

	A. State-State Dispute Settlement Procedure	157
	B. Investor-State Dispute Settlement Procedures	161
VII.	Exceptions to the MAI	165
	A. General Exceptions	165
	B. Temporary Safeguard	168
	C. Country Specific Exceptions	169
VIII.	Financial Services	171
IX.	Taxation	173
X.	Concluding Remarks on the Substance of the MAI	175

CHAPTER SIX. THE FAILURE OF THE OECD MAI TREATY

I.	Reasons of the Failure of the MAI	178
	A. The Impact of the NGOs on the MAI	178
	B. Lost of Interest by Business Community to the MAI	181
	C. Political Changes in the MAI Negotiating Countries	182
II.	Lessons From the MAI	185
	A. The Need for Procedural Changes in the Negotiation of the Agreement	
	1. General Arguments	185
	2. The Legal Status of NGOs in International Law	187
	a. Civil society and the UN	187
	b. Code of Conduct For NGOs	192
	3. Concluding Remarks on Negotiation Process	195
	B. The Content of the Agreement	198
	C. The Flexibility for Negotiating on Investment Treaties	199

	D. The Ripeness of the Multinationalization of the Investment Regime	200

CHAPTER SEVEN. THE WORLD TRADE ORGANIZATION (WTO) AGREEMENTS RELATED TO INVESTMENT

I.	Historical Background for Investment within the GATT Framework	202
	A. The Havana Charter	203
	B. The FIRA Case	206
II.	Investment Issues Within the WTO	209
	A. Agreement on Trade-Related Investment Measures (TRIMs)	210
	B. General Agreement on Trade in Services (GATS)	214
	C. Agreement on Trade-Related Aspects of Intellectual Property Rights TRIPs)	220
	D. Agreement on Subsidies and Countervailing Measures (ASCM)	223
III.	Developments on Investment Issues After the Uruguay Round	227
	A. The Establishment of Working Group on the Relationship between Trade and Investment: First Ministerial Conference in Singapore	227
	B. The Failure of Launching New Round: The Seattle Ministerial Conference	231
	1. Reasons of the Failure of the Conference	231
	a. Disagreement among member states regarding various issues	232
	b. The Impact of NGO Activities on Seattle Ministerial Conference	234
	2. Lessons From the Failure of the Seattle Conference...	235
	a. The Need for Procedural Changes in the Negotiation of Any Agreement at the WTO Framework	235

            b. Implementation Problems of Existing Agreements   239

            c. The Content of the Future Agreement   240

      C. The Doha Ministerial Conference: Is it New Era for Multinational Agreement on Investment   240

IV.   The Future Agenda: Is the WTO appropriate forum for the Multilateral Investment Issues   246

CHAPTER EIGHT.
EFFECTIVENESS OF THE MULTILATERAL INVESTMENT GUARANTEE AGENCY (MIGA)

I.   General Knowledge   250
II.   MIGA's Guarantee Activities   251
      A. Risk Covered by MIGA Insurance   251
            1. Currency Transfer Risk   252
            2. Expropriation and Similar Measures   252
            3. Breach of Contract Risk   253
            4. War and Civil Disturbance Risk   254
            5. Broad Other Political Risk Coverage   254
      B. Eligibility for MIGA Insurance   255
            1. Eligible Investment   255
            2. Eligible Countries and Investors   256
      C. Coinsurance Activities   258
      D. Dispute Settlement Activities   259

III.	MIGA's Technical Assistance Activities	260
IV.	MIGA's Activities in Turkey	262
	A. General Knowledge	262
	B. Example Cases	263
	1. Siemens A.G, Turkey	264
	2. Issues Guarantee for Financial Institutions in Turkey	264
V.	Shortcoming of MIGA's Activities: Environmental impact	265
VI.	Effectiveness of MIGA	267

    A. The Growth of MIGA's Activities and Their impact on Host Countries   267

B. The Limits to MIGA's Effectiveness   269

    C. Future Prospects for MIGA's Effectiveness   271

CHAPTER.9 NATIONAL LAW ON FOREIGN INVESTMENT: FOREIGN INVESTMENT IN TURKEY   273

I. The Development of Foreign Investment In Turkey   274

    A. Foreign Direct Investment Policies in Turkey   274

        1. Regulatory Policies   274

            a. The First Period: Unfriendly Environment for FDI   274

            b. The Second Period: Try to promote and regulate FDI   276

            c. The Third Period: The proliferation of FDI, but not enough   277

            d. The Fourth Period: The Implementation of a More Open and Flexible Foreign Investment Policy   278

            e. The Fifth Period: Legal changes on Foreign Investment Law and Privatization Program   281

		e1. Privatization Program	283
		2. Trends in Sectoral Pattern of FDI in Turkey	285
		3. Promotional Policies	290
		a. Investment Incentives	290
		a1. The Nature and Importance of Investment Incentives	290
		a2. Organization and Procedure for the Investment Incentives	291
		b. Free Trade Zones in Turkey	293
II.		Legal Basis For Foreign Investment	296
A.		Regulation Regarding Foreign Investment	296
B.		Law No. 6224 Regarding the Encouragement of Foreign Capital (Foreign Investment Law)	298
		1. Scope and Application	298
		a. Aim of the Law No. 6224 (herein after TFIL) Regarding the Encouragement of Foreign Capital	298
		b. Definition of Foreign Capital	299
		c. Scope of Law	299
		d. Right to Private Ownership and Establishment	300
		e. Permit requirement for foreign investment	301
		f. Employment of foreign personnel	302
		2. Non-Discrimination Principle (National Treatment Principle)	303
		3. Investment Protection Obligations	304
		a. Transfer of Funds	304
		b. Expropriation and Compensation	304
		4. Performance Requirements	305

5. Dispute Settlement Process: New Development in International Arbitration on Concession Agreements   306

6. Concluding Remarks on Foreign Investment Law   315

III.   International Policies: Bilateral And Multilateral Agreements Relating To the Protection of Investment in Turkey   316

       A. Bilateral Investment Treaties   319

       B. International Agreements on Arbitration   320

       C. Relationship Between International Organizations and Turkey With Respect To Foreign Investment   322

       1. The World Trade Organization (WTO)   322

       2. The Organization for Economic Co-Operation and Development   323

       3. Turkey-European Community (EC) Relationship   330

             a. Intellectual Property Rights   333

             b. Competition Law   335

VI.   Concluding Remarks on Turkish Foreign Investment Policies   338

CHAPTER TEN.   CONCLUSION   343

BIBLIOGRAPHY   349

CHAPTER ONE. INTRODUCTION

Recently one of the most important aspects of international economics, foreign investment is growing among countries all around the world, and it seems that it will keep increasing in the near future. Even though some distrust of foreign investment still remains among some of the developing countries, the world community has recognized that foreign direct investment is central to the process of international economic integration, namely globalization. Foreign direct investment offers recipient countries the opportunity to upgrade productivity and competitiveness, to benefit from the transfer of technical and managerial expertise, and to promote integration into the international economy. [1]

The essential thing that the parties in this foreign investment movement have is different interests and rights, which are controversial. Those interests are, profit-based on ownership of property for investor and development based on the sovereign rights for the host country.[2] Generally, "if the interests and the rights are different, there will be a conflict. The most effective way to avoid conflicts is through the law."[3] Therefore, this dissertation will explain the development of international law on foreign investment with respect to customary international law and treaty law. Especially the role of bilateral and multilateral treaties on foreign investment will be scrutinized in order to purpose what the newest and most effective approach of a multilateral treaty on investment would be.

---

[1] Magnus Blomstrom, Ari Kokko, *How Foreign Investment Affects Host Countries*, The World Bank, Policy Research Working Paper, Mar. (1997), at Summary findings.

[2] Omar Enrique Garcia-Bolivar, *Issues for International Law of Foreign Investment*, (http://www.geocities.com/CapitolHill/3421/fiart.htm) (visited by 3/1/1999).

[3] *Id.*

The purpose of dissertation is to make a contribution to the interaction between national and international rules on FDI. This dissertation proposes to examine the adequacy of the role of domestic and international legal principles used to reach economic liberalization and economic development. Economic liberalization is a policy that reduces or eliminates restrictions on foreign trade and investment. A liberal investment regime can be defined as follows: "{it} is one in which States permit the market to determine allocations of capital, ensure the proper functioning of the market, and provide legal protection for investment against wrongful injury by public or private agents."[4]

On the other hand, due to the fact that this task is rather complex and extensive in its scope, this dissertation proposes to focus only on foreign direct investment, not portfolio investment. FDI differs from portfolio investment in that FDI embodies control of the asset, while portfolio investors are passive investors, motivated only by rate or return on the asset. Foreign direct investment provides better domestic competition and access to markets. Investment in research and development creates new products and processes that will increase productivity and competitiveness internationally. Moreover, international trade and economic growth are improved when inputs such as capital, technology and managerial skills are facilitated.

The principal aim of this dissertation is to study the emerging international regulation of cross border direct investment and its impact on Turkey. Apart from being a Turkish legal scholar, there are many striking reasons I have chosen Turkey as a case study. Turkey is an extraordinary state that provides an ideal framework for the analysis of the interaction between national law and international law on foreign investment, due to its geographic and strategic

---

[4] Kenneth J. Vandevelde, *Sustainable Liberalism and the International Investment Regime*, 19 MICH. J. INT'L L. 373 (1998).

location in Euro-Asia, and its alliances with the East and the West. In addition, even though 99 % of the Turkish population is Muslim, Turkey has a secular and democratic regimen that differentiates her from with almost all other countries with Muslim majorities. Since the introduction of western reforms by Mustafa Kemal Ataturk, founder of modern Turkey, Turkey has been a model country for the modernization process of other developing countries.[5]

This study analyses following international legal instruments in order to illustrate the interaction between international rules and Turkish legal framework on FDI: Bilateral investment treaties, international organization activities. The number of bilateral investment treaties has increased constantly during the first half of the 1990s.[6] Bilateral investment treaties classically contain provisions guaranteeing fair and non-discriminatory treatment for investment, protecting investment against expropriation and other forms of non-commercial risk, and resolving dispute through settlement process. Many international legal scholars claim that BITs typically address the same topics in much the same terms, although there are significant differences among them.[7]

This dissertation tries to find out the role of bilateral investment treaties in the development of national law and international law. In order to do that, there are number of questions that need to be considered: What are the main reasons for which individual countries have decided to conclude BITs? What issues do these treaties cover? What would be BITs

---

[5] Bernard Lewis spells out that " Twice before in the course of history, the Turks have set an example and served as a model for others, under the Ottomans of militant Islam; under Kemal Ataturk, of Secular patriotism. If they succeed in their present endeavor to create, without the loss of character and identity, a liberal economy, and open society, and a liberal democratic policy, they may once again serve as a model to many other peoples." Metin Heper, *Islam and Democracy in Turkey: Toward Reconciliation?* The Middle East Journal, Volume 51, No. 1, at 33, Winter (1997).

[6] UNCTAD, BILATERAL INVESTMENT TREATIES IN THE MID 1990S, at preface (1998).

[7] Muhammed I. Khalil, *Treatment of Foreign Investment in BIT*, ICSID Review, Foreign Investment Law Journal, 339-359 (1992).

implications for the status of customary international law? Moreover, according to the majority opinion of legal scholars, BITs accepted as a *lex specials* that is mutually binding to the parties.[8] This situation has led many countries to establish regional and international organizations deal with trade and FDI. Therefore, this dissertation will also analyze the existing international instruments and activities in the area of investment. Notably the United Nations (UN), the OECD, the WTO, the MIGA are dealt separately in view of their special importance in this study.

The activities of the international organizations have contributed to establishing an international legal framework in foreign investment through binding and non-binding legal instruments. This study will explain the UN' and the OECD' activities on foreign investment. The UN provides technical assistance and other services for the promotion of foreign direct investment in developing countries through the UNDP, UNCTAD, and its regional commissions.

The existing network of bilateral and regional investment instruments is effective to some degree in creating a favorable climate for foreign investment. On the other hand, provisional differences of these instruments may create more complicated problems and distort investment flows. Multilateral investment rules can solve such problems and promote foreign investment. The world community needs truly comprehensive and binding international rules on foreign investment. For many years, international organizations like the UN, the WTO, and OECD have been searching for a new investment agreement which will facilitate the unique needs of a global economy. In other words, many proposals have been made for creation of a multilateral agreement on investment (MAI). One was discussed within the organization for

---

[8] UNCTAD, *supra* note 6, at 4.

economic cooperation and development (OECD).[9] Even though the MAI has failed to materialize comprehensive multilateral investment agreement, it is still important to understand further multileratization process of investment, so this dissertation will examine why MAI failed. In addition, this dissertation demonstrates some lessons from the MAI negotiations and their application to a possible multilateral agreement on investment.

Some countries have asserted that multilateral investment agreement should be negotiated and concluded under the WTO. There is a complex interaction between trade and investment policies.[10] Trade barriers can influence investment decisions. Likewise, investment measures can affect the flow of goods and services. Considering the relationship between trade and investment, investment is an issue that should be negotiated by the WTO. The paper will analyze the framework for negotiations in the WTO for an agreement on direct investment and the conflicting interests of developed and developing countries regarding such an agreement. The most significant part of the Uruguay Round dealt with new issues, including services, trade related investment measures (TRIMS), and intellectual property protection. Each of these issues will be analyzed briefly in this paper so as to understand the framework for negotiations in the WTO for an agreement on FDI.

This study will evaluate provisions and effectiveness of the MIGA and the pertinence of the principles and standards of the MIGA to Turkey. The Multilateral Investment Guarantee Agency (MIGA) was created to provide political risk insurance to foreign investors in developing countries. MIGA was established by an international convention on 12 May 1988

---

[9] OECD, POLICY BRIEF, No. 2, (1997).

[10] Mr. Renato Ruggiero, ex WTO Director-General, at the UNCTAD seminar on foreign direct investment and multilateral trading system in Geneva on 12 February 1996,said that : " Indeed, in today's economy, trade and investment are not merely increasingly complementary, but also increasingly inseparable as two sides of the coin of the process of globalization." WTO PRESS/42, 13 February 1996, http://www.wto.org (visited 3/12./1999).

as one of the World Bank Group's financial institutions designed to encourage the flow of investment to member countries and, in particular, to developing member countries.[11]

Domestic foreign investment law is one of the legal sources on foreign investment disputes since foreign investors and investments are subject to the host country's national law. The foreign investor cannot just trust domestic laws to protect its interests. The only acceptable legal concept is the national law consistent with international law on foreign investment. Recently, most developing countries have enacted new liberal national investment law. This dissertation will evaluate Turkey's foreign investment policy as a case study.

Turkey has been pursuing liberal and outward oriented economic policies since the 1980s.[12] Turkey views FDI as vital to its economic development and prosperity. This study will analyze the legal framework of foreign investment in Turkey, particularly, of existing regional commitment and applicable international treaties.

In Turkey developments in foreign investment occurred in the early fifties. During this period, with the formation of rapid development strategies and international economic cooperation, "Turkish Foreign Investment Law (herein after TFIL)" was enacted. Since the 1980s, the Turkish Government has followed liberalized, outward-oriented economic policies. The foreign investment law was amended. There were rapid changes in the economic and social structure of Turkey. For example, the deregulation of interest rates, the establishment of organized markets for money, foreign exchange, stocks and securities were some of the changes.[13] Following these measures, one of the major policy decisions was the adoption of liberal and flexible foreign investment policy. As a result of the changes in the TFIL, the

---

[11] The Convention Establishing the Multilateral Investment Guarantee Agency, 24 I.L.M. 1598 (1985).

[12] DAVID BARCHARD, TURKEY INVESTING IN THE FUTURE, 113-117 (1990).
[13] *Id.* at 116.

investment climate was made more efficient and suitable for potential investors.[14] Furthermore, Turkey amended its Constitution provision pertaining to international arbitration on concession agreement, which was a very controversial issue, in summer 1998. This study will focus on Turkish point of view on international arbitration in international investment disputes. In summary then, this study will examine Turkey's policies on foreign investment and the role played by foreign investment in the Turkish economy. It will also explain legal structures and policies affecting foreign investment in Turkey.

This dissertation does not completely deal with all of the developments on FDI. It deals with current changes taking place in this field. Thus, the BITs, OECD and the WTO are the main investment instruments examined critically in this dissertation. International rules on foreign investment protection contribute to create a favorable investment climate that benefits both international investors and host countries. Chapter Two examines the sources of international investment law. Chapter Three analyzes the proliferation of the BITs and the impacts of the BITs on customary international law. Chapter Four analyzes international organizations activities on foreign investment, specifically, the UN, and the OECD instruments. Chapter Five analyses the OECD MAI draft treaty in terms of its substantive and procedural provision by comparing it with BITs. Chapter Six analyzes failure of MAI so as to help future negotiations on multilateral investment agreement. Chapter Seven analyzes the framework for negotiations in the WTO for an agreement on FDI. Chapter Eight examines the MIGA's provisions and activities. Chapter Nine is devoted to an overview of Turkish foreign investment law policy. It shows the state's interest and attempts in changing its legal system in line with its international commitments in order to provide better protection for FDI. It also

---

[14] Eric Schneider, Alev Bilgen, *Foreign Investment laws in the Republic of Turkey: A Model for Reform*, 5 TRANSNAT'L LAW. 99, Spring, 101-102 (1992).

underscores the implementation of European Community's regulations on Turkish foreign investment policy. Chapter Ten is the conclusion of the dissertation.

CHAPTER TWO. THE SOURCES OF INTERNATIONAL INVESTMENT LAW

I. The International Legal Framework for FDI

The international legal framework for FDI encompasses various national and international law rules, "differing in form, strength and coverage."[1] Many countries have regulations dealing with FDI. It is a well-recognized general principle that a host government has the right to exercise its sovereignty to regulate all aspects of the FDI in its country. Therefore, ideally the national law of a host country is the primary law to apply in international investment. It should be mentioned that even though many countries have regulations on FDI, most foreign investors may not rely on national laws to protect their investments, therefore the international law could be the "only alternative structure" to shortcomings and ambiguities of national laws.[2]

The rules of any legal system deduce their validity and "authority from their source."[3] Unlike domestic law, which has specific "law-giving" sources, international law does not have "principal organ" to make legislation.[4] International scholars have generally utilized Article 38(1) of the Statute of International Court Of Justice (I.C.J) to identify sources of international law. The dissertation will therefore focus mainly on an analysis of the provisions of Article 38(1).

---

[1] UNCTAD, TRENDS IN INTERNATIONAL INVESTMENT AGREEMENTS: AN OVERVIEW 35 (1999).

[2] Andrew T Guzman, *Why LDCS Sign Treaties That Hurt Them: Explaining the Popularity of Bilateral Investment Treaties*, 38 VA. J. INT'L. L. 639, 659 (1998).

[3] REBECCA M.M. WALLACE, INTERNATIONAL LAW 7 (1997).

[4] L.C. Green, *The Raw Materials of International Law*, INT'L & COMP. L. Q 187 (1980) ; M.N. SHAW, INTERNATIONAL LAW 57 (1986).

The world community today is certainly very different from the one for which Article 38(1) was adopted.[5] Indeed, the world community has recognized the importance of international organizations' activities on the development of international law. The essential issue is whether or not the activities of these organizations form sources of law. The fourth chapter of this dissertation will thus also analyze other possible sources of law, in particular the resolutions and recommendations of the United Nations and the OECD.

It is essential to quote Professor Oppenheim's approach to Article 38 of the ICJ. He asserts that: "Article 38 cannot be regarded as a necessarily exhaustive statement of international law for all time, but it remains a good starting point for the discussion of the subject and provides a convenient list."[6] I agree with Professor Oppenheim statement pertinent to the Article 38 that the provision should not be considered as an "exhaustive statement" of international law, it should be served as a "starting point" for what the sources of international law in general are. This is because Article 38 does not use the word "sources", but rather describes "how the court is to decide disputes which may come for it for settlement."[7] In addition, the development of international law cannot be achieved through only applying the sources that are stipulated in Article 38. R Jennings supports this idea in the following statement:

> We cannot reasonably expect to get vary far if we try to rationalize the law of today society solely in the language of Article 38 of the Statute of International Court of Justice, framed as it was in 1920. It too needs urgent rethinking and elaboration...To use Article 38 as it stands, as we constantly do still, for the

---

[5] *Id.* at 5.

[6] OPPENHEIM, INTERNATIONAL LAW 45 (1992).

[7] WALLACE, *supra* note 3, at 8.

purposes of analyzing and explaining the elements and categories of the law today has a strong element of absurdity.[8]

Therefore, it can be argued that the development of international investment law is linked as a "starting point" with some sources that set forth in Article 38(1) the Statute of the ICJ. Article 38 states that:

1-international conventions, whether general or particular, establishing rules expressly recognized by the contesting states.

2-international custom, as evidence of a general practice accepted as law.

3-the general principle of law recognized by civilized nations.

4-judicial decisions and the teachings of the most highly qualified publicists of the various nations, as subsidiary means for the determination of rules of law.[9]

II. International Conventions

Basically, an international convention or treaty is any agreement governed by international law.[10] Treaties create law governing virtually every aspect of international social life. Treaties, like contracts, are sources of law of only parties who participate in, not for everyone. Treaty law is for the most part non-controversial. It is essential to note that the "1969 Vienna Convention on the Law of Treaties" is the primary source for the

---

[8] R. Jennings, *The Identification of International Law*, in Cheng, B (ed), International Law: Teachings and Practice, 1982, London, at 9 ; TIMOTHY HILLIER, PRINCIPLES OF PUBLIC INTERNATIONAL LAW 32 (1999).

[9] Statute of the International Court of Justice, The Statute, annexed to the Charter of the United Nations, is set forth in 59 Stat. 1055 (1945), T.S. No. 993 (at p.25).

[10] "Treaty is the generic term used to embrace *convention, agreement, arrangement, protocol,* and *exchange of notes*. International law does not distinguish between agreements identified as treaties and other agreements.".

law of treaties.[11] The Convention, which entered into force in January 1980, was the product of 20 years work by the International Law Commission. The Convention is regarded as essentially codifying customary international law through some of the provisions were, at least at the time the Vienna Convention on the law of Treaties was adopted.

The Convention itself is confined to treaties in writing between States. It acknowledges and does not purport to affect the validity of agreements entered into by other international persons. On the other hand, the "Vienna Convention on the Law of Treaties between States and International Organizations or between International Organizations (1986)" states that the convention applies to treaties between one or more States and one or more international organizations, and treaties between international organizations.[12]

Even though treaties have been used for centuries and many have been concluded since World War II, there are no pertinent treaties which provide comprehensive principles of international investment law. However, many international agreements such as the OECD instruments, General Agreement on Tariffs and Trade, are only related to foreign direct investment, but do not deal primarily with foreign investment. Since these instruments are related to foreign direct investment it is worthwhile to discuss them more detail in coming chapters.

---

[11] The Vienna Convention sets forth a basic definition for a treaty as " an international agreement concluded between States in written form and governed by international law, whether embodied in a single instrument or in two or more related instruments and whatever its particular designation…" Vienna Convention on the Law of treaties, U.N Doc. A/Conf. 39/27, art 2, 8 I.L.M. 679, 681.

[12] Vienna Convention on the law of Treaties Between States and International Organizations or Between International organizations, 21 March 1986, A/CONF.129/15, 25 ILM 543.

III. Customary International Law

A. General Knowledge

International custom, as evidence of general practice accepted as law, is considered as one of the sources of international law. Customary international law is essential for its general application to states not parties to treaties. In spite of its recognized importance, customary international law is subject to much controversy for its establishment.[13]

One may rightly claim that there are "material" and "physiological" elements to customary international law.[14] The material elements encompass state practice and consistency of state practices.[15] States in the practice of their international relations tacitly consent to the creation and application of legal rules. State practice may be determined from a wide variety of sources: treaties, legislation, court decisions, etc.[16] Furthermore, consistency of state practice is important to establish custom. However, there is no set standard to ascertain when such practice transforms into law.

Besides the material factors, international scholars often refer to the subjective element of *opinio juris sive necessitatis* (*opinio juris*).[17] In Northern See Continental Shelf Case, the ICJ precisely spells out: "Not only must the acts concerned amount to a

---

[13] Bernard Kishoiyian, *The Utility of Bilateral Investment Treaties in the Formulation of Customary International law*, 14 NW. J. INT'L L. & BUS. 327, 335-336 (1994).

[14] HENRY J. STEINER & DETLEV F. VAGTS & HAROLD HONGJU KOH, TRANSNATIONAL LEGAL PROBLEMS 240 (1994).

[15] *Id.*

[16] MARK W. JANIS, AN INTRODUCTION TO INTERNATIONAL LAW 46-47 (1993).

[17] *Id.* at 46.

settled practice, but they must also be such, or be carried out in such a way, as to be evidence of a belief that this practice is rendered obligatory by the existence of a rule of law requiring it. . . . The States concerned must therefore feel that they are conforming to what amounts to a legal obligation. The frequency, or even habitual character of the acts is not in itself enough."[18] *Opinio juris* is the feeling of legal obligation compelling states to follow a certain practice. It should be noted that the important problem is the proof of *opinio juris* since most states rarely proclaim that they are acting "under a sense of legal obligation rather than an as a matter of courtesy or convenience."[19]

Pursuant to the customary international law, the ability of a foreigner to make an investment in host country is subject exclusively to the territorial sovereignty of that host country.[20] In other words, a State has the right to control the movement of capital into its territory and to control the entry and activities of aliens.

Under international law, the doctrine of State responsibility for injuries to aliens and their property has long held that a State is entitled to exercise diplomatic protection for its nationals who are injured by acts contrary to international law committed by another State, from which they have been unable to obtain satisfaction through local remedies.[21] Especially developed countries argue that developing countries do not

---

[18] Northern Sea Continental Shelf Case (F. R. G. v Den.; F. R. G. v. Neth.), 1969 I.C.J. 3, 44.

[19] The I.C.J Stated that "...They are many international acts. . . which are motivated only by considerations of courtesy, convenience or tradition, and not by any sense of legal duty." (North Sea Continental Shelf Case, 1969 I.C.J. 4).

[20] UNCTAD, BILATERAL INVESTMENT TREATIES IN THE MID-1990S 46 (1998).

[21] R.Y. DON, PROTECTION OF FOREIGN INVESTMENT UNDER INTERNATIONAL LAW 396 (1979).

respect the minimum standard of protection required by customary international law with respect to the treatment of investment.

Fair and equitable treatment is a classic standard in customary international law.[22] According to Dolzer and Stevens, this treatment provides a basic and general standard which is detached from a host state's domestic law.[23] On the other hand, there is no precise meaning of this treatment. There is a debate whether fair and equitable treatment is similar to the minimum standard required by international law or not. According to F.A. Mann, fair and equitable treatment goes beyond the minimum standard required by international law.[24] On the other hand, like NAFTA investment Chapter stipulation, I contend that fair and equitable treatment is included under the minimum standard of customary international law.[25]

Developing countries such as Latin American countries asserted that States are required to grant foreign investor the same treatment they grant their own nationals under national law. In addition foreign states may not enforce their citizens' private claims by violating the territorial sovereignty of host states, either through diplomatic or forceful intervention. The above-mentioned principles are the framework of the Calvo doctrine.[26]

---

[22] UNCTAD, *supra* note 20, at 53.

[23] RUDOLF DOLZER AND MARGRETE STEVENS, BILATERAL INVESTMENT TREATIES 58 (1995).

[24] *Id.* at 59.

[25] *Id.* at 60.

[26] So as to comprehend the Calvo Doctrine, one must first examine the historical environment that originated it. Argentine jurist Carlos Calvo developed the doctrine in 1868 as Latin America's response to foreigners who exploited the region's natural resources. The French intervention in Mexico in 1861-62, the combined German, British and Italian action against Venezuela in 1902-1903, and the numerous instances of United States intervention in Central America throughout the late nineteenth and early twentieth centuries contributed to the suspicious and hostile attitude toward foreign investment.

The Calvo doctrine holds that jurisdiction in international investment disputes lies with the country in which the investment is located. The principle, named after an Argentinean jurist, has been applied throughout Latin America and other areas of the world.

B.   Hull Rule and the New Development on FDI

One may argue that there was a customary international law that had been applied to expropriation of investors' assets.[27] This law is so called "Hull Rule" which required "prompt, adequate and effective" compensation.[28] This rule is derived from the confiscation without compensation issued by Mexican Government in 1930s.[29] Especially, United States nationals suffered from these acts of expropriation, and the United States demanded compensation for its nationals. In 1932, Cordell Hull, American Secretary of State, asserted that:

> The Government of the United States merely adverts to a self-evident fact when it notes that the applicable precedents and recognized authorities on international law support its declaration that, under every rule of law and equity, no government is entitled to expropriate private property, for whatever purpose, without provision for prompt, adequate, and effective payment thereof.[30]

This statement is known as the Hull rule. Namely, the requirement of "prompt, adequate, and effective" compensation has been recognized as the Hull Rule. One may question to what extent the Hull statement could operate as a rule of customary

---

[27] Guzman, *supra* note 2, at 640.

[28] *Id.*

[29] *Id.* at 645.

[30] Notes exchanged between the United States and Mexico during the 1938 dispute reprinted in 3 Green H. Hackworth, *Digest of International Law*, at 658-59.

international law. In order to discuss whether this rule is customary international law or not, we should look at developing countries' point of view regarding the Hull Rule.

The Hull Rule was challenged by developing countries through United Nations Resolutions. They claimed that they had a right to determine treatment standards for investors and their investment, and the standards of compensation in the case of expropriation according to their domestic law. Specifically, the United Nations adopted many resolutions to support developing countries' position during the 1960s and mid 1970.s. The sovereignty of nations principle was the essential principle accepted by United Nations Resolutions. First, the "Resolution on Permanent Sovereignty over Natural Resources" (Resolution 1803) was enacted.[31] This resolution utilized word "appropriate" compensation. Developing countries argued that "appropriate" means something less than the hull rule. However, the United States opted to construe "appropriate" to mean "prompt and, adequate, and effective".[32]

Second, the UN adopted the Resolution on Permanent Sovereignty over Natural Resource (Resolution 3171) in 1973.[33] The Resolution stated that:

> "The application of the principle of nationalization carried out by States, as an expression of their sovereignty in order to safeguard their natural resources, implies that each State is entitled to determine the amount of possible compensation and the mode of payment, and that any dispute which might arise should be settled in accordance with the national legislation of each State carrying out such measures…"[34]

---

[31] General Assembly Resolution 1803, U.N. GAOR, 17th Sess., Supp. No.17,, at 15, U.N. Doc. A/5217 (1962).

[32] Stephen Schwebel, *The Story of the U.N's Declaration on Permanent Sovereignty Over Natural Resources*, 49 A.B.A.J., 1963, at 463-66.

[33] G.A. Res. 3171, U.N. GAOR, 28th Sess., Supp. No.30, at 52, U.N. Doc. A/9030 (1974), reprinted in 13 I.L.M. 238 (1974).

[34] *Id.* at 239.

This resolution reflects the developing countries' points of view since developing countries asserted that compensation should be determined under the national law. Thus, it is not reasonable to argue that the Hull Rule was accepted as a customary international law.

Finally, in 1974, The UN adopted two essential resolutions which clarified developing countries position against the Hull rule. The first one was the New International Economic Order, Resolution 3201.[35] This Resolution stated that:

> "... Full permanent sovereignty . . . over its natural resources and all economic activities...Each State is entitled to exercise effective control over them and their exploitation with means suitable to its own situation, including the right to nationalization or transfer of ownership to its nationals... No State may be subjected to economic, political or any other type of coercion to prevent the free and full exercise of this inalienable right."[36]

This resolution approved the State sovereignty over its natural resources and prohibited any form of sanction on a country that has expropriated the property of an investor. Moreover, like other resolutions, this resolution did not recognize the international obligation of repayment.[37]

The second one was Resolution 3821, the Charter of Economic Rights and Duties, adopted in 1974.[38] This resolution stated that:

"Each State has the right;

---

[35] G.A. Res. 3201, U.N. GAOR, 6th Special Sess., Supp. No. 1, at 3, U.N. Doc. A/9559 (1974), reprinted in 13 I.L.M. 715 (1974).

[36] *Id.* at 717.

[37] Guzman, *supra* note 2, at 650.

[38] G.A Res. 3281, U.N GAOR, 29th Sess., Supp. No. 31, at 50-55, U.N. Doc. A/9631 (1974), reprinted in 14 I.L.M. 251 (1975).

> a- To regulate and exercise authority over foreign investment within its national jurisdiction in accordance with its laws and regulations and in conformity with its national objectives and priorities…..
> b- To nationalize, expropriate or transfer ownership of foreign property, in which case appropriate compensation should be paid by the State adopting such measures, taking into account its relevant laws and regulations and all circumstances that the State considers pertinent. In any cases where the question of compensation gives rise to a controversy, it shall be settled under the domestic law of the nationalizing State and by its tribunals, unless it is freely and mutually agreed by all States concerned that other peaceful means be sought on the basis of the sovereign equality of States and in accordance with the principle of free choice of means."[39]

Resolution 3281 reemphasized the sovereignty of State with respect to its treatment of foreign investors.

Overall, the above resolutions assert that developing countries have control over foreign investment and the investor. Namely, they want to posses the sovereignty over the natural resources and to regulate foreign investment in accordance with their domestic law, not international law. Especially, they would rather use domestic court as a dispute settlement resolution system rather than international one. Thus it follows that it is not reasonable to support the Hull rule as a customary international law. [40]

It is essential to note that the role of international organizations, resolutions and recommendations in establishing custom, specifically the General Assembly of the United Nations resolutions, is controversial.[41] General Assembly resolutions are not a form of international legislation and are not legally binding. On the other hand, Security Council decisions are binding.[42] One may argue that General Assembly Resolutions may

---

[39] *Id.* at 264.

[40] Guzman stated "the U.N . Resolutions provide evidence of the demise of the Hull Rule, not of the rise of an alternative rule of customary international law" Guzman, *supra* note 2, footnote 39, at 688.

[41] JANIS, *supra* note 16, at 50.

[42] STEINER, *supra* note 14, at 299-300.

be used as evidence of customary international law since the votes of the world community may show a consensus or lack of consensus on a particular issue. For example, Professor Rene-Jean Dupuy, acting as the sole arbitrator in Texaco v Libya Arbitration case, held that the requirement of "appropriate compensation" should be the standard accepted by developed and developing countries.[43] Professor Dupuy applied only the Resolution 1803 in this case. However, as we mentioned before, the majority of developing countries changed their opinion pertinent to expropriation of foreign assets in further resolutions since former colonies became sovereign states and their opinions became relevant to the formulation of customary international law. Thus, in my point of view, Professor Dupuy should have applied other resolutions which represent majority opinions.

C. **Findings on Customary International Investment Law**

It is quite difficult to establish what customary international investment law exists. What is clear under the customary international law is that it recognizes that the state has an exclusive right to make decisions, and it seems to control the circumstances of those investments once they are in place.[44] Foreign investors and their home countries often concerned that these sovereign rights of nation states would create barriers to foreign investment. International norms of the treatment of aliens and the state responsibility for injuries to aliens and their property are controversial issues that are still

---

[43] International Arbitral Tribunal: Award on the Merits in the Dispute Between Texaco Overseas Petroleum/California Asiatic Oil Company and the Government of the Libyan Arab Republic, 17 I.L.M. 329 (1978), 53 I.L.R. 389 (1979).

[44] A.A. Fatourus, *Towards an international Agreement on Foreign Direct Investment in* TOWARDS MULTILATERAL INVESTMENT RULES, OECD 50 (1996).

disputed in the world community. Another weakness of customary international law is that it does not provide an effective and binding method for resolving investment disputes.

According to the UNCTAD study, "Customary international law distinguishes between expropriation and the destruction of property due to military necessity. The general consensus that no compensation is due for losses caused by military necessity."[45] On the other hand, most bilateral investment treaties have some provisions relating to such losses.[46] These provisions generally provide MFN and national treatment with respect to losses caused by war and civil disturbance.[47] Namely, a host state does not need to pay compensation unless it signed a treaty to provide compensation for losses caused by war and civil disturbances.

---

[45] UNCTAD, *supra* note 20, at 73.

[46] BIT between Hungary and Norway (1991), Article V provides that: "investors of one Contracting party whose investment suffers losses in the territory of the other Contracting Party owing to war, revolution, or other armed conflict, state of national emergency or other similar events shall be accorded treatment no less favourable than that accorded to investors of any third State as regards restitution, indemnification, compensation or other valuable consideration, such payments shall be freely transferable." *Id.* at 74.

[47] Like many BITs signed between Turkey and other nations, Turkey - Tunisia BIT, Article 3 provides that : "... (3)- Nationals or companies of either party whose investments suffer losses in the territory of the other party owing to war, insurrection, civil disturbance or other similar events shall be accorded treatment by such other Party not less favourable than that accorded to its own nationals or companies or to nationals or companies of any third country, whichever is the most favourable treatment, as regards any measures it adopts in relation to such losses." Agreement Between The Republic of Tunisia and The Republic of Turkey Concerning The Reciprocal Promotion and Protection of Investments, 1991, ICSID, at 4.

IV.   **General Principles of Law**

A.   **General Knowledge**

General principles of law are principles so fundamentally used in all legal system that they form part of the international law.[48] International dispute settlement bodies have utilized general principles of law as gap fillers.[49] It should be noted that due to their incorporation in customary international law and international agreements, general principles of law lost their significance in contemporary international law.

General principles of law are rules concerning liability for damages, unjust enrichment, the sanctity of contract, etc.[50] These are related to the international investment law. According to Professor Sornarajah, the payment of full compensation upon the expropriation of foreign property is based on arguments relating to idea of unjust enrichment and acquired rights being general principles of law.[51] On the other hand, Professor Sornarajah claims that these arguments have to be evaluated very carefully since there is a high degree of subjectivity to ascertain the general principles of law.[52]

---

[48] JANIS, *supra* note 16, at 55.

[49] *Id* Janis, at 57. For example, In the Corfu case, the International Court, in order to justify its use of circumstantial evidence, arguing that such evidence was 'admitted in all systems of law.'". In the AMCO case, in 1984, an international arbitral tribunal used a comparative analysis of Indonesian, Dutch, Belgian, Italian, German, Danish, English, and United States laws to find a general principle of law applicable in international law defining a "contract" as "an agreement based on meeting of minds and wills and creating obligations".*Id*. at 57-58.

[50] M. SORNARAJAH, THE INTERNATIONAL LAW ON FOREIGN INVESTMENT 77-78 (1994).

[51] *Id.* at 77-78.

[52] *Id.* at 78.

B. The Principle of Pacta Sunt Servanda

Professor Joel P.Trachtman asserts, "the primary traditional public international law issue is that of legal stability, identified with the tension between *pacta sunt servanda* and *rebus sic stantibus*. Thus, investors seek protection from expropriation or repudiation."[53] I agree with Professor Trachtman's opinion that the *Pacta Sunt Servanda*, the sanctity of contracts, is the most vital general principle of law relating to international investment. Article 26 of the Vienna Convention on the Law of Treaties articulates it as "every treaty in force is binding upon the parties to it and must be performed by them in good faith."[54] That is to say that according to this principle, the parties of any treaty are obligated to perform the obligation into which they sign.

Many countries have adopted the principle of *pacta sunt servanda* in their national laws.[55] Moreover, *pacta sunt servanda* is considered a cornerstone of the *lex mercatoria*.[56] Indeed, the UNIDROIT principles deal with the principle of *pacta sunt servanda* in Article 1.3 indicates, "a contract validly entered into is binding upon the parties. It can only be modified or terminated in accordance with its terms, by agreement,

---

[53] Joel P. Trachtman, *Foreign Investment, Regulation and Expropriation: A Debtor's Jubilee?*, in *Capitalism in Transition: The Role of International law*, (Mulan Ashwin ed., American Society of International law Proceedings, April 5-8, at 107 1995).

[54] Vienna Convention on the law of Treaties, adopted May 23, 1969 23 May 1969, 1155 United Nations Treaty Series 331 ("the Vienna Convention"), reproduced in 8 I.L.M. 702 (1969).

[55] Arbitrators often have recognized the principle of *pact sunt servanda* by reference to a specific national law. As one arbitrator held: "The principle of the sanctity of contacts has always constituted an integral part of most legal systems. These include those systems that are based on Roman law, the Napoleonic Code (e.g. article 1143) and other European civil codes, as well as Anglo-Saxon Common Law and Islamic Jurisprudence, Sharia", Liamco v Libya, April 12, 1977, Yb. Comm. Arb., 1981, 89 at 101.

[56] M. Mustill, *The New Lex Mercatoria: The First Twenty-five years*, Arbitration International, 110-111 (1988).

or as otherwise provided in these principles".[57] That is to say that, modification or the termination of the contract may be allowed only when in line with the terms of the contract. In addition, a contract may be modified or terminated if the parties so agree. The principle of *pacta sunt servanda*, sanctity of contract, has to be recognized by the world community, but this recognition must be consistent with the principle of changed circumstances so as to balance the respective interest of the parties.

C. The Principle of Rebus Sic Stantibus

The *rebus sic stantibus* (the doctrine of changed circumstances) is another general principle of law relating to international investment. *Rebus sic stantibus* is also considered a principle of lex mercatoria. It derives from the *"Civilist maxim coventio omnis intelligitur rebus sic stantibus"*.[58]

Rebus sic Stantibus is determined as a general principle of international Treaty Law by the 1969 Vienna Convention on the Law of Treaties, Article 62 states:

> "1-A fundamental change of circumstances which has occurred with regard to those existing at the time of the conclusion of a treaty, and which was not foreseen by the parties, may not be invoked as a ground for terminating or withdrawing from the treaty unless:
> (a) The existence of those circumstances constituted an essential basis of the consent of the parties to be bound by the treaty: and
> (b)The effect of the change is radically to transform the extend of the obligations still to be performed under the treaty......".[59]

---

[57] Dr. Maria Del Piar Perales Viscasillas, *UNITROIT Principles of International Commercial Contract: Sphere of Application and General Provisions*, 13 Arizona Journal of International and Comparative Law 381 (1996).

[58] WESTBERG JOHN A, INTERNATIONAL TRANSACTION AND CLAIMS INVOLVING GOVERNMENT PARTIES CASE LAW OF IRAN-USA TRIBUNAL CLAIM (1998).

[59] VIENNA CONVENTION, art. 62.

If we interpret Article 62, we will find out easily that this article is subordinate the principle of *pacta sunt servanda*. The change in circumstances has to be fundamental. It has to jeopardize the survival of the state. As the international Court of Justice stated in the Fisheries Jurisdiction Case, the changes must be vital; they have to "imperil the existence or vital development of one party". Furthermore, the change in circumstances has to be unforeseeable.[60] These types of stipulations are also required in the Article 6.2.2. of the UNIDROIT principles[61]

Many countries have adopted the principle of *Rebus sic stantibus* in their national laws. For example, Polish Civil Code art 269 (1935), Turkish Civil Code art 21 (1926), the United States U.C.C. 2-615 (1990), and in various Latin American countries, such as Argentina, Civil Code art. 1198, which recognized this principle. [62]These laws permit the alteration of contractual terms as a result of unforeseen circumstances.

The doctrine of changed circumstances is also recognized in the Iran- USA claims Tribunal.[63] Article V of the Declaration specifies that the Tribunal can utilize the doctrine of changed circumstances as a source of law.

---

[60] "Arbitral decisions found that rebus sic stantibus only concerns unforeseeable changes. Consequently arbitrators denied relief for shortage on the crude oil market and for the rise in oil prices after the outbreak of the Israeli-Egypt war in Autumn 1973 as its consequences could have been foreseen when the contract was concluded in February 1974." (Ad Hoc Award July, 1983, Yb. Comm, Arb., 1984, 69 at 70 , Transnational Rules in International Commercial Arbitration, ICC, (1993).

[61] General Principles of International Commercial Law, *Special Section Seminar Proceeding*, World Arb. &Mediation Rep, May (1996), at 133.

[62] Hernany Veytia, *The requirement of Justice and Equity in Contracts*, 69 TUL. L. REV. 1191 (1995).

[63] The 1981 Algiers Declarations provided for the creation of the Iran- US Claims Tribunal and resulted in the release of the fifty-two US. Hostages from Iran. The purpose of the tribunal was to adjudicate claims brought by the U.S. nationals against Iran, by Iranian nationals against the U.S, and by one government against the other. Professor Richard Lillich, an expert on international claims tribunal, described the Tribunal as "the most significant arbitral body in the history". Judge Abraham D. Sofaer, the former legal adviser to the U.S State Department, stated that the Tribunal has" produced more international law than any law making body in the history of mankind." Furthermore, because the tribunal utilized adaptations of the United Nations Commission on International Trade Law (UNCITRAL) Arbitration Rules, "the Tribunal

The applicable law provision of the Claims Settlement Declaration, Article V, states: "The Tribunal Shall decide all cases on the basis of respect for law, applying such choice of law rules and principles of commercial and international law as the Tribunal determines to be applicable, taking into account relevant usage's of the trade, contract provisions and changed circumstances." The US wanted to include the doctrine of changed circumstances in the Declaration in order "to authorize the Tribunal to disregard Iranian law that might give effect to an Iranian-forum clause."[64] Iran also wanted to have this principle in the Declaration in order to justify its termination of contracts due to the fact that the revolution brought about radical political and social changes in Iran.[65]

The Tribunal found that the doctrine of changed circumstances is a general principle of law. However, apart from the Questech Award, the Tribunal did not find the revolution as changed circumstances that could excuse the termination of a contract by Iran.[66] For example, the Mobil Oil and Amoco International Finance Awards of Chamber Three, and the Phillips Petroleum award of Chamber Two concluded that the

---

has encountered and resolved procedural issues that might have taken decades to arise in the normal course of commercial arbitration."
Richard M. Mosk, *Book Review*, 24 VAND. J. TRANSNAT'L L. 587-590 (1991).

[64] John R. Crock, *Applicable Law in International Arbitration: The Iran-U.S. Claims Tribunal Experience*, 83 AM. J. INT'L L. 278, 280 (1989).

[65] *Id.*

[66] WESTBERG, *supra* note 58, at 176. The Arbitral Chamber decided "The fundamental changes in the political conditions as a consequence of the revolution in Iran, the different attitude of the new government and the new foreign policy especially towards the United States which had considerable support in large sections of the people, the drastically changed significance of highly sensitive military contracts as the present one, especially those to which the United States companies were parties, are all factors that brought about such a change of circumstances as to give the respondent (the Iranian government) a right to terminate the contract. When the Ministry of Defense decided not to go on…it opted for the termination of a contract which the parties probably would not have entered into had it been known that such fundamental changes occur." (Hans van Houtte, *Changed Circumstances and Pacta Sunt Servanda*, in Transnational Rules in International Commercial Arbitration, ICC, 1993, at 118.).

Iranian Revolution did not constitute changed circumstances that could excuse the termination of a contract by Iran.

V. Judicial Decisions and Publicists

Judicial decisions and the teachings of highly qualified publicists are recognized as subsidiary sources in accordance with Article 38 of the Statue of the International Court of Justice. Article 59 of the Statue of the International Court of Justice states that " the decision of the Court has no binding force except between the parties and in respect to that particular."[67] Although article 59 reflects that there is no doctrine of binding *stare decisis* in international law, the court does in fact take into account previous decisions.

The ICJ has delivered two significant judgments which have been influential in their contributions to the development of international investment law: concerning foreign investment. First, the Barcelona Traction Case relates to corporate nationality and diplomatic protection of foreign investment. Second, the Elsi Case is related to nationalization of property and protection of shareholder rights in foreign investment.[68] The implications of these cases will be analyzed below. Apart from ICJ decisions, there are also international arbitrational awards regarding international investment disputes..[69] For example, Texaco, the Iran-US Claims Tribunals are the important ones which are dealt with in this dissertation.

---

[67] Statute of the International Court of Justice, The Statute, annexed to the Charter of the United Nations, is set forth in 59 Stat. 1055 (1945), T.S. No. 993 (at p.25).

[68] SORNARAJAH, *supra* note 50, at 79-80

[69] *Id.*

The work of scholars is a subsidiary source of international law. The writings of highly qualified publicists influence the international legal system. International law scholars such as Grotious and Oppenheim play an important role in the development of international law.[70]

A. **Implication of Barcelona Traction Case**

The facts of this case are explained briefly in the following. Belgian nationals were shareholders in the Barcelona Traction, Light and Power Company, Ltd (hereinafter Barcelona Traction, or company), which was incorporated in Toronto, Canada, in 1911. The company produced and distributed electric service in Spain through its Spanish subsidiaries. The company issued bonds in pesetas and sterling. As a result of the Spanish Civil War in 1936, the payment of interest on both types of bonds was suspended. Even though the Spanish government authorized the company to resume payment of interest on peseta bonds in 1940, the government did not authorize the company to resume payment of interest on sterling bonds. As a result of the company's failure to pay the interest on sterling bonds, three Spanish shareholders who had bought sterling bonds sued the company for bankruptcy. On 12 February 1948, the Spanish bankruptcy court declared the company bankrupt. The court ordered seizure and liquidation of the assets of the company. The Spanish court authorized "the issuance of new shares for the subsidiaries which were then sold in 1952 by public auction and purchased by a newly formed Spanish corporation."[71] Before starting to analyze the ICJ

---

[70] *Id.*

[71] STEINER, *supra* note 14, at 205.

proceeding pertaining to the Barcelona Traction case, it should be mentioned that there were many judicial proceedings initiated with respect to the bankruptcy judgment in Spain and in Canada.[72]

Belgium filed a case against Spain to the ICJ, seeking compensation for damages to its national shareholders in Barcelona Traction. Belgium claimed that unlawful acts committed by Spanish government caused injury to the financial interests of its national shareholders in the company. Spain challenged this claim in its third Preliminary Objections, noting that:

> Since the Belgian government is without capacity in the present case, having regard to the fact that the Barcelona Traction company, which is still the object of claim referred to the Court, does not possess Belgian nationality; and having regard also to the fact that no claim whatsoever can be recognized in the present case on the basis of the protection of Belgian nationals being shareholders of Barcelona Traction, as the principal of these nationals lacks the legal status of a shareholder of Barcelona Traction, and as international law does not recognize, in respect of injury caused by a State to a foreign company, any diplomatic protection of shareholders exercised by a State other than the national State of the company.[73]

The ICJ analyzed the issue of standing in terms of nationality of the company and Spain's municipal law for the rights of shareholders. The ICJ held the corporation was a Canadian corporation since it was incorporated there. Due to the fact that the corporation has a Canadian nationality, Canada could exercise its right of diplomatic protection on behalf of the Barcelona Traction. Belgium lacked standing to represent Belgian shareholders under customary international law. The court decision was based on the municipal law since Spanish law denied rights to shareholder to bring a suit either on behalf of the company or in his name. The court found that

---

[72] DON, *supra* note 21, at 398.

[73] I.C.J Reports 1964, p. 15, (Id. at 405).

In this field international law is called upon to recognize institutions of municipal law that have an important and extensive role in the international field. . . . whenever legal issues arise concerning the rights of States with regard to the treatment of companies and shareholders, as to which rights international law has not established its own rules, it has to refer to the relevant rules of municipal law.[74]

The ICJ concluded that foreign shareholders in foreign investment had no right under customary international law to submit a damage claim on their own behalf against the state of incorporation. The court stated that:

The mere fact that damage is sustained by both the company and shareholder does not imply that both are entitled to claim compensation.... Thus whenever a shareholder's interests are harmed by an act done to the company, it is to the latter that he must look to institute appropriate action; for although two separate entities may have suffered from the same wrong, it is only one entity whose rights have been infringed....[75]

It is worthwhile to note that the ICJ recognized remedies in two exceptional situations for foreign shareholders[76]. First, if the direct rights of shareholders are infringed, "the shareholder has an independent right of action". The court granted some examples of "direct rights": "the right to any declared dividend, the right to attend and vote at general meetings, the right to share in the residual assets of the company on liquidation."[77] Second, the ICJ acknowledged that if the case involved the breach of international treaty, the Belgium government could be entitled to bring a claim on behalf of its national shareholders.[78] The Court spelled out that "The Belgian Government

---

[74] Excerpts from the opinion of the Court P. 38, (STEINER, *supra* note 14, at 207).

[75] Stephen A. Kubiatowski, *The Case of Elettronica Sicula S.P.A: Toward Greater Protection of Shareholders' Rights in Foreign Investments*, 29 COLUM. J. TRANSNAT'L. J. 215, 222-223 (1991).

[76] *Id.* at 223.

[77] Excerpts from the opinion of the Court P. 47 (STEINER, *supra* note 14, at 209).

[78] Excerpts from the opinion of the Court P. 86-90 (STEINER,*supra* note 14, at 214-216).

would be entitled to bring a claim if it could show that one of its rights had been infringed and that the acts complained of involved the breach of an international obligation arising out of a treaty or a general rule of law."[79]

The Barcelona Traction Case has impact on the protection of shareholder rights in foreign investment. The court concluded that a state could not assert claim on behalf of its shareholders in foreign investment disputes. However, the court recognized the importance of investment treaties for the protection of shareholders' rights in foreign investment. The court pointed out that:

> Thus, in the present state of the law, the protection of shareholders requires that recourse be had to treaty stipulations or special agreements directly concluded between the private investor and the State in which the investment is placed. States ever more frequently provide for such protection, in both bilateral and multilateral relations, either by means of special instruments or within the framework of wider economic arrangements. Indeed, whether in the form of multilateral or bilateral treaties between States, or in that of agreements between States and companies, there has since the Second World War been considerable development in the protection of foreign investments.[80]

Bernard Kishoiyian rightly points out that "this decision contributed significantly to the impetus leading to the conclusion of BITs as it created doubt as to whether and when diplomatic protection of the interests of shareholders is permissible in international law."[81] The Court decision encourages countries to negotiate and conclude international investment agreements that expand the rights of their nationals as shareholders in foreign investment. Otherwise, the general principle on the protection of shareholder rights and corporate nationality determined by the I.C.J in the Barcelona Traction case remains.

---

[79] STEINER *supra* note 14, at 214.

[80] *Id.* at 215.

[81] Kishoiyian, *supra* note 13, at 349-350.

B. **Implication of ELSI Case**

The facts of this case are explained briefly in the following. Two United States companies (Raytheon and Machlett) purchased all the shares of ELSI, an Italian corporation, between 1955 and 1967. Due the fact that the ELSI had financial difficulties during the 1960s, the two United States corporations commenced planning "to close and liquidate ELSI". [82] The liquidation plan was approved by the shareholders on March 28, 1968. In response, the Mayor of Palermo issued a requisition order on ELSI's plant for a period of six months to protect "the general economic public interest and public order."[83] ELSI appealed the Mayor's order to the Prefect of Palermo, the Mayor's administrative superior. ELSI filed a voluntary petition in bankruptcy on April 25, 1968 citing the requisition as the reason for the bankruptcy. An Italian bankruptcy court issued a bankruptcy decree. It should be noted that the Italian government established state enterprise (Industria Ellettronica Telecommunicaioni S.p.A (ELTEL)) to take over ELSI's plant through the bankruptcy process. Indeed, ELTEL bought the ELSI plan in the fourth auction.[84] Interestingly enough the Prefect of Palermo abrogated the requisition after the ELSI was purchased by ELTEL.

---

[82] Sean D. Murphy, *The Elsi Case: An Investment Dispute at the International Court of Justice*, 16 YALE J. INT'L L. 391, 399-400 (1991).

[83] Kubiatowski, *supra* note 75, at 219.

[84] Sean D. Murphy explains the situation as follows: " The bankruptcy court began its effort to liquidate ELSI soon after the formation of ELTEL. The first auction of ELSI's plant and equipment occurred on January 18, 1969, with a minimum bid of a five billion lire (U.S. $ 8.000.000). No buyers appeared at the auction. (no buyers appeared at the second auction as well). ELTEL proposed to the trustee that it be allowed to lease and reopen the plant for eighteen months. The trustee recommended this course of action, and the judge agreed to grant ELTEL the lease. In April 1969, ELTEL proposed to trustee that it be allowed to buy ELSI's work in progress. ....On May 27, ELTEL offered to buy the remaining plant, equipment, and supplies for four billion lira (U.S. $6.400.000)). With the approval of the creditors'

The United States filed a suit against Italy with the ICJ. The ELSI case submitted to the court on the basis of a "compromissory clause" set out in the Treaty of Friendship and Commerce and Navigation between the United States and Italy. This case demonstrates that even though the United States has no longer accepted compulsory jurisdiction of the ICJ, it can apply to the ICJ on the basis of a "compromissory clause". The United States asserted that Italy had violated their bilateral 1948 Treaty of Friendship, Commerce and Navigation treaty, and the Supplementary Agreement by actions and omissions that deprived two United States corporations (Raytheon and Machlett) of their right to manage and control an Italian corporation (ElSI) that they owned.[85] As Wendy Huey elaborated, the United States' claim was the result of the "three events: the Mayor of Palermo's requisition of ELSI, the Italian subsidiary of Raytheon and Machlett; ELSI's bankruptcy; and the acquisition of ELSI by Italian state-owned entity."[86]

The court found that Italy did not violate the Article II, III, V, and VI of US- Italy FCN and Articles I, and V of the Treaty supplement. The court rejected the US's claims on merits that the requisition order did not deprive ELSI of any rights of control and management guaranteed by the treaty. Furthermore, the court held that the Mayor's requisition order did not constitute "arbitrary or discriminatory" conduct within the

---

committee, the bankruptcy court scheduled a fourth auction on these terms, and the sale was consummated.", Murphy, *supra* note 82, at 403.

[85] Case Concerning Elettronica Sicula S.p.A (ELSI) (U.S. v Italy) , 1989 I.C.J. 15 (July 20), (hereinafter ELSI), reprinted in 28 I.L.M. 1109.

[86] Wendy Huey, *International Litigation: United States and Italy FCN Treaty and I.C.J. Jurisdiction over Disputes- United States v Italy, 1989 I.C.J. 15 (1989)*, 32 HARV. INT'L L. J. 236 (1991).

meaning of Article 1 of the treaty supplement since the mayor did not utilize his power "unreasonably or capriciously" in his attempt to resolve the situation.

The ELSI case has some important implications in international investment law. Indeed, Peter D. Trooboff notes that the ELSI case is "an important decision in what is ostensibly a relatively unimportant case."[87] The following issues are the legal significance of the case: the proving facts, the recognition of importance of the BITs and the utilizing clear language, the applicability of the exhausted local remedies rules, and the protection of shareholders.

It is important to note that the ICJ found the US' claims unacceptable since the US could not prove the facts of the dispute. Judge Schwebel, in his dissenting opinion states that the United States lost the case not because the ICJ "found against the United States on the law of the treaty," which was "largely interpreted to give effect rather than to deprive of effect," but because the ICJ found against "the practical and legal significance to be attached to the facts of the case."[88]

There are some lessons to be learned from the ELSI decision with respect to treaty law. One of the lessons that we can draw from the case that the BITs should be drafted well to entitle the foreign investor to submit disputes to the international dispute settlement body. As we analyzed the ELSI Case, we can conclude that the court strictly construed treaty provisions with regard to "arbitrary measures" and "indirect expropriation". Thus, these strict interpretations of the treaty can adversely affect future

---

[87] Kurt J. Hamrock, *The Elsi Case: Toward An International Definition of 'Arbitrary" Conduct*, 27 TEX. INT'L L. J. 837 (1992). He footnotes Peter D. Trooboff's opinion. Peter D. Trooboff, International Decisions, 84 Am. J. Int'l. 249, 257 (1990).

[88] Kubiatowski, *supra* note 75, at 243.

decisions dealing with FDI. In order to avoid having the same kind of problem, countries should negotiate and draft well the international investment agreements, especially BITs. Indeed, many BITs which were signed after the ELSI decision provide a broad investment definition to prevent any kind of problem as to whether the protection of shareholder rights is recognized or not. The problem, however, still exists on the interpretation of "arbitrary measures" and "indirect expropriation".

In the ELSI case, the ICJ reiterated its previous opinions pertaining to the exhausted local remedies issue.[89] The ICJ held that in order to have recourse to international dispute, foreign investor must exhaust the local remedies that available in the host states' national law. This is well-recognized customary international law. The only exception to this rule is that parties can lodge exceptions in the treaties. Thus, foreign investors can get lesson from the ELSI case that if they want to submit the dispute directly to international dispute mechanisms, they should exclude the exhausted local remedies rule.

The court granted to the United States the right to protect American shareholder's investments. This case has contributed to the security of shareholder rights in foreign investment. Namely, the state can intervene for the protection of its national's investment. Like Christopher N. Camponovo, Seen D. Murphy rightly claims that even though the ELSI case was based on the treaty protection, the ICJ ostensibly retreated from its prior decision in Barcelona Traction Case "which restricted states' standing

---

[89] ELSI Case, *supra* note 85.

under customary international law to espouse the claims of its nationals who own shares in a foreign corporation."[90]

In the light of the foregoing discussion, I contend that in spite of the I.C.J. factual findings, the ELSI case underscores not only the importance of signing international investment treaties but also particularly the need of precise terminology on investment instruments to protect investment.

---

[90] Christopher N. Camponovo, *Dispute Settlement and the OECD Multilateral Agreement on Investment*, 1 UCLA Journal of International Law and Foreign Affairs. 181, 187-188 (1996); Murphy, *supra* note 82 at 393.

CHAPTER THREE.

ANALYSIS OF THE BILATERAL INVESTMENT TREATIES

I. General Knowledge

Bilateral investment treaties (BITs) control investment relationships only between two countries. These treaties are typically signed between developed and developing countries.[1] However, recently they have been also signed between two developing countries, or a developed and less developed countries. This chapter analyses BITs provisions and their role in the development of international investment law.

The most important purpose of bilateral investment treaties for capital importing countries is to attract foreign investment in the interest of development. On the other hand, the most important purpose of bilateral investment treaties for capital exporting countries is to protect their investment abroad. If benefits can flow in both directions, both parties to a BIT may follow these two objectives simultaneously. It is essential to note that in practice capital importing countries (mostly developing countries) do not participate in drafting BITs, but merely approve the BITs that already been drafted by the capital exporting countries [2]

---

[1] Pursuant to the data contained in the UNCTAD World Investment Report 1997, the countries with the largest number of bilateral investment treaties are Germany (111), the United Kingdom (87), Romania (82), Switzerland (81), China (80), France (74), the Netherlands (58), Poland (58), Italy (53), the Republic of Korea (49), Argentina (44), Egypt (43), Hungary (43), Turkey (42), Belgium-Luxembourg (40), Malaysia (40), the United States (39), Denmark(38), Ukraine (38), Bulgaria (37), Spain (37), Chile (36), Indonesia (35), Sweden (35), and Vietnam (32).

[2] Turkey-US BIT contains in its Article 6 (1) a definition of an "investment Dispute" fully in line with the US model treaty. (Turkey-United States: Treaty Concerning The Reciprocal Encouragement and Protection of Investments, December 3, 1985, International Legal Materials, January 1986, 25 I.L.M. 85.

II. The Origin of the BITs

BITs can be considered as a successor to the Friendship, Commerce and Navigation Treaties (FCNs). The BITs program started during and after the War of Independence of the USA.[3] Thomas Jefferson, John Adams, and Benjamin Franklin were authorized by the Congress to negotiate a series of FCNs with many European states, including France, Netherlands, and Spain. These FCNs are the origin of the modern BITs[4]. It is necessary to explain FCNs so as to understand origin of the BITs.

The first FCN was signed with France in 1778.[5] Later, theUnited States and newly independent Latin American States negotiated and signed FCNs with each otherin order to improve and to protect foreign trade relations.[6] At the outset, FCNs generally provided international legal standards for the protection of natural and juridical persons. Later on, signatories added a couple of provisions to protect property or facilitate investment.[7] For example, they provided a clause prohibiting expropriation of property belonging to aliens without payment of compensations. A UN study showed that FCNs had a very broad coverage including such important provisions as

> "entry and freedom of movement, protection of persons, right to counsel and prompt trial, national treatment in application of local laws, enforceability of arbitration awards, protection of acquired property, right to lease and purchase land freely, patents, trademarks, equal tax treatment, administration and exchange controls, transit of goods and persons, import and export duties and taxes, right to

---

[3] Kenneth J. Vandevelde, *The BIT Program: A Fifteen-Year Appraisal, The Development and Expansion of Bilateral Investment Treaties*, 86 American Society of International Law Proceedings. 532, 533 (1992).

[4] *Id.*

[5] Todd Shenkin, *Trade Related Investment Measures in Bilateral Investment Treaties and The GATT: Moving Toward a Multilateral Investment Treaty*, 55 U. PITT. L.REV. 541, 571 (1994).

[6] Vandevelde, *supra* note 3, at 533.

[7] *Id.*

compete with local monopolies, consultations on restrictive business practices, freedom, commerce and navigation and freedom of transit of person.".[8]

After realizing the need to address investment related issues in the international instruments, most European countries begin to sign bilateral investment treaties with developing countries. The first modern bilateral investment treaty signed between Germany and Pakistan in 1959.[9] After recognizing success of the European BITs program, The United States launched a new American BITs program on August 15 of the 1977.[10] The success of the European BITs program was not the only reason to launch this program: there were legal, economic and political considerations.[11] The number of BITs, and the number of countries to these treaties have increased in recent years.

---

[8] UNITED NATIONS CENTRE ON TRANSNATIONAL CORPORATIONS, BILATERAL INVESTMENT TREATIES (1988).

[9] Treaty for the Promotion and Protection of Investments, Nov. 25, 1959, Pak. -F.R.G., 457 U.N.T.S. 23, Elihu Lauterpacht, *International Law and private Foreign Investment,* 4 Indiana Journal of Global Legal Studies. 259, 266 (1997).

[10] The US BIT program's main aims are to:
"1-protect U.S investment abroad in those countries where U.S. investor's rights are not protected through existing agreements such as our treaties of Friendship, Commerce and Navigation;
2-encourage adoption in foreign countries of market-oriented domestic policies that treat private investment fairly; and
3-support the development of international law standards consistent with these objectives."
www.state.gov/www/issues/economic (visited 2/8/1998)

[11] Vandevelde, *supra* note 3, at 532. The United States Government was also under political pressure from member of Congress and business people who were concerned about the lack of protection of United States foreign direct investment from host country regulation or interference. Even though the Charter Administration did not begin actual BITs negotiations, it formulated the basic policy for future administration. Thus, Reagan, Bush and Clinton Administration pursued this objective in order to provide free market competition in foreign investment.

III. Analysis of BITs Provisions

Almost every BIT covers the same issues. However, there are many exceptions, and reservations.[12] This section will review of the most basic provisions of BITs. Professor Kenneth J. Vandevelde analyzes the substance of the BITs based on three aspects: "investment security", "investment neutrality", and "market facilitation", so as to figure out the position of BITs as instruments of liberalization.[13] I will also use the same methodology in order to find out the place of BITs in international foreign investment law. Furthermore, it is necessary to notice that bilateral investment treaties for the promotion and reciprocal protection of investments should be differentiated from other similar agreements, such as treaties of economic and trade cooperation or treaties forming binational enterprises.[14] The most important among other bilateral treaties pertaining to investment are bilateral treaties for the avoidance of double taxation.[15]

---

[12] A typical list of the issues in virtually all BITs include the following:
Preamble, scope of application, Admission of investment, promotion of investment, general Standards of treatment (Fair and equitable treatment, national Treatment, Most favored nation treatment), Standards of treatment with regard to specific issues (Dispossession of the investor, Losses due to armed conflict or internal disorder, Transfer of payments and repatriation of capital, operational conditions of investment, subrogation, settlement of disputes).

[13] Kenneth J. Vandevelde, *Investment Liberalization and Economic Development: The Role of Bilateral Investment Treaties*, 36 COLUM. J. TRANSNAT'L L. 501, 507-514 (1998).

[14] Jose Luis Siqueiros, *Bilateral Treaties on the Reciprocal Protection of Foreign Investment*, 24 CAL. W. INT'L L. J.255, 258 (1994).

[15] This dissertation will not cover double taxation treaties.

A. **The Provisions of BITs Pertaining to the Investment Security**

Most of the BITs have a number of provisions that provide security to foreign investment. BITs consist of substantive and procedural rules that secure foreign investment.[16]

1. Substantive Rules:

a. **Expropriation and Compensation Provision**

Almost all BITs have one uniform provision about expropriation. In this provision, each contracting party agrees not to take any measures, directly or indirectly, for expropriation or nationalization, or any other comparable measures affecting foreign investment made in its territory by nationals of the other contracting party.[17] First, there is broad agreement that the exercise of right should not be discriminatory and should have a basis in public purpose or be of national interest. Some treaties with European countries use the concept of "common good". Secondly, the measures must be imposed in accordance with procedures previously established in international law. Thirdly, the agreements are subject to payment of adequate and effective compensation. Some agreements require "prompt" payment. Others merely regulate that the payment be fair or appropriate.

---

[16] See *supra* note 13, at 507.

[17] Like many BITs signed between Turkey and other nations, Turkey-Netherlands BIT, Article 5 states that: "Neither Contracting party shall take any measures depriving, directly or indirectly, investors of the other Contracting Party of their investments unless the following conditions are complied with:
a) the measures are taken in the public interest and under due process of law
b) the measures are not discriminatory; ..." Agreement on Reciprocal Encouragement and Protection of Investments Between The Republic of Turkey and The Kingdom Of the Netherlands, Turkish Official Gazette, September 1989, at 7

b.   **Protection from Strife Provision**

Most treaties provide for compensation in the event of damage to the foreign investor as a result of war, civil unrest or other national emergency. According to the national treatment principle, if nationals of states get compensation from its losses from those events then the foreign investor also has the right to get compensation.

c.   **Non-discrimination Provision**

Most BITs contain provisions that each contracting party ensures that the investments and investment activities of the nationals and companies of the other party receive either national treatment or most favored nation treatment.[18]

d.   **Rules on currency transfers**[19]

d.1.   **General knowledge of the transfer of payments**

Currency transfer is an area where the interest of the host state and the foreign investor clash. Foreign investors regard the timely transfer of income from their investments as the key factor for the investment. On the other hand, balance of payment difficulties of many host countries can reduce the opportunity to provide free transfer of payments to the foreign investor.[20]

---

[18] For example Article 3 of the Turkey -United Kingdom BITs stated that: "1-Neither Contracting Party Shall in its territory subject investments or returns of nationals or companies of the other Contracting party to treatment less favourable than that which it accords to Investments or returns of its own nationals or companies or to investments or returns of nationals or companies of any third State.
2-Neither Contracting party shall in its territory subject nationals or companies of the other Contracting party, as regards the management, maintenance, use, enjoyment or disposal of their investments, to treatment less favourable than that which it accords to its own nationals or companies or to nationals or companies of any third State."(Agreement Between the United Kingdom and The Republic of Turkey For the Promotion and Protection of Investments, 1991, ICSID)

[19] See *supra* note 13, at 507.

[20] UNCTAD stated that "For host countries, including most developing countries, the sudden repatriation of large profits or the proceeds from sale or liquidation can have an adverse affect on their balance of payments, thereby hindering economic development and defeating the objective of the BIT. However, foreign investors regard the timely transfer of income, capital, and another payments as an indispensable

The rules on currency transfer are important provisions that provide investment security for foreign investor. The protection of the right to repatriate profits becomes an investment security provision of the treaties. Most BITs have a provision on the transfer of payments, but there are important differences among them.[21] Most agreements precisely provide the obligation of each contracting party to guarantee the free transfer of liquid assets in freely convertible currency without delay.[22] However treaties usually provide some exceptions of this rule. For example many of the British treaties guarantee that the free transfer of fund subjects to the right of the host government "in exceptional economic or financial circumstances to exercise equitably and in good faith power conferred by its laws."[23] Especially, if unforeseen circumstances arise, the rule will not apply. This is acceptable under the rule of *rebuc sic stantibus*. Therefore, apart from exceptions, transfer of funds provision provides secure environment for investors.

d.2 Exchange rate

Most BITs require that the transfer of currency must be affected in "freely convertible currency."[24] Some BITs stipulate that the currency should be the same as the

---

requirement to operate and benefit from their investment projects, and to meet their obligations visa-visa shareholders, contractors, creditors or licensors. " UNCTAD, BILATERAL INVESTMENT TREATIES IN THE MID-1990s, 75 (1998).

[21] *Id.*

[22] Bergman Mark S., *Bilateral Investment Protection Treaties: An Examination of the Evolution and Significance of the U.S. Prototype Treaty*, 16 N. Y.U. J. INT'L L & POL. 1, 10 (1983).

[23] See Agreement for the Promotion and Protection of Investments, July 22, 1975, Great Britain- Northern Ireland-Singapore, 1975 Gr. Brit. T.S. No. 151 (Cmnd. 6300) (Id. at 10).

[24] For example, Article 4 of the Turkey- Netherlands BITs stated that: " Each Contracting Party shall permit, to the extent permitted by and in conformity with its relevant laws and regulations, the transfer, without unreasonable restriction or delay, into its country or to the country of the other Contracting Party and in the currency of that country or in any freely convertible currency of payments resulting from investments and in particular of the following items:
a) Profits, dividends, capital gains and similar payments;

capital originally invested or any other convertible currency agreed to by the investor and the contracting party concerned.

The broadest applicable limitation on the right of countries to impose controls on currency exchanges is found in the Article of Agreement of the International Monetary Fund (IMF), (Article VIII (2)).[25] This limitation applies only to controls on currency exchanges for current, as opposed to capital, transactions.[26] Moreover, the majority of IMF member countries have reserved the right under this article. So, the IMF articles provide little protection for foreign investors. The developed countries continue to insist on the provision of the right of free transfer in BITs.

2. Procedural Rules (Dispute Settlement Process)

Like substantive rules, procedural rules provide security for investors. BITS contain provisions for settlement of disputes between the contracting parties and also between the host state and investor. Each agreement provides that the settlement of disputes between contracting parties be submitted to arbitration upon the request of either

---

b) the proceeds of sale or liquidation of all or any part of the investment;
c) principal and interest payments arising under a loan agreement;
d) management, technical assistance, personnel or other fees;
e) royalty payments.
(Agreement on Reciprocal Encouragement And Protection of Investments between The Republic of Turkey and the Kingdom of Netherlands, September 1989, Turkish Official Gazette, at 7)

[25] Articles of Agreement of the International Monetary Fund, Article VIII, Section 2 stated that: "*a*) Subject to the provisions of Article VII, Section 3(*b*) and Article XIV, Section 2, no member shall, without the approval of the Fund, impose restrictions on the making of payments and transfers for current international transactions.
(*b*) Exchange contracts which involve the currency of any member and which are contrary to the exchange control regulations of that member maintained or imposed consistently with this Agreement shall be unenforceable in the territories of any member. In addition, members may, by mutual accord, cooperate in measures for the purpose of making the exchange control regulations of either member more effective, provided that such measures and regulations are consistent with this Agreement."
(http://www.imf.org/external/pubs/ft/aa/aa08.htm#2) (visited 10/10/2001)

[26] UNCTAD, *supra* note 20, at 75.

party if the dispute cannot be settled through diplomatic channels.[27] The provision for settlement is often provided in two separate articles in the BITs. However, there is no uniformity with respect to dispute settlement provisions of the various BITs. Due to the fact that disputes are settled by different methods, it would be convenient to discuss them under separate title.

a. **Disputes between Contracting Parties**

Parties are required to try to settle the dispute amicably between them before instituting formal proceedings. If they fail to do so, their disputes are submitted at the request of either party to an ad hoc tribunal. The tribunal will be composed of two arbitrators, each appointed independently by each party, and third arbitrator, who is to be from a third country appointed by agreement of the parties or the party appointed arbitrators.[28] If the parties fail to reach an agreement for appointment of arbitrators, the President of the International Court of Justice is invited to make the necessary appointments.[29] Many BITs signed between Turkey and other countries show that dispute settlement provisions contain almost the same language and the same procedure.[30] So, there is uniformity with respect to this provision.

---

[27] See *supra* note 13, at 508.

[28] Article 7 of the Turkey-US BITs provides settlement disputes between contacting parties (Turkey-United States: Treaty Concerning the Reciprocal Encouragement and Protection of Investments, December 3, 1985, International Legal Materials, 25 I.L.M 85, at 96.).

[29] *Id.* Art 7.

[30] Turkey-United States: Treaty Concerning the Reciprocal Encouragement and Protection of Investments, December 3, 1985, International Legal Materials, 25 I.L.M 85, at 96, Article 7, Turkey- United Kingdom, Agreement for the Promotion and Protection of investments, 1991, ICSID, Article 9, Turkey-Tunisia, Agreement for Investment Promotion and Protection, 1991, ICSID, Article 8, Turkey-Romania, Agreement on the Reciprocal promotion and Protection of Investments, 1991, ICSID, Article 10, Agreement Between The Republic of Turkey and The Republic of Kazakhstan, 1995, Turkish Official Gazette, Number 22199, at 8, Article 8, Agreement on Reciprocal Encouragement And Protection of Investments Between The Republic of Turkey and The Kingdom of the Netherlands, 1989, Turkish Official Gazette, at 9, Article 10,

b. **Disputes between a Contracting Party and an Investor**

Many BITs include provisions to settle disputes between the host government and the investor by referring the dispute to an institution. Most of them refer cases to the International Centre for Settlement of Investment Disputes (ICSID).[31] However, there is a significant number which refer cases to arbitration under the rules of the United Nations Commission on International Trade Law (UNCITRAL) or the court of arbitration of the Paris International Chamber of Commerce.[32] It should be noted that many BITs also grant rights to parties to choose from among arbitral proceedings.[33] On the other hand, some agreements, like Turkey-United Kingdom BITs, stipulate that ICSID arbitration is the only acceptable dispute resolution mechanism.[34]

Agreement between the Republic of Turkey and the Swiss Confederation on the Reciprocal Promotion and Protection of Investments, 1989, Turkish Official Gazette, At 7, Article 9, Agreement Between The Republic of Turkey and the Kingdom of Spain on the Reciprocal Promotion and Protection of Investments, 1997, Turkish Official Gazette, at 29, Article 10.

[31] Turkey- United Kingdom, Agreement for the Promotion and Protection of investments, 1991, ICSID, Article 8 states that: "...(2) Each contacting party hereby consents to submit to the International Centre for the Settlement of Investment Disputes (hereinafter referred to as "the Centre") for settlement by arbitration under the Convention on the Settlement of Investment Disputes between States and Nationals of other States, opened for signature at Washington on 18 March 1965 any legal dispute arising between that Contacting party and national or company of the other Contracting party concerning an investment of the latter in the territory of the former......"

[32] Agreement Between The Republic of Turkey and the Kingdom of Spain on the Reciprocal Promotion and Protection of Investments, 1997, Turkish Official Gazette, at 29, Article 9 states that "... the dispute shall be submitted, as the investor may choose, to:
(a) the Court of arbitration of the Paris International Chamber of Commerce,
(b) an ad hoc court of arbitration laid down under the Arbitration Rules of Procedure of the united Nations Commission for International Trade Law (UNCITRAL),..."

[33] Such as, Agreement Between The Republic of Turkey and The Republic of Kazakhstan, 1995, Turkish Official Gazette, Number 22199, at 8, Article 8, Agreement Between The Republic of Turkey and the Kingdom of Spain on the Reciprocal Promotion and Protection of Investments, 1997, Turkish Official Gazette, at 29, Article 9.

[34] Turkey- United Kingdom, Agreement for the Promotion and Protection of investments, 1991, ICSID, Article 8.

According to the Turkey-Romania BIT, each party consents in advance to the submission of legal disputes to conciliation or arbitration under the ICSID convention, which gives direct access to individuals, and natural legal persons, in their claims against a State.[35] In the event of a dispute, the State and the company concerned may resolve the conflict through pursuit of local remedies. If no agreement is reached within three months, the complainant company may then consent in writing to submit itself to the jurisdiction of ICSID.[36] Unlike the Turkey-United Kingdom BIT, the Turkey-Romania agreement, stipulates that the exhaustion of local remedies is the first step to procedure dispute settlement. If the conflict cannot be resolved within twelve months, either party can transfer it to ICSID for settlement.[37] The problem of the ICSID is that there is no compulsory jurisdiction, so if the disagreement occurs, the powerful party has a right to make a decision which way they will follow.[38]

Overall, it is evident that most BITs refer to ICSID arbitration while others refer to the optional facility of the ICSID or to some ad hoc arbitration. The different provisions of the dispute settlement create security for the investor.

---

[35] Agreement Between Romania and The Republic of Turkey on the Reciprocal Promotion and Protection of Investments, ICSID, at 7-9, Article 6. (1991).

[36] *Id.* Article 6.

[37] Turkey- United Kingdom, Agreement for the Promotion and Protection of investments, 1991, ICSID, Article 8 stipulates ICSID procedure without mentioning local remedies. On the other hand, Agreement Between Romania and The Republic of Turkey on the Reciprocal Promotion and Protection of Investments, 1991, ICSID, at 7-9, Article 6 stated exhausted of local remedies.

[38] Turkey-US BIT contains in its Article 6 (1) a definition of an "investment Dispute" fully in line with the US model treaty.

B. The Provisions of BITs Pertaining to the Investment Neutrality

Most BITs comprise market access and non-discrimination provisions in order to promote "investment neutrality".[39] Firstly, BITs may contain provisions requiring each party to permit investors of the other party to establish investments in its territory and requiring each party to permit its own investors to establish investments in the territory of the other party. The aim of those provisions is to guarantee free movement of investment across borders.[40] Namely, those provisions would remove both investment and investor barriers. Secondly, a non-discrimination principle provides that foreign investment will receive national treatment and most favored nation treatment, in other words, the host state will not discriminate among investments based on the nationality of ownership.[41]

There are also exceptions that vitiate "investment neutrality". Non-discrimination principle will apply to the investor after the establishment of investment.[42] The host state has discretionary power to discriminate against or among foreign investors regarding to the establishment of investment within its territory, since the pre-establishment phrase is still under control of the host state. Furthermore, most BITs contain some exceptions to the National treatment and most favored nation treatment obligations. For example tax exemptions and regional economic integration agreement, such as customs union, and

---

[39] See *supra* note 13, at 510.

[40] *Id.*

[41] *Id.*

[42] *Id.* at 512.

free trade area, are the most important exceptions that undermine the non- discrimination provisions.[43]

The BITs provisions that provide protection to investment apply only to foreign investors.[44] Unfortunately, BITs do not protect domestic investors. However, foreign investors are getting more favorable treatment than domestic investors. For example, most BITs embodied dispute settlement provisions which is the main one for just foreign investors. Thus, this situation will attenuate investment neutrality.

C. **The Provisions of BITs Pertaining to the Market Facilitation**

BITs generally do not include provisions that provide "market facilitation".[45] Some BITs have provisions requiring the parties to promulgate their laws and regulations with respect to investment.[46] Moreover, some BITs embodied that parties have to create a mechanism for making investors aware of investment opportunities in the territory of the other party.[47] These are transparency provisions relating to the market facilitation. Unfortunately these transparency provisions are rare.

---

[43] For example Article 2 of the Turkey-Tunisia BITs states that: "....4- The Provisions of this Article shall have no effect in relation to following agreements entered into by either of the Contracting Parties: a) relating to any existing or future customs Unions, regional economic organization or similar international agreements. b) relating wholly, or mainly to taxation c) bilateral agreements for the purposes of facilitation cross-border trade." (Agreement Between The Republic of Tunisia and The Republic of Turkey Concerning The Reciprocal Promotion and Protection of Investments, 1991, ICSID, at 3.)

[44] See *supra* note 13, at 513.

[45] *Id.*

[46] For example Article 2 of the USA- Turkey BITs states: "...9- Each party shall make public all laws, regulations, administrative practices and procedures, and adjudicatory decisions that pertain to or affect investments."(Turkey-United States: Treaty Concerning The Reciprocal Encouragement and Protection of Investments, December 3, 1985, International Legal Materials, 91 Jan. (1986).

[47] See *supra* note 13, at 514.

IV. The Impact of BITS on Customary International Law

The question may arise as to what extent BITs can be considered as part of customary international law. This question is debated among legal scholars. There is no conformity among legal scholars with respect to the relationship between BITs and customary international law.

Some scholars argue that BITs are important treaties that establish strong customary international law on international investment. For example E. Denza and S. Brooks assert, "BITs give important support for those standards of customary international law which had seemed to be slipping away." Like these two British writers, F.A. Mann also claims "these treaties establish and accept and thus enlarge the force of traditional conceptions of the law of state responsibility for foreign investment."[48]

On the other hand, many legal scholars contend that BITs do not create a customary international law. For instance, Bernard Kishoiyian claims that: "each BIT is nothing but a *lex specialis* between parties designed to create a mutual regime of investment protection". In his point of view, a *lex specialis* is indispensable due to the uncertainty in the law on international investment. Like Kishoiyian, Professor Sornarajah argues that BITs are *lex specialis* as between the parties and they are likely to remain so. Both of these scholars analyze the most essential provisions of BITs in the formulation of customary international law.

In this debate, Oscar Schachter is the most popular proponent of the view that BITs should not be considered to create customary international law. He claims that: "the repetition of common clauses in bilateral treaties does not create or support an

---

[48] F.A. Mann, *British Treaties For the Promotion and Protection of Investment*, 52 Brit. Y. B. Int'l L. 241, 249 (1981).

inference that those clauses express customary law. Extradition and air transit treaties are notable examples of bilateral agreements with standard clauses that are widely used, yet it is not claimed that those provisions are either declaratory or constitutive of customary law binding on third states."[49] Similar views were reflected in the detailed studies of BITs by Migliorino. Migliorino reviewed approximately 250 BITs to point out relevant evidence of customary international law. He argues that BITs do not constitute sufficient evidence of principles of customary international law.[50] He concludes that state practice does not confirm any part of the substance of the treaty provisions to be a principle of customary international law.[51] According to these legal scholars, BITs are contractual agreements that result from negotiation between countries. In this contractual relationship, developing countries get benefits in exchange for agreeing to pay full compensation.

Unlike Schachter, Andrew Guzman asserts that BITs represent evidence of state practice. He explains it as follow: "Although one might ask if a single BIT is enough to demonstrate the practice of a state and argue that one must look to the actual practice of states rather than their obligations under treaties, for our purposes it is sufficient to simply assume that the general practice requirement is met."[52] Guzman elaborates the relationship between BITs and customary international law in terms of *opinio jurist* in his

---

[49] Oscar Schachter, *Compensation for Expropriation,* 78 AM.J. INT'L. L. 121, 126 (1984).

[50] Luigi Migliorino, *GLI Accordi Internazionali Sugli Investment,* Reviewed by Patrick Del Duca, and Detlev F. Vagts, 85 AM. J. INT'L. L. 240, 241 (1991).

[51] *Id.*

[52] Andrew Guzman, Explaining The Popularity of Bilateral Investment Treaties: Why LDCS Sign Treaties That Hurt Them, 26 August 1997, (visited 9/6/1999) (http://www.law.harvard.edu/Programs/JeanMonnet/papers/97/97-12-VII.html)

well-written and comprehensive article pertaining to BITs. He asserts that "the popularity of BITs should not be taken as evidence in support of customary international law. Indeed, it suggests that BITs have come about because developing countries successfully challenged the Hull standard. Once the standard of full compensation was undermined, developing states, as a group were better off."[53] He further claims that developing countries attain a competitive advantage against other countries by signing BITs.[54]

As a matter fact this view is completely true. If we look at many BITs, we can find out that many developing countries provide better protection of investment rules then the Hull Rule. The reason for signing BITs is to resolve economic problems. I strongly agree with Guzman's opinion that developing countries should sign these treaties so as to attain an advantage in the competition for investment. Therefore, they are not signing BITs because they have to provide these rules for international investment. Namely, they are not signing these treaties due to the fact that they have a sense of legal obligation (*opinio jurist*).

In the light of foregoing analysis of BITs as a possible tool for the formation of customary international law, I contend that BITs constitute *lex specialis*, establishing treaty rights and obligations for the parties. Although most BITs generally address the same topics in much the same provisions, there are also differences among them. Therefore, they do not constitute state practice and *opinio jurist*. For example, in the Asylum case, the I.C.J found that there is "so much uncertainty and contradiction, so

---

[53] *Id.*

[54] *Id.*

much fluctuation and discrepancy in the rapid conclusion of BITs, and the practice has been so much influenced by considerations of political expediency in the various cases, that is not easy to discern in all the treaties any constant and uniform usage, accepted as law regulating foreign investment."[55] One may also argue that the rejection of concluding multilateral investment treaty can be considered a rejection of *opinio jurist*.[56] As mentioned before, customary international law itself is the most problematic area of international law. Apart from this problem, there is another issue that should be mentioned. If BITs are considered as a part of customary international law, this means that developing countries have to comply with the principles laid down in BITs, regardless of whether they signed BITs or not. Furthermore, the recently published UNCTAD report also illustrates that developing countries accept foreign investment rules established by bilateral investment treaties as *lex specialis* between two contracting parties.[57]

Even though BITs may not be considered to create customary international law, they do have some impact since many BITs provisions reflect traditional principles of customary international law regarding the treatment of foreign investment. For example, provisions reflecting the right of states to control entry of foreign investors and their investments into their territories, the principle of fair and equitable treatment, and some of the legal requirements for expropriation of foreign investment are the main principles of customary international law set out in the BITs.

---

[55] Asylum (Colom. V. Peru), 1950 I.C.J. Rep. 266, at 277.

[56] Bergman, *supra* note 22, at 33.

[57] UNCTAD, *Bilateral investment treaties and their relevance to a possible multilateral framework on investment: issues and questions*, TD/B/COM.2/EM.1/2, 21 March 1997, at 11.

V. The Benefit of BITs to the World Community

As pointed out before, the network of BITs extended considerably during the first half of the 1990s, the number of such treaties having reached 1, 160 in June 1996.[58] Countries from all regions have concluded BITs. Many questions will be raised as to why many countries signed BITs and what roles they play in international investment law. Namely, "What are the benefits that they provide to the world community?" is the question that should be answered so as to define their significance in international investment law.

The goal of developing countries signing BITs is to attract foreign direct investment as a means of fostering economic growth and development. Capital importing countries sign BITs in an effort to attract foreign investment in the interest of development, by protecting it and thereby demonstrating their commitment to providing a favorable investment climate. On the other hand, the purpose of BITs for the developed countries is to obtain legal protection for investment under international law and so preclude non-commercial risks facing foreign investors in host countries. Most BITs do not specify which contracting party is the source of the investment or which is the recipient. Therefore, the promotion and protection of the investment is reciprocal.[59]

Little is known about how the influence of BITs on FDI inflows to the world community has contributed to the growth of FDI, since BITs are only one among several confidence-building measures that can be used to improve a host country's investment

---

[58] Two thirds of these BITs were concluded during the 1990s alone. The number of countries parties to these treaties has also increased in recent years, having reached 158 in June 1996.

[59] Siqueiros, *supra* note 14, at 271.

climate. For example, there is a close relationship between the significant growth of Peru's outward FDI since the mid- 1980s and the conclusion of BITs.[60] On the other hand, looking at the trend of investment authorizations according to the country of origin, it can be argued that BITs have no remarkable effect on the growth of FDI inflows to Turkey.[61] Overall, there is a lack detailed information on and analysis of the application of BITs.

It is asserted that signing BITs enhances the investor's confidence to make a decision to invest in a host country. But this may not be the only reason; for example, in spite of the fact that there are no BITs between the USA and China, major investments have been made by the United States in China.[62] Regarding efficiency of protection standards brought by BITs, there is very little practical experience to make an evaluation of the use of BITs. Overall, the analysis of the world community's experience with BITs reveals that BITs do not automatically produce an increase in FDI inflows. However these agreements are essential for inducing foreign firms at least to consider undertaking investments in a given country. Furthermore, BITs may not increase FDI flows, but they may support the existing level of investment or prevent it from decreasing.[63]

BITs have contributed to develop international investment law in two issues: the subject matter of international law, and the protection of shareholders. Even though

---

[60] WTO Report 1998 of the Working Group on the Relationship Between Trade and Investment to the General Council, WT/WGTI/2, 8 December 1998, Paragraph, 136.

[61] See Communication From Turkey, Working Group on the Relationship between Trade and Investment, WT/WGTI/W/51, 18 September 1998 (98-3573).

[62] Table of Countries/Territories that have concluded BITs, end 1996, shows that there is no BITS between China and USA., UNCTAD, *supra* note 20, at 11.

[63] UNCTAD, *supra* note 20, at 142.

international law does not formally recognize private firms as international subjects, it does, through BITs, allow states to bind themselves to agreements with such firms.[64] Furthermore, BITs create special regime for the protection of shareholders which do not have any protection in international law.[65]

The BITs do not prohibit States from enacting investment laws, but provide that any such laws should not interfere with any rights in the treaty. With regard to the interaction between BITs and national law, the BITs can affect national legislation. The countries enacted or amended to their national laws in order to make them consistent with the BITs. For example Professor Mutharika's analysis of this issue states that in 1993, Zambia revoked the 1991 code and enacted a new code that allows remittances similar to those provided in the Germany-Zambia BIT.[66]

The contents of BITs have played a role as a source of inspiration in negotiations of recent regional and multilateral agreements. For example, BITs were influential in the formulation of the World Bank Group Guidelines on the Treatment of Foreign Direct Investment, issued in September 1992 by the Joint Ministerial Development Committee of The World Bank and the IMF.[67] Moreover, the North American Free Trade Agreement Investment Chapter provisions provide much the same ground as BITs. BITs' contribution to the regional and multilateral instruments of investment is notable

---

[64] Lauterpacht, *supra* note 9, at 272.
[65] Bernard Kishoiyian, *The Utility of Bilateral Investment Treaties in the Formulation of Customary International Law*, 14 NW. J. INT'L & BUS. 327, 350 (1994).

[66] A. Peter Mutharika, *Creating an Attractive Investment Climate in the Common Market for Eastern and Southern Africa (COMESA) Region*, Foreign Investment Law Journal, ICSID Review, at 272. (1997).

[67] RUDOLF DOLZER & MARGETE STEVENS, BILATERAL INVESTMENT TREATIES (1995).

since there is no precise consensus in the world community regarding international law on foreign direct investment.[68]

There are also many investment issues that are generally not provided in BITs. According to the UNCTAD latest study regarding BITs enumerates these issues in the following: "

    1-Obligations regarding progressive liberalization;
    2-The treatment of foreign investment during privatization;
    3-Contol of restrictive business practice;
    4-Private management practices that restrain investment and trade;
    5-Consumer protection;
    6-Enviromental protection;
    7-Taxation of foreign affiliates;
    8-Avoidance of illicit payments;
    9-Protection against violations of intellectual property rights;
    10-Labour standards;
    11-Provisions concerning the transfer of technology;
    12-Specific commitments by home countries to promote investments;
    13-Social responsibilities of foreign investors in host countries;
    14-Obligations of subnational authorities."[69]

---

[68] *Id.* at Xiii.

[69] UNCTAD, *supra* note 20, at 138-139.

CHAPTER FOUR.

INTERNATIONAL ORGANIZATIONS AND INTERNATIONAL INVESTMENT

This chapter and following chapters will examine essential international organizations with respect to their law making and development functions on FDI. Apart from the treaty making power, international organizations make decisions and resolutions on FDI issues. It is really difficult to enumerate all international instruments regarding FDI since their legal status, their coverage and their effects are different. Thus, this study examines only the UN, OECD, MIGA, and WTO activities pertaining to FDI.

I. The United Nations and International Investment

A. General Knowledge

The United Nations has power to work on FDI issues. Thus, the UN has produced both binding and non-binding international instruments regarding FDI. Secretary General Kofi A. Annan states, "Only universal organizations like the United nations have the scope and legitimacy to generate principles, norms and rules that are essential if globalization is to benefit everyone."[1] We can observe from many world investment reports that trade and FDI are the central factors in the globalization. So, this statement clearly explains how UN activities are important on FDI issues.

One objective of the United Nations, as set out in its Charter, is to "achieve international cooperation in solving international problems of an economic and social

---

[1] Secretary- General Kofi A. Annan, 1998. Partnerships for Global community: Annual Report on the work of the Organization 1998 (New York: United Nations), P.81, (MARK W. ZACHER, THE UNITED NATIONS AND GLOBAL COMMERCE, UNITED NATIONS 10 (1999)).

character, and to be a center for harmonizing the actions of nations in the attainment of these common ends."[2] In order to achieve this objective, many UN organs are working on global commerce issues. In addition, Article 13 of the UN Charter is used as the basis for providing power to the General Assembly to study and make recommendations on FDI.[3]

The UN is composed of its main organs, the Security Council, the General Assembly, the Secretariat, the International Court of Justice, and its fourteen specialized agencies and its sub-bodies of the main organs.[4] The most important UN specialized agencies concerned with economic issues are the International Monetary Fund (IMF) and the World Bank Group. The World Trade Organization (WTO) is not formally specialized agency of the UN, but it is a de facto UN specialized agency because it participates in some studies with the agencies.[5]

The most important UN bodies on FDI issues are the General Assembly, the UN Commission on International Trade Law (UNCITRAL) and UN Conference on Trade and Development (UNCTAD).[6] UNCITRAL was established in 1967 in order to

---

[2] UN. CHARTER, art. 1, 3.

[3] Article 13 of the UN Charters states that: "The General Assembly shall initiate studies and make recommendations for the purpose of: a-promoting international cooperation in the political field and encouraging the progressive development of international law and its codification; b-promoting international cooperation in the economic cooperation in the economic, social, cultural, educational, and health fields, and assisting in the realization of human rights and fundamental freedoms for all without distinction as to race, sex, language, or religion."

[4] Article 7 of the UN Charter states that: "1-There are established as the principal organs of the United nations: a General Assembly, a Security Council, an Economic and Social Council, a Trusteeship Council, an International Court of Justice, and a Secretariat. 2- such subsidiary organs as may be found necessary may be established in accordance with the present Charter."

[5] ZACHER *supra* note 1, at 12.

[6] The UN homepage (www.un.org).

harmonize international trade law.[7] UNCITRAL has been working on international trade issues since its establishment.[8] In FDI issues, UNCITRAL works on international dispute settlement systems have to be taken into account. UNCITRAL has become a major impetus in the promotion of arbitration and conciliation of international commercial disputes.[9] It supervises and promotes the 1958 Convention on the Recognition and Enforcement of Foreign Arbitral Awards, the substantial treaty signed on international dispute settlement system. Furthermore, it creates UNCITRAL Arbitral Rules that have been utilized by world community through BITs.

B. The UN Work on Transnational Corporations

Even though this dissertation will not precisely focus on transnational corporations and their contribution to development, it is important to note that the activities of transnational corporations have to be regulated in international investment law. Professor Peter Muchlinski analyzed the reasons to regulate transnational corporations as follows:

> The global organization, size and technological superiority of TNCs could threaten the sovereignty of the host State through the ability of the TNC to evade national regulation and taxation, to abuse its competitive power by distorting

---

[7] Before the establishment of the UNCITRAL, International Institute for the Unification of Private Law or UNIDROIT, the Hague Conference on Private International law, and the Council for Mutual Economic Assistance in Moscow are three intergovernmental organizations have worked to unify international law. Furthermore, International Chamber of Commerce (ICC), non-governmental agency, has still quite effect on global commerce issues. For example, ICC reviewed bilateral investment treaties in 1979.

[8] The UN Sales Convention of 1980 and 1967 UN Convention on the Carriage of Goods by Sea are the most valuable work done by UNCITRAL.

[9] Gerald R. Aksen, *Legal Principles and Practices Relating to Private Foreign Investment*, Reporter, Matthew P. Jaffe, 77 American Society of International Law Proceedings. 292, 209 (1983).

market conditions, and to exploit the lack of technological know-how of the host where the latter needed modern technology to ensure the growth of its economy.[10]

Transnational corporations should comply with the rules relating with the exercise of sovereignty by states. It is well-recognized customary international law that states have the right to regulate economic activities within their territories in accordance with their national objectives.

The work at the UN on FDI and transnational corporations started on July 2, 1972 with the adoption of ECONSOC Resolution 1721 (LIII).[11] The Resolution requested the Secretary General to establish a "group of eminent persons…to study the role of multinational corporations and their impact on the process of development, especially that of the developing countries."[12] The General Assembly and the Group of Eminent Persons urged the creation of the Commission and the Centre on Transnational Corporations as a subsidiary body of the Economic and Social Council.[13] ECONSOC established the Commission and the Centre on Transnational Corporations by its Resolution 1913(LVII) in December 5, 1974.[14] The Commission and the Centre had the following objectives:

---

[10] Peter T. Muchlinski, *Attempts to Extend the Accountability of Transnational Corporations: The Role of UNCTAD*, in LIABILITY OF MULTINATIONAL CORPORATIONS UNDER INTERNATIONAL LAW 99-100 (Menno T. Kamminga & Saman Zia Zarifi eds., 2000).

[11] KENNETH R. SIMMONDS, LEGAL PROBLEMS OF MULTINATIONAL CORPORATIONS 43 (1977).

[12] SIDNEY DELL, THE UNITED NATIONS AND INTERNATIONAL BUSINESS 63 (1990).

[13] United Nations Conference on Trade and Development, *Bilateral Investment Treaties and their relevance to a possible multilateral framework on investment: issues and questions*, TD/B/COM.2/EM.1/2, 21 March 1997, at 8.

[14] UNCTC CURRENT STUDIES, THE UNITED NATIONS CODE OF CONDUCT ON TRANSNATIONAL CORPORATIONS 6 (1988).

To enhance the understanding of the nature and the impact of [transnational corporations] activities in political, social and economic spheres of the international and domestic relations of home and host countries, developed and developing;

To obtain effective international arrangements for {transnational corporations} operations which promote their contribution to national goals while minimizing their costs:

To strengthen negotiating capacity of host governments (especially of developing nations) in their dealings with multinational firms.[15]

The United Nation Centre on Transnational Corporations carried out this program from December 5 1974 to the 1992. In 1992, the name was changed to Transnational Corporations and Management Division of the United Nations Department of Economic and Social Development. In 1993, UNCTAD created the Division on Transnational Corporations and Investment to continue to work on the same issues.[16]

The drafting of the United Nations Code of Conduct on Transnational Corporations was one of the main tasks of the Commission.[17] The Commission drafted the Code of Conduct to regulate the behavior of transnational corporations. For example

---

[15] THOMAS L. BREWER & STEPHEN YOUNG, MULTILATERAL INVESTMENT SYSTEM AND MULTINATIONAL ENTERPRISES 87 (1998).

[16] UNCTAD, WORLD INVESTMENT REPORT (1995).

[17] The history of the negotiation of the Code of Conduct can be explained as follows "The preparation of the text of the Draft Code was entrusted first to an Ad Hoc Inter-Governmental Working Group. The Group submitted its report to the Commission at its eight session in 1982 (United Nations document E/C.10/1982/6). The next stage of the negotiations was entrusted to a special session of the Commission on Transnational Corporations which began deliberations in 1983 and was open to the participation of all States. The special session was reconvened a number of times between 1983 and 1990. In 1988, the Chairman of the reconvened special session and the Secretary-General of the United Nations prepared a text of a draft code (E/1988/39/Add.1), drawing upon discussions and proposals presented over the years. In an effort to facilitate compromise while preserving the already agreed texts, the Chairman, at the meeting on 24 May 1990, transmitted to the Economic and Social Council a revised text of the draft code of conduct, based on the 1988 draft. The text of the draft Code of Conduct on Transnational Corporations reproduced in this volume reflects the status of negotiations as at 1986." (visited 05/18/2002) http://www.attac.org/fra/libe/doc/unctad.html

the Code of Conduct prohibits corruption and encourages environmental protection.[18] One may argue that the Code has no legal effect since it remains incomplete and not approved by UN organs. On the other hand, one may also rightly argue that the Code of Conduct could be regarded as "writings" under Article 38 of the I.C.J Statute, since many prominent international legal scholars have participated in negotiations on the Code of Conduct and they have submitted legal papers in the negotiating process.

Although the negotiations towards a draft Code of Conduct for Transnational Corporations were discontinued, the UN has been still working on transnational corporations. This work is generally on technical issues and voluntary basis.[19] In addition, there were also negotiations within the UNCTAD to create a Restrictive Business Practices Code. However, those negotiations also were not completed.[20] Recently, the principal center of activity on FDI issues related to transnational corporations within the UN is the UNCTAD Division on Investment Technology and Enterprise Development (DITE).[21] DITE continues the extensive research and publishing program on FDI.[22] The programme contributes better knowledge concerning FDI to any

---

[18] General Assembly, *Code of conduct on transnational corporations*, A/RES/45/186. General Assembly, 71st plenary meeting 21 December 1990.

[19] Thomas L. Brewer, *International Investment Dispute Settlement Procedures: The Evolving Regime for Foreign Direct Investment*, 26 LAW & POL'Y INT'L BUS. 633, 650 (1995).

[20] *Id.*

[21] Peter T. Muchlinski elucidates, "A new Division on Transnational Corporations and Investment (DTCI) was established. This has since been re-named the Division on Investment Technology and Enterprise Development (DITE). In the meantime, the UN Commission on TNC was wound up and replaced by the Commission on Investment Technology and Related Financial Issues (the "Commission") which reports to the Trade and Investment Board of UNCTAD as the body supervising the development of the UN TNCs programme." Muchlinksi, *supra* note 10, at 97.

[22] UNCTAD, *supra* note 16.

negotiations with UNCTAD experience on FDI related issues.[23] Thus, before beginning any negotiations at bilateral, regional or multilateral level, the participant countries or groups can get significant information regarding legal and economic aspects of FDI.

It is worthwhile to emphasize an initiative on transnational corporations called the Global Compact, proposed by Kofi Annan, UN Secretary-General, at the 1999 World Economic Forum in Davos.[24] The Compact comprises nine principles in the areas of human rights, labor and environment, and recommends transnational corporations to follow them.[25] These principles are derived from the Universal Declaration of Human Rights, the Rio Declaration of the United Nations Conference of Environment and Development held in 1992, and the ILO's Fundamental Principles on Rights at work.[26]

Many corporations have participated in the global compact by sending a letter to the Secretary-General and by issuing public statements. The effectiveness of the compact

---

[23] Muchlinksi, *supra* note 10, at 104-105.

[24] George Kell and John Gerard Ruggie, *Global Markets and Social Legitimacy: The Case for the "Global Compact"*, Transnational Corporations, 103 (1999).

[25] The followings are the nine principles of the Global Compact: "
Human Rights, The Secretary General asked world business to:
Principle 1: support and respect the protection of international human rights within their sphere of influence; and
Principle 2: make sure their own corporations are not complicit in human rights abuses.
Labour, The Secretary-General asked world business to uphold:
Principle 3: freedom of association and the effective recognition of the right to collective bargaining;
Principle 4: the elimination of all forms of forced and compulsory labour;
Principle 5: the effective abolition of child labour; and
Principle 6: the elimination of discrimination in respect of employment and occupation.
Environment, The Secretary-General asked world business to:
Principle 7: support a precautionary approach to environmental challenges;
Principle 8: undertake initiatives to promote greater environmental responsibility; and
Principle 9: encourage the development and diffusion of environmentally friendly technologies."
The UN GLOBAL COMPACT, The Nine Principles,
http://www.unglobalcompact.org/un/gc/unweb.nsf/content/thenine.htm (visited 05/18/2002)

[26] Ambassador Betty King, *The UN Global Compact: Responsibility For Human Rights, Labor Relations, And the Environment in Developing Nations*, 34 CORNELL INT'L L. J. 481,482 (2001).

can be criticized since it is not a legally binding instrument.[27] However, it can be considered as a soft law since it is a voluntary initiative.

C. The Resolutions and Recommendations of the UN Dealing with FDI

The UN General Assembly (G.A.) has adopted various resolutions and recommendations on FDI. Even though article 38 of the Statute of the International Court of Justice does not list G.A. resolutions as a source of international law, G.A resolutions are frequently used as evidence of customary international law.[28] The ICJ spells out the legal status of G.A Resolutions as follows:

> The court notes that General Assembly resolutions, even if they are not binding, may sometimes have normative value. They can, in certain circumstances, provide evidence important for establishing the existence of a rule or the emergence of an opinio juris. To establish whether this is true of a given General Assembly resolution, it is necessary to look at its content and the conditions of its adoption; it is also necessary to see whether an opinio juris exists as to its normative character. Or a series of resolutions may show the gradual evolution of the opinio juris required for the establishment of a new rule.[29]

Most G.A. resolutions on FDI deal with expropriation of foreign investment. The G.A. resolutions state differing views regarding the amounts and types of compensation.[30] For example G.A. Resolution 1803, states that host nations shall pay

---

[27] "The Global Compact is not a regulatory instrument, a legally binding code of conduct or a forum for policing management policies and practices. Nor is it a "safe-harbour" allowing companies to sign-on without demonstrating real involvement and results. The Compact is a voluntary initiative that seeks to provide a global framework to promote sustainable growth and good citizenship through committed and creative corporate leadership." *The Global Compact, Corporate Leadership in the World Economy*, www.unglobalcompact.org (visited 05/30/2002).

[28] MARK W. JANIS, AN INTRODUCTION TO INTERNATIONAL LAW 50 (1993).

[29] Advisory opinion on Legality of the threat or use of nuclear weapons, ICJ Reports 1996, at Paragraph 70.

[30] Eduardo A. Wiesner, *ANCOM: A new Attitude Toward Foreign Investment?*, 24 U. MIAMI INTER-AM. L. REV. 435, 444 (1993).

investors appropriate compensation in accordance with the host state's law and international law.[31] However, G.A Resolution 3281 states a standard of appropriate compensation in accordance with only host state's law.[32]

Even though the G.A seeks to encourage the progressive development of international investment law, the role of the G.A resolutions and recommendations in establishing custom is controversial.[33] The resolutions are useful as evidence since the votes of the UN members may show a consensus on a particular issue. As evaluated in the second chapter, in the Texaco-Libya arbitration case, Professor Dupuy rejected three 1974 UN resolutions because of the opposition of Western countries and relied on 1963 UN resolution when the majority represented a wide array of developed and developing countries. This shows how difficult is to accept the UN resolutions as a customary international law.

In the Nicaragua Case, the ICJ pointed out that UN resolutions might constitute opinio juris and thus go towards the establishment of customary international law.[34] Even if other legal scholars may not accept that UN resolutions can be utilized as evidence of customary international law, the resolutions and recommendations of G.A may be regarded as a forum of soft international law[35], that is to say that rules which are neither strictly binding nor completely void of any legal significance.[36]

---

[31] *Id.*

[32] *Id.*

[33] JANIS, *supra* note 28, at 50.

[34] V.D. DEGAN, SOURCES OF INTERNATIONAL LAW 194-195 (1997); TIM HILLIER, PRINCIPLES OF PUBLIC INTERNATIONAL LAW 42 (1999).

[35] A.A.Fatouros, *Towards an International Agreement on Foreign Direct Investment?*, ICSID REVIEW, 190 (1995).

D. UNCTAD and International Investment

1. General Knowledge

UNCTAD has very special responsibility to assist developing countries in the area of international investment agreements. The first aim of UNCTAD's work on international investment agreements is to enhance the understanding of the major issues and concepts involved on FDI.[37] The second aim is to show the development dimension of FDI to the developing countries.[38]

UNCTAD, according to its mandate, has been pursuing a number of activities relating to international investment agreements. In order to carry out its aims, UNCTAD has organized seminars, negotiation forums and working groups on multinational investment agreement. Its work programme aims at helping developing countries to participate as effectively as possible in discussions on international investment arrangements.[39] International deliberations in various forums have given a new momentum to the involvement of developing countries in discussions on the FDI.[40]

---

[36] JANIS, *supra* note 28, at 51

[37] Pedro Roffe, Inter-Regional Advisor, UNCTAD, Opening Speech, at the Regional Symposium Arab Countries: The Government of Egypt, the United Nations Conference on Trade and Development and the Inter Arab Investment Guarantee Corporation with the Participation of the League of Arab States: *International Investment Agreements and Their Implications for Arab Countries*, 17-18 May 1999

[38] *Id.*

[39] Rubens Ricupero, Secretary- General of UNCTAD, Opening, Geneva, 17 May 1999.

[40] Regional Symposiums are financially supported by UNCTAD's trust fund on a possible multilateral framework on investment to which the European Commission, France, the Netherlands, Norway, Switzerland and the United Kingdom have contributed., UNCTAD, Developing Countries to Discuss Regional Impact of International Investment Agreements, 2 December 1999, at 31.

2. **Hosting Bilateral Investment Treaty Negotiations**

Recent way of achieving those aims is hosting bilateral investment treaty negotiations. UNCTAD provides organizational meetings for developing countries to sign BITs among themselves. In other words, UNCTAD brings developing countries together to negotiate BITs. This is a new programme launched on January 7 1999.[41] UNCTAD launched this programme so as to help members of the Group of Fifteen (G-15) developing countries strengthen investment cooperation among themselves.[42] According to UN News Release: apart from chief negotiators of G-15, the G-15 Technical Support Facility, the United Nations Development Programme (UNDP), Special Unit for Technical Cooperation among Developing Countries (TCDC) and the UNCTAD secretariat joined the meeting on BITs between G-15.[43]

Seven G-15 countries participated in this new programme and negotiated eight BITs among themselves. It was financially supported by the Technical Cooperation among Developing Countries (TCDC) Unit of UNDP and the Government of Switzerland.[44] In this programme, seven countries had very intensive discussions with respect to BITs provisions such as the definition of FDI and scope of the agreements, standards of treatment and dispute settlement provisions. At the end of the programme, three BITs were negotiated between India and Zimbabwe; Sri Lanka and Zimbabwe, and

---

[41] UN Press Release, TAD/1864, 8 January 1999. This program derives from the Seventh Summit Meeting of Group of Fifteen (G-15) heads of State and government in Kuala Lumpur, Malaysia, in November 1997. In this meeting, they decided to improve South-to-South cooperation over FDI and promote FDI flows among developing countries.

[42] Total Outward FDI stock of G-15 Countries grew at annual average rate of 17 per cent between 1995-1996, and was estimated at $44 billion in 1996. Despite this constant increase, FDI flows between G-15 countries have been relatively limited, and there is considerable scope for enhancement.

[43] *Id*. UN Press Release, TAD/1864, 8 January 1999.

[44] UNCTAD Home Page, www.unctad.org (visited 1/20/2000).

Egypt and Jamaica.[45] At the end of the meeting, the Deputy Secretary- General of UNCTAD, Mr.Carlos Fortin stated that, "We are pleased that this effort has yielded concrete results that further the interests of developing countries."[46] Overall, the seven participating countries will have a BIT with every other participating country if all BITs signed and ratified by their government.

I think the programme of hosting BITs negotiations between developing countries should continue since the BITs are one of the international investment law sources.[47] This provides the possibility of exchanging information among developing countries and benefiting from the advice of experts from UNCTAD. Thus, it helps to further the negotiating capacity of the participating countries involved in respect to the negotiation of any international investment agreements, including at the multilateral level.[48] Moreover, this program shows developing countries' commitment to provide a transparent, predictable and stable legal environment for FDI.

3. UNCTAD Works on Possible Multilateral Investment Treaty

The dramatic increase of FDI in recent years and the central role that transnational corporations play in globalization are the driving force of the multilateral investment rule-making in various international organizations. UNCTAD's work on a possible

---

[45] *Id.*

[46] UN Press Release, TAD/INF/2787/, 14 January 1999.

[47] Ambassador Anthony Hill of Jamaica, Chairperson of the G-15 Personal Representatives stated that: "The conclusion of BITs will facilitate FDI between member countries of the G-15, in the mutual interest of promoting our development.", UN Press Release, TAD/1864, 8 January, 1999.

[48] Pursuant to UNCTAD's Secretary General, Rubens Ricupero: "one of the main attractions of this format for negotiating BITs is that it gives developing countries the opportunity to share negotiating experiences. If successful, this type of exercise can be replicated and involve more developing countries." UN Press Release, TAD/1864, 8 January 1999.

multilateral investment treaty stems from the Midrand Conference of UNCTAD IX. Paragraph 89(b) of the Midrand Document states that "identifying and analyzing implications for development of issues relevant to a possible multilateral framework on investment, beginning with an examination and review of existing agreements, taking into account the interests of developing countries and bearing in mind the work undertaken by other organizations."[49] This conference urges UNCTAD to provide a forum for international dialogue on FDI issues. UNCTAD underscores that any negotiations on international agreements on investment should include the full and effective participation of all countries.[50]

The main purpose of UNCTAD's work in this area is to help developing countries and economies in transition to participate as effectively as possible in international discussions on investment rule-making. In order to do that, UNCTAD analyses implications for development of FDI issues relevant to a multilateral investment agreement. It examines and reviews existing agreements so as to supply necessary legal information that needs to be considered in international investment rule making.

The main forum for UNCTAD's to facilitate intergovernmental debate on issues related to investment is the Commission on Investment, Technology and Related Financial Issues, one of the subsidiary bodies of the Trade and Development Board. The Commission draws on the findings of expert meetings that serve as a forum for the exchange of experiences and debate on existing agreements and their implications for

---

[49] UNCTAD Midrand Declaration and a Partnership for Growth and Development, adopted by the UNCTAD at its ninth session, Midrand 27 April 1996, TD/377, 24 May (1996), Paragraph 23-24.

[50] For example Association of Southeast Asian Nations (ASEAN), said that a multilateral investment agreement should first be thoroughly studied by the UNCTAD and only then addressed by the WTO, UN Press Release, GA/EF/2748, 7 November 1996.

development. Especially, the meetings address the nature and implications of these agreements, the range of issues addressed by them, the extent to which issues arising in the context of these agreements are relevant, from a development perspective. The Commission on Investment, Technology and Related Financial Issues decided, during its November 1996, January 1997 meeting, to convene three expert group meeting in 1997. These three meetings are:

1-) a meeting on competition law and policy, as called for in the report of the Expert Meeting on Competition Law and Policy

2-) a meeting to examine and review existing agreements on investment, taking into account the interests of developing countries, and bearing in mind the work undertaken by other organizations, in pursuance of the mandate of paragraph 89(b) of "A partnership for Growth and Development" to identify and analyze implications for development of issues relevant to a possible multilateral investment agreement

3-) a meeting on investment promotion and suggested measures in this respect that further development objectives.[51]

The first expert meeting held on 28-30 May 1997, dealt with BITs, their development dimension and implications for a possible multilateral investment agreement.[52] The second meeting took place on 1-3 April 1998 and focused on regional

---

[51] A Statement made by the Observer from UNCTAD at the meeting of the Committee on Trade-Related Investment Measures on 17 March 1997, World Trade G/TRIMS/W/8, 14 April 1997, 97-1527.

[52] UNCTAD, Trade and Development Board Commission on Investment, Technology and Related Financial Issues, Expert Meeting on Existing Agreements on Investment and Their Development Dimensions, Geneva, 28-30 May 1997, Bilateral Investment Treaties and their relevance to a possible multilateral framework on investment: issues and questions, TD/B/COM.2/EM.1/2, 21 March 1997.

and multilateral investment agreements.[53] The aim of both expert meetings was to examine and review existing agreements on investment and their social and economic development. The Commission on Investment, Technology and Related Financial Issues at its third meetings from 14 to 18 September 1998 examined issues related to the development dimension of international investment agreements.[54] Furthermore, the main issue for expert meeting held from 24 to 26 March 1999, was the determination of the features of international investment agreements that provide for flexibility in these agreements in the interest of development.[55] Overall, these meetings can contribute to a better understanding of the development implications of international investment agreements and the need for multilateral investment agreement. After these meetings, the Secretariat of UNCTAD has prepared and published series of issues papers concerning FDI.

UNCTAD has been working together with WTO with respect to FDI. The WTO, at its first Ministerial conference held in Singapore in December 1996, agreed to establish a working group to examine the relationship between trade and investment. This group was requested to join work with UNCTAD. UNCTAD has special observer status in the WTO working group on the relationship between trade and investment, as well as the

---

[53] UNCTAD Trade and Development Board Commission on Investment, Technology and Related Financial Issues, Expert Meeting on Existing Agreements on Investment and Their Development Dimensions, Held at the Palais des Nations, Geneva, from 1 to 3 April 1998, TD/B/COM.2/11, TD//B/COM.2/EM.3/3, 22 April 1998.

[54] UNCTAD, Trade and Development Board Commission on Investment, Technology and Related Financial Issues, Report of the Commission on Investment, Technology and Related Financial Issues on its third Session, held at the Palais des Nations, Geneva, from 14 to 18 September 1998, TD/B/45/9, Td/B/COM.2/15, 26 October 1998.

[55] Trade and Development Board Commission on Investment, Technology and Related Financial Issues, Expert Meeting on International Investment Agreements, Geneva, 24-26 March 1999, TD/B/COM.2/Em.5.L.1).

WTO working group on the interaction between trade and competition policy. UNCTAD contributed to the discussions of the Working group with the submission of some documents pertaining to FDI.[56]

In order to achieve its aims, UNCTAD prepares and publishes technical papers with respect to international investment agreements, such as "foreign direct investment and development", "scope and definition", "admission and establishment" and "investment- related trade measures".[57] Rubens Ricupero, Secretary-General of UNCTAD, pointed out that the topics selected for the publication were among the core issues affecting international investment agreements. "They will fill the evident need for greater information and transparency, as well as proper economic and legal analysis, of these subjects."[58] Indeed, the main aim of the UNCTAD series on issues in international investment agreement is to address key concepts and issues pertaining to international investment agreements and to present them to the world community.

UNCTAD has organized seminars, and regional symposiums. The first regional symposium took place in Morocco, for African countries in June 1997.[59] After that, the UNCTAD organized symposiums in Asia, Latin America and the Caribbean, Eastern

---

[56] UNCTAD prepared a document on "Transnational Corporations, Foreign Direct Investment And Development".

[57] According to UNCTAD publication services, a series of publications on issues in international investment agreements, designed to address key concepts and issues relevant to international agreements. The new publications are the following: Foreign Direct Investment and Development, Transfer Pricing, Scope and Definition, Admission and Establishment, Most Favoured Nation Treatment, Fair and Equitable Treatment, Investment-Related Trade Measures, National Treatment. <www.unctad.org> (visited 11/27/1999).

[58] UNCTAD Press Release, Educating Policymakers on International Investment Issues: A New Tool From UNCTAD, TAD/INF/2793, 18 February 1999.

[59] UNCTAD, Regional Symposiums, (www.unctad.org).

Europe and Central Asia from 1998 to 2000.[60] Regional symposiums are intended to familiarize government officials from that region with existing investment arrangements, especially the understanding of major issues and concepts in face of future international negotiations is the main purpose of these regional symposiums. Furthermore, these symposiums will continue to provide an opportunity for policy makers from the region to reflect on FDI issues in informal settings. The symposiums also provide an opportunity for interested groups from civil society to discuss issues related to international investment.[61] The UNCTAD also offers training courses on FDI for governmental officials in order to give the participants significant knowledge about FDI.[62]

I think that UNCTAD's work on multilateral investment agreement is more constructive than the work of other international organizations, because UNCTAD's work does not just take into account the interests of developed countries, but also takes into account the interests of developing countries. For example as mentioned before, UNCTAD has organized seminars and symposiums in developing countries in order to provide their participation in discussion on FDI issues. At these seminars, developed countries, policy-makers and participants will draw lessons that will be helpful for future negations on FDI since developing countries have reflected their views on FDI issues in an informal setting.

---

[60] *Id.*

[61] For example, Over 300 government officials, business executives, non-governmental organizations, trade union representatives, academics and other civil society representatives participated in the one day Global Investment Forum on FDI and Development organized by the UNCTAD on 10 October 1996, UN Press Release, TAD/1837, 16 October 1996.

[62] More knowledge regarding Training courses will be found in the UNCTAD home page.

E.   **United Nations Regional Economic Commissions**

The UN established the regional commissions in order to enhance its role in the economic and social areas.[63] It should be noted that even though all the regional commissions' priorities have specific differences due to the their respective regions' conditions and needs, this study analyzes them generally. There are five regional economic commissions within the United Nations system:

1-Economic Commission for Europe (UNECE)

2-Economic and Social Commission for Asia and the Pacific (UNESCAP)

3-Economic Commission for Latin America and the Caribbean (UNECLAC)

4-Economic Commission for Africa (UNECA)

5-Economic and Social Commission for Western Asia (UNESCWA)[64]

The regional commissions play an important role in implementing and creating economic and social policies of the UN at the regional level. It should be noted that the regional commissions' activities are very broad, including among others sustainable

---

[63] Parley W. Newman, Jr, *Regionalism in Developing Areas: United Nations Regional Economic Commissions and Their Relations With Regional Organizations, in* REGIONALISM AND THE UNITED NATIONS 339-341(Berhanykun Andemicael ed., 1979).

[64] The Economic Commission for Europe (UNECE) was established in 1947. It is the forum for countries of North America, western, central and Eastern Europe, and central Asia to come together to promote economic cooperation. See more information at http://www.unece.org (visited 05/20/2002),
The Economic and Social Commission for Asia and the Pacific (ESCAP) was established in 1947 and is the main organization for United Nations activities in the Asian and Pacific region. Located in Bangkok, ESCAP is the largest of the five UN Regional Commissions, comprising 51 members and 9 associated members and representing some 60 per cent of the world's population, or 3.5 billion people. See more information at http://www.unescap.org (visited 05/20/2002),
The Economic Commission for Latin America and the Caribbean (ECLAC) was established in 1948 and is located in Santiago, Chile. See more information at http://www.eclac.cl/default.asp?idioma=IN (visited 05/20/2002),
The United Nations Economic Commission for Africa (ECA) was established in 1958 and is located in Ethiopia. Its member states include 53 African nations, represented by their ministers of finance and planning. See more information at http://www.uneca.org (visited 05/20/2002),
The Economic and Social Commission for Western Asia (ESCWA) was established in 1973 and is located in Lebanon. See more information at http://www.escwa.org.lb/ (visited 05/20/2002).

environment development, social development, macro economic policies, and water resources management. The ECOSOC states firmly the role of regional commissions in the following:

> As part of the United Nations, the regional commissions are well placed to facilitate the promotion and implementation, both regionally and, through appropriate backstopping, at the national level, of global commitments within the United Nations framework. As part of their respective regions, the commissions enable member countries to bring their perspective to global forums, and allow each and every country to participate on an equal footing in the discussions and decision-making process. Further, the commissions offer neutral forums in which policy debates can take place, drawing on multisectoral analysis focused on the specific situations and needs of their respective regions.[65]

The regional commissions' aim is to promote economic development and to bring about a better understanding on foreign trade and investment policies in their respective regions.[66] The regional commissions offer various services in order to co-ordinate and implement the work on trade and investment promotion. They have special sub-bodies that deal with trade and investment. For example, the UNESCAP has a sub-body called "Trade Promotion and Facilitation Section", whose aim is to "develop trade and investment information services network."[67] The UNECA also has a sub-program to enhance domestic and FDI and liberalize trade.[68]

One may assert that the regional commissions have the following functions to carry out their objectives:

---

[65] UN Economic and Social Council, Regional Cooperation, Regional Cooperation in the economic, social and related fields, Report of the Secretary General, Substantive session of 1997, 16 May 1997, E/1997/40.

[66] Parley W. Newman spell outs " In a practical sense the economic commissions represent a regionalization of ECOSOC's activities." NEWMAN, *supra* note 53, at 348.

[67] International Trade and Industry Division, www.unescao.org/itid/TRPROM.HTM (visited 05/20/2002).

[68] ECA Programmes, Regional Cooperation and Integration Division, www.uneca.org/rcid/index.htm (visited 05/20/2002).

a) to provide advisory services and technical assistance in the preparation of development programs to member states;

b) to undertake studies and surveys that provide information and policy guidelines for regional development;

c) to serve as a link between regional organizations and the United Nations;

d) to propose policies directly to member states and regional and multinational organizations;

e) to seek ways to include non-governmental organizations (NGOs) in their intergovernmental machinery.[69]

They provide advisory services to review and discuss economic and social issues. The regional commissions carry out studies and programs in collaboration with the governments of the region. In addition, the regional commissions have organized conferences, intergovernmental meetings, and seminars in order to provide a forum for debate within the regions of their economic and social development. In these arrangements, member states and civil society groups have discussed the changes that need to be introduced in FDI policies. For example, the ESCWA held a Regional Seminar on "Foreign Direct Investment (FDI) National Strategies and Policies in the ESCWA Region", on 12-13 June 2001 at the Beirut.[70]

Many international agreements have been negotiated under the auspices of the regional commissions. For example 1961 European Convention on International

---

[69] Regional Economic Commissions, www.surfsouthasia.org/RelPrg/RegEcon/regecon.shtm (visited 05/20/2002), and Homepages of five regional commissions.

[70] Activities of the Regional Commissions, Economic and Social Commission for Western Asia (ESCWA), Regional Commissions Development Update, Eleventh Issue, November 2001, http://www.un.org/Depts/rcnyo/newsletter/nl11/actescwa.htm (visited 05/20/2002).

Commercial Arbitration was negotiated under the UNECE guidance.[71] The regional commissions can adopt resolutions and guidelines to promote foreign investment flows. As an example, the UNECE "has issued guidelines on the creation of viable real estate markets in Central and Eastern Europe and the Commonwealth of Independent States (CIS)."[72]

In addition, the regional commissions have been a powerful impetus for establishing sub-regional organizations. For instance, the UNECA was the leading party in establishing the African Development Bank (ADB), which is the main investment loan center in Africa. In addition, the UNEACA helped establish the Economic Community of West African States (ECOWAS) and the Community of Eastern and Southern Africa (COMESA).[73]

The regional commissions also work in close collaboration with regional organizations not affiliated with the UN such as the Inter-American Development Bank (IDP), and Organization of American States (OAS). The interaction between the regional commissions and regional organizations has been an effective factor for the preparation of conferences held to address trade and investment issues. Furthermore, they jointly work with regional organizations on providing technical support to respective members

---

[71] The Convention was prepared and opened for signature on 21 April 1961 by the Special Meeting of Plenipotentiaries for the purpose of negotiating and signing a European Convention on International Commercial Arbitration, which was convened in accordance with resolution 7 (XV) 1 of the Economic Commission for Europe, adopted on 5 May 1960. European Convention on International Commercial Arbitration of 1961 Done at Geneva, April 21, 1961 United Nations, Treaty Series , vol. 484, p. 364 No. 7041 (1963-1964).

[72] UN Economic and Social Council, Regional Cooperation, Regional Cooperation in the economic, social and related fields, Report of the Secretary General, Substantive session of 1997, 16 May 1997, E/1997/40, Paragraph 88.

[73] Overview of the ECA, www.uneca.org/about_eca/overwiev_of_eca.htm (visited 05/21/2002).

regarding investment development, and undertaking studies and research programs on FDI issues.

With their cooperation and coordination programs, they work to strengthen regional economic integration for promoting not only trade but also foreign investment flows. According to the May 2000 report of the ECOSOC, "the regional commissions have intensified their cooperation with other regional organizations. In Economic and Social Council resolution 1998/46, annex III, the Council called for close cooperation between the commissions and other relevant bodies in their respective regions."[74] The following two examples show the cooperation between the regional commissions and regional organizations. Firstly, UNESCAP have an annual consultative meeting with sub-regional organizations such as the Association of Southeast Asian Nations (ASIAN), the South Asian Association for Regional Cooperation (SAARC) so as to work jointly in trade and investment areas.[75] Secondly, the UNECA worked closely with the Organization of African Unity (OAU) in "organizing technical backstopping for African member States with regard to the negotiations of a new cooperation agreement between the European Union (EU) and the African Caribbean and Pacific Group of States and for the preparatory process for the World Trade Organization Ministerial Conference in Seattle."[76]

One may argue that the regional commissions help developing countries to participate actively in international investment rule-making at the regional levels. Indeed,

---

[74] United Nations, Economic and Social Council, E/2000/10?Add.1, 9 May 2000, at Paragraph 1.

[75] *Id*. Paragraph 6.

[76] *Id*. Paragraph at 17.

the regional commissions provide a forum where agreements are negotiated, and convene "capacity building seminars" and regional symposiums where all member states work together on policy issues concerning trade and foreign investment development. By submitting their recommendations and guidelines to the ECOSOC, the regional commissions directly induce the UN to adopt resolutions and decisions on investment policies at the global level. Moreover, one may rightly argue that these commissions' study findings on economic, environmental and social problems can compel negotiating countries to include environmental provisions in investment treaties.

II. Regional Organizations

The number of regional investment agreements has increased dramatically in recent years. Regional investment agreements have found a place either incorporated into a broader framework of regional trade agreement or as separate instruments. Most of the regional agreements create regional organizations that will monitor agreements and provide services in order to carry out the objectives that are determined in regional agreements. It is very difficult to evaluate all the regional organizations that deal with FDI. However, it is worth to note some of the organizations activities.

The following are the some of the regional organizations that deal with investment issues. The European Community, the Association of South East Asian Nations (ASEAN), the Asia- Pacific Economic Co-operation (APEC), the Common Market for Eastern and Southern Africa (COMESA). In South America, members of the Southern Cone Common Market (MERCOUSUR) approved the Colonial Protocol for the Promotion and Protection of Investments in MERCOUSUR on January 17, 1994.

Regional organizations' activities regarding investment instruments can be divided into two categories: a) binding investment instruments, b) non- binding instruments. One may claim that the majority of regional instruments are binding in nature. They are applicable only to participant countries.[77]

For example, ASEAN member states adopted the "Framework Agreement on the ASEAN Investment Area" that is a binding instrument. Its main objective is to promote investment in the region through the cooperation of the countries. ASEAN was founded to provide a framework and mechanism for regional cooperation.[78] ASEAN has adopted the following main regional investment instruments which complement each other in order to protect and promote foreign investment in the region: a) the 1987 ASEAN Agreement for the Promotion and Protection of Investments, b) the 1996 Protocol to Amend the 1987 Agreement for the Promotion and Protection of Investments, c) the 1996 Protocol on Dispute Settlement Mechanism, d) the Framework Agreement on the ASEAN Investment Area.[79] Due to the fact that these agreements are legally binding agreements, they will enhance investors' confidence in the region. The Framework Agreement on the ASEAN Investment Area is considered the main instrument to govern FDI in the region.[80] Indeed, the ASEAN countries agreed to gradually liberalize their

---

[77] UNCTAD, TRENDS IN INTERNATIONAL INVESTMENT AGREEMENTS: AN OVERVIEW 42 (1999).

[78] According to the Organizations' homepage "Indonesia, Malaysia, the Philippines, Singapore and Thailand signed the ASEAN Declaration of 8 August 1967. Thirty-two years later-on 30 April 1999- ASEAN encompassed all ten countries of Southeast Asia by admitting Cambodia. (Brunei Darussalam had been admitted in 1984, Viet Nam in 1995, and Laos and Myanmar in 1997)." http://www.aseansec.org (Visited 10/16/2001).

[79] ASEAN, HANDBOOK OF INVESTMENT AGREEMENT IN ASEAN, it can be found in ASEAN Homepage. http://www.aseansec.org (Visited 10/16/2001).

[80] *Id.*

investment regime through the opening of all industries and granting national treatment to ASEAN investors. The objective of the agreement is to substantially increase the flow of direct investment from ASEAN and non-ASEAN sources by making the region a more competitive, open and liberal investment area. The Handbook of Investment Agreements in ASEAN briefly summarizes the provision of the Framework Agreement on the ASEAN Investment Area as follows:

> i) opening up all industries, with some exceptions as specified in the Temporary Exclusion List (TEL) and Sensitive List (SL), for investment to ASEAN investors by 2010 and to all investors by 2020;
>
> ii) granting national treatment, with some exceptions as specified in the TEL and SL, to ASEAN investors by 2010 and to all investors by 2020;
>
> iii) involving the private sector actively in the AIA development process;
>
> iv) undertaking joint investment facilitation activities that will help bring down transaction cost and adopting coordinated investment promotion programme to facilitate greater awareness of the opportunities within the AIA;
>
> v) promoting freer flow of capital, skilled labour and professionals, and technology amongst the ASEAN countries;
>
> vi) providing transparency of investment policies, rules, procedures and administrative processes; and

vii) providing a more streamlined and simplified investment process.[81]

This regional agreement can create liberal investment regime through granting national treatment and providing transparency of members' investment policies.

On the other hand, some regional and inter-regional instruments are non-binding such as the APEC Non-Binding Investment Principles. This instrument can be considered inter-regional investment instrument since APEC encompasses countries from

---

[81] *Id.*

different continents.[82] APEC was established in 1989 "to advance Asia-Pacific economic dynamism and sense of community."[83] Alan M. Rugman rightly states, "Investment is on the regular agenda for APEC because it is a line item in each member's annual individual action plan report and also because of the ground breaking work of the investment experts group in advocating a set of non-binding investment principles."[84] Furthermore, Mr. C. Phasukavanich examined the principles under negotiation for the Investment Area of ASEAN and then non-binding investment principles adopted by the APEC, in terms of their development objectives.[85] He pointed out that a transition period was necessary for developing countries entering into a liberalized investment regime.[86] Indeed, these instruments designate that developing countries have in need of the economic and technical cooperation to liberalize their investment regimes.

---

[82] Riyaz Dattu, *A Journey From Havana To Paris: The Fifty- Year Quest For The Elusive Multilateral Agreement on Investment*, 24 FORDHAM INT'L L. J.275 , 311 (2000).

[83] Followings are the member countries of APEC: Australia, Brunei Darussalam, Canada, Indonesia, Japan, Republic of Korea, Malaysia, New Zealand, Republic of the Philippines, Singapore, Thailand and Unites States, People's Republic of China, Hong Kong China and Chinese Taipei, Mexico and Papua New Guinea, Chile, Peru, Russia and Vietnam. http://www.apecsec.org (visited 10/16/2001).

[84] Alan M. Rugman, *Towards and investment agenda for APEC*, Transnational Corporations, 123 (1997).

[85] WTO, Working Group on Relationship between Trade and Investment, *Report of the Expert Meeting on Existing Regional and Multinational Investment Agreements and Their Development Dimension*, WT/WGTI/W/46, 29 July 1998.

[86] *Id.*

III. OECD and International Investment

The Organization for Economic Cooperation and Development (herein after OECD) has a long and successful history in the area of international investment.[87] Member countries have agreed to "pursue their efforts to reduce or abolish obstacles to the exchange of goods and services and current payments and maintain and extend the liberalization of capital movements".[88] Thus, FDI issues have been central to the program of the OECD since its inauguration in the early 1960s.[89] In other words, the OECD, an organization of thirty developed nations, has produced an invaluable framework for the liberalization of foreign investment.[90] The OECD has adopted some instruments that are related to FDI. The most important of these are the Code of Liberalization of Capital Movement (Capital Movements Code) and the Code of Liberalization of Current Invisible Operations (Invisible Code), and the 1976 Declaration on International Investment and Multilateral Enterprises with its four elements: the instrument of National Treatment, the Guide for Multilateral Enterprises, the instrument on Incentives and Disincentives for Investment and the instrument on Conflicting Requirements.[91]

---

[87] The OECD, an international organization with 29 member countries, is a unique forum permitting governments of the industrialized countries to study and formulate the best policies possible in all economic and social fields, particularly international investment. (www.oecd.org).

[88] *Id.*

[89] Brewer, *supra* note 19, at 648.

[90] Paul Bryan Christy III, *Negotiating Investment in the GATT: A Call For Functionalism*, 12 MICH. J. INT'L L. 743, 764 (1991).

[91] William H. Witherell, *The OECD Multilateral Agreement on Investment*, Transnational Corporations, 3-4 (1995).

A. **The OECD Codes of Liberalization**

The OECD Capital Movements Code[92] and Invisible Code[93] are the sources of liberalization of economic environment of the OECD member States. These two codes both adopted in 1961, have the same binding power on OECD members. The reason for adopting these two codes was that there were still remaining national restrictive measures on international investments from the Second World War.[94] The Codes constitute stipulating; progressive, non- discriminatory liberalization of capital movements, the right of establishment and current invisible transactions.[95] Furthermore, the Codes continue to be used as a standards and requirements of OECD membership.[96]

1. **Capital Movements Code**

The Capital Movements Code was adopted in December 1961. Accepting this Code, OECD Member countries have undertaken to remove restrictions on specified lists of capital movements between residents of different member countries.[97] At its beginning, the Code provided only a limited number of capital movements. The 1984

---

[92] OECD, Code of Liberalization of Capital Movements (1986).

[93] OECD, Code of Liberalization of Current Invisible Operations (1986).

[94] BREWER & YOUNG, *supra* note 15, at 73.

[95] www.oecd.org (visited 1/27/2000).

[96] BREWER & YOUNG, *supra* note 15, at 73

[97] Article 1 of the OECD Code of Liberalization of Capital Movements states that: ' a-Members shall progressively abolish between one another, in accordance with the provision of Article 2, restrictions on movements of capital to the extent necessary for effective economic cooperation. Measures designed to eliminate such restrictions are hereinafter called " measures of liberalization". ."Article 2 states; " a- Subject to the provisions of paragraph (b) (iv), Members shall grant any authorization required for the conclusion or execution of transactions and for transfers specified in an item set out in List A or List B of Annex A to this Code".

revision, the Code's scope has enlarged the definition of FDI. Especially, the principle of non-discrimination embodied in Article 9 of the Code became applicable to the pre-establishment stage.[98] In 1992, the Code was amended again to widen its scope to include all kinds of capital movements. The Code applies both FDI and portfolio investment. Overall, the Code provides free admission of investments between member States.[99]

The most important provisions of the Code are the following:

1-Article One of the Code provides that Members shall apply any measures without discrimination among OECD Members.[100]

2-Pursuant to the Code, Members are required to notify the Organization of any existing measures affecting capital movements.[101]

3-Members pledge to liberalize all the operations specified on the liberalization lists of the Code, except with respect to items against which reservations are lodged.[102]

4-Members shall endeavor not to introduce any new restrictions which would not be covered by reservations.[103] This provision embodies the standstill principle.[104]

---

[98] Article 9 of the Code states: "A member shall not discriminate as between other Members in authorizing the conclusion and execution of transactions and transfers which are listed in Annex A and which are subject to any degree of liberalization.".

[99] Patrick Juillard, *MAI: A European View*, 31 CORNELL INT'L L. J. 477, 478 (1998).

[100] Article 1 Of the OECD Code.

[101] Article 11 of the OECD Code, states that "Members shall notify the organization, within the periods which the later may determine, of the measures of liberalization which they have taken and of any other measures which have a bearing on this code, as well as of any modifications of such measures".

[102] Article 2 of the OECD Code.

[103] Article 1 of the OECD Code states that: "...e- members shall endeavor to avoid introducing any new exchange restrictions on the movements of capital or the use of non-resident-owned funds shall endeavor to avoid making existing regulations more restrictive.".

The OECD Capital Movements Code is the only multilateral instrument promoting liberalization of wide range of international capital movements. The Code has the legal status of an OECD Decision which is binding on all the members. Consequently, the members are expected to take some measures so as to fulfill the requirements. The implementation of the code is being reviewed by the OECD Committee on Capital Movements and Invisible Transactions. Moreover, the Code serves as a reference point for the liberalization process.

2.   Invisible Code

The Invisible Code promotes the liberalization of current payments and transfers. In addition, it ensures that the underlying transactions are not frustrated by legal or administrative regulations.[105] The invisible Code requires members to eliminate all restrictions on specified current invisible operations of other member countries.[106] In particular, the invisible Code requires members to allow the transfer of profits, dividends, interest payments, and other remittances associated with FDI. Covered Operations are listed in an annex under headings as follows: business and industry, foreign trade, transport, insurance, films, income from capital, travel and tourism, personal income and

---

[104] Pierre Poret, *The Experience of the OECD with the Code of Liberalization of Capital Movements*, OECD, Paper presented in May 1998 in IMF Seminar on Current legal Issues Affecting Central Banks.

[105] "Invisible is the general term applied to all exchanges in which no merchandise is involved. Within this group there are current and capital operations and most of these consist of a transaction between two parties and related transfer of money. The OECD has not attempted to give theoretical definitions of current and capital operations and distinguishes them by reference to lists." (www.oecd.org/daf/investment/legal-instruments/codes.htm) (visited 1/27/2000).

[106] OECD, OECD Code of Liberalization of Current Invisible Operations, Article 1 states that: 'a-Members shall eliminate between one another, in accordance with the provisions of Article 2, restrictions on current invisible transactions and transfers.....".

expenditure, public income and expenditure, and 'general' which includes advertising, professional services, and the registration of patents and trademarks.[107] Countries lodged some reservations to these obligations, particularly for insurance, air, land and sea transport and films.

The invisible Code was amended four times to broaden its scope. Four amendments provide detailed treatment of insurance, tourism, and audiovisual works, and banking and financial services. Paul Bryan Christy asserts that these amendments overlap the Capital Movements Code.[108] He further evaluates the insurance agreement so as to show why he is thinking in this way. I agree with his evaluation and opinion since the insurance agreement provides not only types of insurance but also endeavors to discipline the use of financial and prudential requirements on the insurer and on the insurer's investments and deposits.[109] In particular, Annex I to Annex A of the Invisible Code regarding Insurance, Item D/6 states that "1. All statutory and administrative controls of insurance shall ensure equivalent treatment for national insurers and insurers from other Member States so that the latter shall not be liable to heavier burdens than those imposed on national insurers."[110] With respect to national treatment for establishment authorizations to branches or agencies, the same article states that "2- Where the establishment of insurers in a Member State is made subject to authorization:

---

[107] Operations Covered by the OECD Code of Liberalization of Current Invisible Operations.

[108] Christy, *supra* note 90, at 769.

[109] *Id*.

[110] OECD Invisible Code, at 39, Part III.

a) That Member shall accord insurers from other Member States treatment equivalent to that applied to national insurers..."[111]

3. Evaluation of Both Codes

The general principles that govern the Invisible Code and Capital Movements Code are almost the same. Adopting both Codes, Members undertake to remove restrictions on specified lists of current invisible operations and capital movements. According to OECD documents, the ultimate objective of adopting these codes is that "residents of different Member countries should be as free to transact business with each other as are residents of a single country."[112]

It should be stressed that both codes provide safeguard measures for members to avoid their obligations. Both Codes allow members to lodge reservations against specific obligations.[113] If a member has a balance of payments problem, a member may temporarily suspend the application of measures of liberalization taken or maintained in accordance with the provisions of Article 2 of both Codes.[114] In addition, members may take action against the Codes' obligations so as to maintain public order, public health, morals and safety, and essential security interest and to fulfill international peace and security obligations.[115] Moreover, both Codes provide exceptions to the principle of non-discrimination.[116]

---

[111] *Id.*

[112] OECD : Introduction to the OECD CODES of LIBERALIZATION 22, 1987, at 12.

[113] OECD Capital Movements Code, Article 2, and OECD Invisible Code art 2.

[114] OECD Capital Movements Code, Article 7, and OECD Invisible Code art 7.

[115] OECD Capital Movements Code, Article 3, and OECD Invisible Code art 3.

B. **The OECD Draft Convention of 1967 on the Protection of Foreign Property**

OECD Council decided for publication of the Draft Convention on the Protection of Foreign Property on October 12, 1967.[117] The 1967 Draft Convention provided "recognized principles relating to the protection of foreign property" and "render more effective the application of these principles".[118] The Draft Convention remains as a draft, and the Draft Convention was never formally adopted. So, it does not have legally binding power. On the other hand, it has been utilized in the preparation and negotiation of other agreements on the FDI. For example it has been served as a reference for BITs.[119]

C. **Declaration on Foreign Investment and Multinational Enterprises (hereinafter the Declaration)**

The Declaration was adopted 1976 and most recently revised 1991. The Declaration contains the National Treatment Instrument, the International Investment and the Incentives and Disincentives Instruments, the Conflicting Requirements and the

---

[116] Article 10 of the OECD Capital Movements Code and OECD Invisible Code state that: "Members forming part of special customs or monetary system may apply to one another, in addition to measures of liberalization taken in accordance with the provisions of Article 2 (a), other measures of liberalization without extending them to other Members. Members forming part of such a system shall inform the organization of its membership and those of its provisions which have a bearing on this Code.".

[117] Georg Schwarzenberger compared between the Draft Convention and the Abs-Shawcross draft convention in his book. GEORG SCHWARZENBERG, FOREIGN INVESTMENTS AND INTERNATIONAL LAW 153-154 (1969).

[118] *Id.* at 154.

[119] Witherell, *supra* note 91, at 17.

Guidelines for Multinational Enterprises.[120] The first two instruments cover investment. The third and fourth instruments cover multinational enterprises.

1. **National Treatment Instrument**

A National Treatment Instrument obliges members to accord foreign investors and investments national treatment.[121] A National Treatment Instrument itself consists of two items:

"1-A declaration of principle, which forms part of the Declaration on International Investment and Multinational Enterprises, adopted in 1976 by the governments of the OECD Member Countries;

2-A procedural Decision by the OECD Council (last revised in December 1991), which obliges OECD Members to notify their exceptions to National Treatment, and establishes follow-up procedures to deal with such exceptions in the OECD."[122]

Member Countries should grant national treatment under their laws, regulations, and administrative practices to the enterprises operating in their territories and owned or controlled directly or indirectly by nationals of another member Country.[123] Pursuant to Article II of the Declaration, members will consider applying such treatment to the

---

[120] OECD, Declaration by the Governments of OECD Member Countries and Decisions of the OECD Council on International Investment and Multinational Enterprises.

[121] National Treatment is the commitment by a country to treat enterprises operating on its territory, but controlled by the nationals of another country, no less favorably than domestic enterprises in like situations.

[122] OECD, The National Treatment Instrument.

[123] OECD, OECD Declaration and Decisions on International investment and Multinational Enterprises, Article II provides national treatment principle.

enterprises of non-member countries.[124] Like other Codes, the National Treatment Instrument provides exceptions to the national treatment principle. Member countries may take measures that will be inconsistent with national treatment principle in order to maintain public order, to protect their essential security interests and to fulfill commitments pertaining to international peace and security.[125]

Unlike Capital Movements Code, the National Treatment Instrument provides and applies the national treatment principle after establishment phase of the foreign controlled enterprises.[126] Paul Bryan Christy illustrates these differences in his article in this way: "for example, a first time creation of subsidiary by a firm of one Member in the territory of another would be covered by Capital Movements Code while both the operations of the subsidiary established and any further investments by it would be covered by the National Treatment Instrument."[127] Unlike Codes, the National Treatment Instrument is not legally binding on OECD Members.[128] The OECD members have voluntarily applied this instrument to the foreign controlled enterprises.[129] The United States has been

---

[124] *Id.* Art.II/2.

[125] *Id.* Art II/1.

[126] *Id.* Art II/4 states that " That this Declaration does not deal with the right of Member Countries to regulate the entry of foreign investment or the conditions of establishment of foreign enterprises.".

[127] Christy, *supra* note 90, at 768.

[128] WTO, Working Group on the Relationship between Trade and Investment, *Bilateral, Regional, Plurilateral and Multilateral Agreements Note by the Secretariat*, WT/WGTI/W/22, 26 January 1998, 98-0269, at 19.

[129] The OECD Publication, National Treatment for Foreign- Controlled Enterprises (Paris, 1993), discusses the interpretation f the national treatment commitment and contains list f measures notified by OECD member countries as exceptions to national treatment.

pressuring other Member countries to adopt national treatment instrument as binding code.[130]

One of the important problems of the national treatment instrument is the exception. "public order" and "essential security interests" are two main exceptions provided by the declaration to the national treatment.[131] These terms are not defined, and they do not have precise meaning. So, in order to apply these exceptions, these terms should be interpreted. The interpretation of these terms depends on the economic and politic situations and culture of the member state which lodged the exceptions.[132] OECD Council decided to follow-up procedures in order to encourage the fullest possible application of national treatment by member countries.[133] According to the follow-up procedures, members shall notify the Organization list of exceptions regarding national treatment.[134] Each exception has to be examined and accepted by the Council.[135] Furthermore, the Committee on International Investment and Multilateral Enterprises

---

[130] Chris Alan Johnson, Protectionism Toward Transplants and obligations under GATT, FCN Treaty and OECD Instruments; Trojan Horse or Engine For Growth?, 4 TRANSNAT'L L. & CONTEMP. PROBS. 279, 300-301 (1994).

[131] OECD, OECD Declaration and Decisions on International Investment and Multilateral Enterprises, Article 2.

[132] Johnson, *supra* note 130, at 300.

[133] OECD, National Treatment Instrument, Third Revised Decision of the Council, adopted by the Council in December 1991.

[134] *Id*. Article 1 states that: " Members shall notify the Organization of all measures constituting exceptions to the National Treatment within 60 days of their adoption and of any other measures which have a bearing on National Treatment. All exceptions shall be set out in Annex A to the Decision.".

[135] *Id* Article 2 States that: " The Organization shall examine each exception lodged by a Member and other measures notified under Article 1 at intervals to be determined by the Organization. These intervals shall, however, be not more than three years, unless the Council decides otherwise.".

periodically examined the exceptions.[136] After examination, the Committee must submit the results and proposals to the Council and the Council has the power to decide whether members withdraw their exceptions or not.[137] In addition, the results of the examinations will be found in the series of OECD Reviews of foreign direct investment.[138].

2. The International Investment Incentives and Disincentives Instrument

Pursuant to the Article IV of the OECD Declaration, member countries recognize the need to strengthen their cooperation in the field of international direct investment, the need to give due weight to the interests of other Members affected by measures providing official incentives and disincentives to international direct investment, and endeavor to make such measures as transparent as possible.[139] It is important to know that incentives and disincentives are not defined by the Instrument. The broad definition of these terms are stated in one of the OECD Surveys that: "An incentive (or disincentives) will be understood as any government measure designed to influence an investment decision, and increasing (or reducing) the profit accruing to the potential investment or altering the risks attaching to it."[140]

---

[136] *Id*. Article4 states that: "a. The Committee on international and Multinational Enterprises (hereinafter called " the Committee" shall consider all questions concerning the interpretation or implementation of the provisions of the Declaration or of Acts of the Council relating to national Treatment and shall report its conclusions thereon to the council.".

[137] *Id*. Article 4 and 5.

[138] OECD Reviews of the Exceptions, OECD Homepage.

[139] *Id*. OECD, Declaration and Decisions on International Investment and Multinational Enterprises, Article IV. (www.oecd.org/daf//investment/guidelines/declarat1.htm) (visited 2/10/2000).

[140] OECD, International Investment and multinational Enterprises: Investment Incentives and Disincentives and the International Investment Process 10 (1983).

The reason for adopting this instrument is to promote cooperation among member countries in this area. In particular, Member countries may be adversely affected by international incentives and disincentives measures, so the member countries need to cooperate with each other.[141]. The instrument provides consultations and review procedures to make cooperation between member countries more efficient.[142]

3. **The OECD Guidelines for Multinational Enterprises (Hereinafter the OECD Guidelines)**

The OECD Guidelines are recommendations to enterprises from thirty-three governments to help ensure that multinational enterprises operate in harmony with government policies.[143] The OECD Guidelines cover a wide range of multinational enterprises' operations: taxation, general policies, employment and industrial relations, disclosure of information, environmental protection, competition, science and technology, and financing.[144] For example, multinational enterprises are encouraged to refrain from actions which would adversely affect competition in the relevant market by abusing a dominant position of market power.[145] They are also encouraged to take

---

[141] Christy, *supra* note 90, at 766.

[142] Witherell, *supra* note 91, at 28.

[143] OECD, OECD Declaration and Decisions on International investment and Multinational Enterprises, Article I states Guidelines for Multinational Enterprises.

[144] OECD, Annex 1 to the Declaration, Text of the OECD Guidelines for Multinational Enterprises.

[145] *Id*, Competition, Article 1, at 3.

appropriate measures in their operations to minimize the risk of accidents and damage to health and environment, and to cooperate in mitigating adverse effects.[146]

The aim of the OECD Guidelines is to facilitate direct investment among OECD Member countries, and to enhance their investment climate.[147] In other words, the OECD Guidelines encourages the positive contributions of multinational enterprises and helps to minimize and resolve the problems which may arise in their operation.[148] Overall, the OECD Guidelines try to promote responsible corporate behavior.

The OECD Guidelines have been reviewed over the years to keep them updated and effective. The aims of the review are to assess the experience of the OECD guidelines and to maintain stability of the OECD Guidelines and to monitor and promote their implementation.[149] It may be argued that the participation of different groups in the review process will be helpful for recognition of the OECD Guidelines by the world community, because of peer pressure. Representatives, who have new and different perspectives, propose solutions for responsible corporate behavior.[150] In addition, this participation provides transparency in the review process.

Like the National Treatment Instrument, the OECD Guidelines are not legally binding instruments. In fact, they are recommendations addressed by signatory countries

---

[146] *Id*, Environmental Protection, Article 3, at 5.

[147] OECD, Text of OECD Guidelines for Multinational Enterprises, Introduction, at 1.

[148] OECD, OECD Guidelines for Multinational Enterprises Frequently Asked Questions, at 2, www.oecd.org/daf/investment/guidelines/faq.htm (visited 1/27/2000).

[149] *Id*. at 4.

[150] For example, in the Conference on the OECD Guidelines for Multinational Enterprises was held in Budapest, Hungary, from 16-18 November 1998, Representatives from governments, business, labour, and other representatives of civil society discussed the influence of the OECD Guidelines on corporate behavior and reflected their view. OECD, Conference on the OECD Guidelines for Multinational Enterprises, Budapest, Hungary, 16-18 November 1998, DAFFE/IME (98) 18, Unclassified, Dist. 23 November 1998.

to multinational enterprises operating in their territories.[151] Thus, signatory countries are willing to observe the behavior and activities of multinational enterprises. Even though this is a voluntarily commitment, the OECD Guidelines are supported by follow-up procedures in the OECD Member countries, and three non-member countries, Argentina, Brazil and Chile[152]. The OECD Council decided that three institutions have responsibility for the follow-up process: the National Contact Points, the OECD's Committee on International Investment and Multinational Enterprises (CIME); and the Advisory Committees of Business and Labour Federations, (BIAC and TUAC).[153]

According to the OECD Council Decision, Member Governments shall establish National Contact points (NCP) to handle the implementation of the OECD Guidelines.[154] The aim of the NCPs is to undertake promotional activities, assist in solving problems that may arise in this connection, handle inquires, discuss all matters related to the guidelines, and collect information on experience with the OECD Guidelines.[155] The NCPs are the central institutions for the follow-up procedures. Any interested parties should use the NCPs as a first step to solve issues at the national level.[156]

---

[151] William H. Witherell, *Towards an International Set of Rules for Investment*, in TOWARDS MULTILATERAL INVESTMENT RULES 28 (OECD ed., 1996).

[152] OECD, Review of the OECD Guidelines for Multinational Enterprises, www.oecd.org/daf/investment/guidelines/index.htm, (visited 1/27/2000).

[153] *Id*. Text of the OECD Guidelines for Multinational Enterprises, The Guidelines for Multinational Enterprises: Second revised Decision of the OECD Council, Amended June 1991, www.oecd.org/daf/investment/guidelines/mnetext.htm, (visited 1/27/2000), at 6.

[154] *Id*. at 6-7.

[155] See *supra* note 152.

[156] *Id*.

The CIME is responsible for clarifications of the interpretation of the OECD Guidelines, exchanging views on them, proposing changes or amendments of the OECD Guidelines, periodically reviewing them, and responding to requests or queries from adhering governments.[157] Namely, the CIME promotes the application of the OECD Guidelines among Member countries.

According to the Second Revised Decision of the OECD Council, the CIME must regularly invite two non-governmental organizations (NGOs), the BIAC and TUAC to OECD to express their views on matters with respect to the OECD Guidelines[158]. In addition without invitation, interested parties (such as other NGOs), and the BIAC and TUAC may raise such issues with the CIME and NCPs.[159] These views have to be taken into account by the CIME.[160]

4. The Instrument on Conflicting Requirements

Pursuant to Article III of the OECD Declaration, Member countries should cooperate with a view to avoiding or minimizing the imposition of conflicting requirements on multinational enterprises.[161] In order to do that, Member countries

---

[157] *Id.*

[158] *Id.* Text of the OECD Guidelines for Multinational Enterprises, The Guidelines for Multinational Enterprises: Second revised Decision of the OECD Council, Amended June 1991, www.oecd.org/daf/investment/guidelines/mnetext.htm, (visited 1/27/2000), at 7.

[159] The BIAC and TUAC have different point of view regarding investment issues. The BIAC statement emphasized that the Guidelines generally reflected the recognition by OECD Governments that enterprises should be treated equitably, with discrimination between public and private sector firms eliminated. In contrast, the TUAC statement noted that the Guidelines would be only a first step to further international arrangements incorporating binding rules. (BREWER AND YOUNG, *supra* note 15, at 94).

[160] *Id.* at 7.

[161] Id. OECD, Declaration and Decisions on International Investment and Multinational Enterprises, Article III. (www.oecd.org/daf//investment/guidelines/declarat1.htm) (visited 2/10/2000).

should take into account the general considerations and practical approaches annexed to the Declaration.[162] The OECD Council has an adopted procedural decision so as to promote co-operation among member countries. Member countries should take into account the sovereignty and legitimate economic, law enforcement and other interests of other Member countries and have respect to relevant principles of international law.[163]

D.   OECD Activities on Combating Corruption

The world community recognizes that the cost of corruption is high. The Preamble to the OECD Combating Bribery of Foreign Officials in International Business Transactions (hereinafter OECD Convention on Bribery) states that: "Corruption raises serious moral and political concerns, undermines good governance and economic development, and distorts international competitive conditions."[164]

This study does not evaluate the effect of corruption on FDI. However it is important to note that corruption discourages investment. For example, Shang- Jin Wei studies the effect of corruption on FDI.[165] Shang- Jin Wei reached three central findings:

> (1) A rise in either the tax rate on multinational firms or the corruption level in a host country reduces inward foreign direct investment (FDI). An increase in the corruption level from that of Singapore to that of Mexico is equivalent to raising the tax rate by over twenty percentage points. (2) There is no support for the hypothesis that corruption has a smaller effect on FDI into East Asian host

---

[162] OECD, Conflicting Requirement imposed on multinational enterprises: General Considerations and Practical approaches, (www.oecd.org/daf/investment/guidelines/conflict.htm) (visited 1/27/2000).

[163] *Id.* at 1.

[164] OECD, Combating Bribery of Foreign Public Officials in international Business Transactions, www.oecd.org/daf/nocorruptiojn/20nov1e.htm (visited 1/27/2000).

[165] Shang- Jin Wei, *How Taxing is Corruption on International Investor?*, National Bureau of Economic Research, NBER Working Paper, 6030. (1997).

countries. (3) American investors are averse to corruption in host countries, but not necessarily more so than average OECD investors, in spite of the U.S. Foreign Corrupt Practices Act of 1977.[166]

Overall, international investors want to make investment in countries where transparency on investment regulations is provided, and where corruption is regulated by law.[167]

Many countries have laws against bribery of their own officials, but only the U.S and Sweden have laws prohibiting their nationals and corporations from bribing foreign officials. In 1977 the United States enacted the Foreign Corrupt Practices Act (FCPA), the first code to combat of bribery in the world. It can be argued that this law discourages the US investors from investing in foreign market since they are placed at competitive disadvantages.

The world community under the leadership of America has taken steps in many international organizations to stop corruption in international business transactions.[168] OECD launched an initiative in 1994 aimed at helping members and non-members alike institute effective measures to prevent corruption. In 1994, the OECD issued a "Recommendations on Bribery in International Business Transactions" which requires member governments to take effective action to deter, prevent and combat bribery of foreign business officials. Such measures include reviewing their criminal, civil, administrative, tax, business accounting and banking laws. However, according to the OECD agreement, this recommendation is not legally binding.

---

[166] *Id.* Abstract.

[167] Nancy Zucker Boswell, *An Emerging Consensus on Controlling Corruption,* 18 University of Pennsylvania Journal of International Economic Law. 1165, 1168 (1997).

[168] For example, the Organisation of American States has negotiated the Inter-American Convention Against corruption in 1996 and which was sign in march 1997 The OAS Convention mandates that signatories enact laws to criminalize bribes to foreign public officials by its domestic companies and other private interests.

In many countries, particularly Germany and France, bribes have been defended as a necessary cost of doing business, and it is widely accepted that they are a legitimate tax deduction. In 1996, the OECD Council adopted a "Recommendation on the Tax Deductibility of Bribes to Foreign Officials", which called on OECD member states to "re-examine such treatment with the intention of denying this deductibility." In 1997 an OECD report on implementation of the 1996 Recommendation observed that Norway and the Netherlands had adopted legislation limiting the deductibility of bribes to foreign officials, and that several other states are actively re-examining the issue.

The Convention was negotiated and signed on 17 December 1997 under the auspices of the OECD; signatories include all 29 member states of the OECD as well as five non-members Argentina, Brazil, Bulgaria, Chile, and the Slovak Republic, and entered into force on 15 February 1999.[169] The aim of the OECD Convention is to prohibit bribery of foreign public officials in international business transactions, specifically international trade and investment.[170] The Convention covers the suppliers, who pay the bribes. It makes it a crime for citizens and companies to bribe officials of another country. In other words, countries have committed themselves to making the bribery of foreign public officials a criminal offense. Article 1 of the Convention states that:

> Each party shall take measures as may be necessary to establish that it is a criminal offense under its law for any person intentionally to offer, promise or give any undue pecuniary or other advantage, whether directly or through intermediaries, to a foreign public officials, for that official or for a third party, in

---

[169] Till now, 20 Signatories have ratified the Convention: Iceland, Japan, Germany, Hungary, United States, Finland, United Kingdom, Canada, Norway, Bulgaria, Korea, Greece, Austria, Mexico, Sweden, Belgium, Slovak Republic, Australia, Spain, Czech Republic.

[170] *Id.* OECD Convention on Bribery, Preamble.

order that the official act or refrain from acting in relation to the performance of official duties, in order to obtain or retain business or other improper advantage in the conduct of international business.[171]

Articles of the Convention have been criticized. In particular Article 1 of the Convention is the most controversial article in the Convention. For example, one of the failings of the Convention is that it does not cover bribes to political parties and their officials. Article 1(1) covers bribes given to a "foreign public official," defined in Article 1(4) as any person holding a "legislative, administrative or judicial office" of a foreign country, a person "exercising a public function" for a foreign country or a "public agency or public enterprise" of that country, or an official of a public international organization. Thus, this definition does not cover officials of political parties or candidates for office, although bribes of political parties and candidates are a serious source of corruption.[172] There are many articles in this convention related to the international criminal law.[173] However, this study does not point them out.

Article 8 provides that signatories must take some measures within the framework of their laws and regulations pertaining to the financial statement disclosures, the maintenance of books and records, and accounting and auditing standards. In addition, signatories must prohibit off-the book accounts and other accounting abuses such as

---

[171] *Id.* Art.1.

[172] Especially, the United States seeks a broader provision on bribes of foreign political parties, but it defends the final text as progress in the right direction. Supporters of the Convention also note that the OECD has pledged to review this issue again in the future.

[173] For example, Article 9 provides for mutual legal assistance in criminal proceedings and in non-criminal proceedings among member states. Article 10(2) provides that the Bribery Convention can serve as the legal basis for extradition in the absence of an extradition treaty. Like most recent multilateral treaties on international criminal law, Article 10(3) of the Bribery Convention obliges a state party either to extradite its own nationals for bribery of foreign officials or to submit the case to its "competent authorities" for prosecution.

inadequately identified transactions.[174] The convention does not include any provision on tax deductions for bribery of foreign officials. On the other hand, the OECD Fiscal Committee surveys compliance with OECD Recommendation on the Tax deductibility of bribes and recently reported that by the end of the 1999, there should be no OECD member left that allows such tax deductibility.[175]

Each signatory must now pass implementing legislation that will put the provisions of the OECD Convention into effect. Article 12 provides "monitoring and follow-up" procedure for the implementation of the Convention.[176] Pursuant to this article, monitoring and follow-up procedures are carried out by the OECD Working Group on Bribery in International Business Transactions, made up of all signatories.[177] The Working Group examines each signatory's legislation to evaluate whether the Convention is effectively implemented or not.[178]

There will be a criticism for this convention.[179] Like other OECD instruments on FDI, it also does not establish effective dispute settlement procedure to solve the problems regarding the implementation of the Convention.[180] Indeed, the treaty should

---

[174] *Id*. OECD Convention on Bribery Article 8, at 4.

[175] OECD, OECD Anti-Corruption Frequently Asked Questions, (www.oecd.org/daf/nocorruption/faq.htm) (visited 2/18/2000)., at 6.

[176] *Id*. OECD Convention on Bribery Article 12, at 5.

[177] *Id*. Article 12-13, at 5.

[178] Geoffrey R. Watson, *The OECD Convention on Bribery*, ASIL, Insight., March (1998).

[179] Mehmet Komurcu and Yusuf Caliskan, *"Yolsuzluk Problemine Karsi Uluslararasi Toplumun Tepkileri ve Ortak Bir Hukuki Duzenleme Olusturma Cabalari, (Global Efforts to Curb Corruption and Towards Multilateral Rules on Combating Corruption)"*, Turkiye Barolar Birligi Dergisi (Journal of Turkish Bar Association), (2000).

[180] *Id*.

include dispute settlement procedure so as to ensure that member countries abide by their obligations under the agreement. Despite the fact that Article 12 regulates monitoring and follow-up procedures of the implementation of the Convention, the Convention does not contain effective enforcement for noncompliance.

E. **Evaluation of the OECD Instruments**

There are many investment instruments, which were adopted, drafted or negotiated by the OECD. Most of these instruments are not legally binding. They are simply political commitments by the signatory countries.

The OECD Codes (Capital Movements Code and Invisible Code) provide for progressive, nondiscriminatory liberalization of capital movements, and the right of establishment and current invisible transactions. The Codes are legally binding according to the OECD Convention and are enforceable under international law. The Codes have been criticized in terms of two shortcomings. First, even though the Codes provide almost all unrestricted capital movements, they allow member states to lodge reservations, which have negative effect on the scope and application of the Codes. Especially, Article 10 of the codes, allows members of customs unions to maintain preferential treatment among themselves.[181] In other words, this article provides special treatment within the European Community. The good thing is that new reservations

---

[181] *Id.* OECD Capital Movements Code, Article 10 states that: "members forming part of special customs or monetary system may apply to one another, in addition to measures of liberalization taken in accordance with the provisions of Article 2 (a), other measures of liberalization without extending them to other Members. Members forming part of such a system shall inform the Organization of its membership and those of its provisions which have a bearing on this Code.".

cannot be lodged to operations in certain listed sectors.[182] The standstill and ratchet effect rules exist in the application of these codes. Second, the Codes have not established dispute settlement procedures. Christy states that:

> The Codes provide no right of retaliation or other means of positive enforcement, but instead seek compliance through a system of notification, examination, and consultation... For those seeking redress against a member for improperly invoking a derogation or for frustrating or violating its liberalization commitments, there exist only a right to notify the Organization, and in the case of improper derogation, to have the situation examined by a 'Special Ministerial Group". The CMIT considers these complaints, but the Codes provide neither "carrot' nor "stick" to ensure compliance.[183]

Unlike the OECD Codes, the OECD Guidelines addressed to the multinational enterprises and they do not have legally binding power on the Member States. Some scholars argue that the OECD Guidelines have become part of customary international law, since they have been applied and accepted widely by the world community.[184] However, this argument is not widely accepted and it only works when the disputed issue is not very controversial.[185]

The effectiveness of the voluntary rules is debated by scholars. As Thomas L. Brewer and Stephen Young explain, the Badger case has been used as a reference for application of the non-binding OECD Guidelines.[186] Badger Company was a subsidiary of US based Raytheon and cooperated in Belgium. In 1976, employees at Badger

---

[182] Alexander Lehmann, *Liberalizing Investment Policies: Prospects After the 1985 Investment Incentives and Performance Requirements.*, Royal Institute of International Affairs, 30 (1995).

[183] Christy, *supra* note 90, at 771.

[184] Michael Hart, *A Multilateral Agreement on Foreign Direct Investment - Why Now? in* Investment Rules for the Global Economy: Enhancing Access to Markets (Pierre Sauvé & Daniel Schwanen eds., Toronto: C.D. Howe Institute, 1996).

[185] *Id*. at 15.

[186] BREWER AND YOUNG, *supra* note 15, at 95.

demanded full compensation pursuant to the Belgian Law, since the Badger Company was nearly closed and bankrupt. Employees did not get compensation and the American company refused to intervene to settle the liabilities of its subsidiary. After that, Belgian Government applied to OECD to consider the case, specifically pointing to the provision on the "employment and industrial relations" in the OECD Guidelines.[187] After consideration of the case, the American company agreed to pay compensation to the employees.[188] Overall, this shows that rules also applied voluntarily, but this relies on the moral value of the companies which is unpredictable.

Thomas L. Brewer and Stephen Young summarized the positive aspects of the OECD Guidelines referencing the Schwann and Germidis's works.[189] They pointed out positive impact of the OECD Guidelines as follows. First, the OECD Guidelines showed an acceptance by mostly developed countries that the activities of multinational enterprises needed to be restricted. Second, the OECD Guidelines provide consensus and harmonization among different groups and countries. Third, they could be utilized as a bridge between the work of the OECD, the UN and its specialized agencies. Fourth, as mentioned above, they could be somehow accepted as a customary international law even though most multinational enterprises never accepted this.[190]

Like Codes, the OECD Guidelines have been criticized in terms of their provisions since their provisions are either general or vague. For example there is no precise definition for "essential interest" provided as an exception to the general

---

[187] *Id.*

[188] *Id.*

[189] *Id.*

[190] *Id.*

principles of the OECD instruments. It is one of the failings of the OECD instruments that their provisions are fragmented.[191] A second failing of the OECD Instruments is that their coverage is not complete. For example, the national treatment instrument does not apply to privatization process, to the behavior of public and private monopolies, and to investment incentives in the establishment phase.[192] In addition, they apply only to the OECD members, and do not address the developing countries point of view.[193]

One of the most important functions of the OECD instruments is to encourage liberalization of member states' national investment policies.[194] It should be noted that acceptance of the OECD instruments by new Members is considered fundamental from the moment of their accession to the OECD. In particularly, the implications of OECD instruments on Turkey will be analyzed in the coming chapters related to the Turkish foreign investment policy.

It is essential to note that the OECD Guidelines regulate the behavior of the multinational enterprises. This provides balanced approach to the FDI which is desired by most developing countries. Thus, if there will be a multilateral investment agreement in the future, this agreement should regulate not only host countries investment policies, but also multinational corporate behavior. In order to do that, drafters of the new agreement should take into account of the OECD guidelines. To sum up, the OECD Instruments have played an important role till now, and they should be used as a reference for the negotiation of the multilateral investment agreement.

---

[191] OECD, OECD Investment Instruments and the MAI, Toronto Speech, (www.oecd.org//daf/cmis/mai/toronto.htm) (visited 1/27/2000).

[192] *Id*.

[193] Hart, *supra* note 184, at 15.

[194] Witherell, *supra* note 91, at 3.

IV.   **The Role of International Organizations on the development of International Investment Law**

The activities of international organizations such as the UN, and the OECD, have played an important role on the development of international legal framework on FDI. The international organizations have negotiated and adopted both binding, and non-binding legal instruments dealing with FDI.

Even though most legal instruments issued by international organizations are considered "soft law", non- binding rules, they can be adopted by states and become legally binding. For example, the UNCITRAL Arbitration Model Law is not a legally binding instrument. However, as many countries did, Turkey enacted a new, and its first, international arbitration law based on the UNCITRAL Arbitration Model Law.[195]

The legal instruments issued by international organizations may not have a legal enforcement mechanism. However, some countries, which adopted the legal instruments, can pressure other countries to change their rules towards the instruments' aim. For example, as we noted before, the OECD Guidelines for Multinational Enterprises are not legally binding instruments. However, OECD member countries, and six non-Member countries, Argentina, Brazil Chile, Estonia, Lithuania and Slovenia, voluntarily adopted the guidelines into their legal systems.[196]

International organizations can provide technical information to promote and to revise bilateral investment treaties and national investment law. As we explained, UNCTAD has continued to work on hosting bilateral investment treaty negotiations. For

---

[195] Turkish Official Gazette No. 24453, dated 5 July 2001; Serdar Bezen, Turkey Adopts the UNCITRAL Model Law, Mealey's International Arbitration Reports, August (2001).

[196] OECD, *About Guidelines on Multinational Enterprises*, http://www.oecd.org/EN/about/0,,EN-about-93-nodirectorate-no-no-no-9,00.html (visited 06/05/2002)

example, like Bolivia, Zimbabwe, and Philippines, many countries negotiated BITs under the auspices of the UNCTAD.

It should be noted that a number of international organizations, such as the UN and the OECD, provide various international instruments to promote FDI in the world. International organizations, like UNCTAD, have been working on investment policies that rely on the balance approach for protecting and promoting FDI at the same time. UNCTAD's works on FDI are based on developing countries' view, mostly their economic and social development concerns. The role of the international organizations on the development of international investment law will be explained in more detail at Chapter 10.

CHAPTER FIVE. ANALYSIS OF THE OECD MULTILATERAL AGREEMENT ON INVESTMENT TREATY

I. Preliminary Remarks: Multilateral Agreement on Investment (MAI)

As already mentioned, the OECD investment instruments have impetus power to liberalize and to govern the investment policy of the OECD member countries. However, there is no comprehensive multilateral agreement on international investment. The OECD countries are convinced of the importance of international investment and the need for transparent and fair rules for investors and investments. Therefore, the negotiations for the Multilateral Agreement on Investment (MAI) were launched under the auspices of the OECD in May 1995.

Negotiations on the treaty had begun in 1995 among the OECD member states and the European communities, in accordance with a mandate granted by the OECD Ministerial in June 1994.[1] The intended completion date of the MAI was the 1997 OECD Ministerial Meeting. This date was never met because of the growing internal dissent and widespread civil society opposition to the MAI draft.[2] In April 1997, OECD Ministers called for a six month discontinuity in negations to allow for a period of assessment and national consultations with civil society, bearing in mind among other things economic concerns and political, social, and cultural sensitivities. The Negotiations were resumed in October 20, 1998; however, the new French government

---

[1] WILLIAM H. WITHERELL, TOWARD AN INTERNATIONAL SET RULES FOR INVESTMENT, OECD, TOWARDS MULTILATERAL INVESTMENT RULES 21 (1996).

[2] UNCTAD, LESSONS FROM THE MAI (1999).

announced its withdrawal from the MAI talks citing conflicts with national sovereignty and protection of France's culture industries.[3] On December 3, 1998, the OECD announced that " Negotiations on the MAI are no longer taking place."[4]

Even though the negotiations on the MAI failed, it is still important to analyze the last draft of the MAI provisions. This chapter explains negotiations on the MAI so as to draw lessons that could be utilized for future negotiations of international investment agreements, whether bilateral, regional or multilateral. First, this chapter analyzes the legal status of Draft treaties under international law. Then, the chapter examines the substantive and procedural rules of the MAI draft treaty by comparing it with BITs.

II. The Legal Status of Draft Treaties Under the International Law

The legal status of draft treaties can be considered as a "writings of publicists", or "soft law" under the international law. The legal status of the draft treaty under the international law should be examined in order to understand the importance of the MAI draft treaty. The draft treaties have an impact on international law. Oppenheim rightly states, "The results of conferences held in such circumstances may have a significant

---

[3] Prime Minister Lionel Jospin said that: "France will not resume talks at the OECD on October 20," notably due to concern that the planned agreement will undermine French sovereignty. He said that: " It does not seem to us that it would be wise to see private interests bite into the sphere of the sovereignty of the state to an extensive extent", and he added that "the World Trade Organization in Geneva is a more appropriate forum for negotiating an international investment agreement." Sue Kendall, *France Pulls Out of International Investment Talks*, Agence France Presse, October 14, 1998, Paris.

[4] OECD News Release, *Informal Consultations on International Investment*, OECD, Paris, 3 December 1998. According to the OECD official statement : "Negotiations on the MAI are no longer taking place. However, the officials agreed on the importance of multidisciplinary work on investment at OECD. There are a number of important issues on which further analytical work and intergovernmental co-operation are needed. The officials agreed that this work should be carried out in a transparent manner and should involve all OECD members as well as interested non-member countries, including those that participated as observers in the negotiations."

effect on the rules of international law. . . . Even if the conference fails altogether to lead to the conclusion of a treaty, this will not be without its effects upon international law, particularly where the conference has been based on the extensive preparatory work."[5]

Many conferences had been held before the negotiation text of the treaty drafted. Legal scholars have been attending these conferences as government representatives, and they have been working many years to have some outcome. One may argue that draft treaties "are not law per se. Yet they may be the best available current expressions of customary law and if so, they may have persuasive influence."[6] Oppenheim spells out the importance of the draft treaty by giving example of the International Law Commissions' work. He says,

> Given the authoritative status of the members of the Commission as individual jurists, the fact that collectively they represent many nationalities, and the close connection of their work with the international political realities of the day, the work of the Commission, even where it does not result in a treaty but particularly so if is does, is itself an authoritative influence on the development of the law and a cogent material source of law."[7]

One may argue that the draft treaties can be accepted as a secondary international law source under the "writings of publicists" stipulated in Article 38 of the I.C.J Statute. The written documents prepared by working parties in negotiation process of the treaty serve as principal sources of evidence of international consent. As justice Gray stated in the Paquete Habana:

> International law is part of our law, must be ascertained and administered by the courts of justice of appropriate jurisdiction, as often as questions of right

---

[5] OPPENHEIM, INTERNATIONAL LAW, VOLUME I PEACE 50 (Sir Robert Jennings, & Sir Arthur Watts eds., 9th ed.), (1992).

[6] VIDAYA DHAR MAHARAJAN, PUBLIC INTERNATIONAL LAW 86 (1972).

[7] OPPENHEIM, *supra* note 5, at 50.

depending upon it are duly presented for their determination. For this purpose, where there is no treaty, and no controlling executive or legislative act or judicial decision, resort must be had to the customs and usages of civilized nations; and as evidence of these, to the works of jurist and commentators who by years of labour, research, and experience have made themselves peculiarly well acquainted with the subjects of which they treat. Such works are resorted to by judicial tribunals, not for the speculations of their authors concerning what the law ought to be, but for trustworthy evidence of what the law really is.[8]

These sources provide guidance on rulemaking. They have been recognized as evidence of international law rather than as independent sources of law themselves. This chapter, as already noted that at the outset elucidates the MAI draft treaty by comparing it with BITs and concludes controversial issues that should be taken into account in future international investment arrangements.

It is also possible to argue that the draft treaties can be considered as soft law instruments. Indeed, many legal scholars argue that conference declarations, resolutions and guidelines issued by organization and draft treaties, are soft law instruments.[9] Even though the term "soft law" has been recognized by international community and has become an important in the development of international economic law, international human rights law and international environmental law, there is no generally accepted

---

[8] The Paqueta Habana, 175 U.S. at 677 (1900). Lori Fisler Damrosch, *Scholars in the Construction and Critique of International Law*, American Society of International Law Proceedings, 317 (2000).

[9] Catherine Tinker spells out that" Commentators frequently refer to international conference statements that represent international consensus or aspiration as "soft law," a legal form that is not actually binding on states." Catherine Tinker, *Is a United Nations Convention the Most Appropriate Means to Pursue the Goal of Biological Diversity? Responsibility For Biological Diversity Conservation Under International Law*, 28 VAND. J. TRANSNAT'L L. 777 (1995); Professor Gunther F. Handl, *A Hard Look at Soft Law*, American Society of International Law Proceedings, April 20-23, 371 (1998); A. Neil Craik,, *Recalcitrant Reality and Chosen Ideals: the Public Function of Dispute Settlement in International Environmental Law*, 10 GEO. INT'L ENVTL. L. REV 551, 573 (1998); Pierre Marie Dupuy, *Soft Law and The international Law of the Environment*, 12 MICH. J. INT'L L 420, 428 (1991).

definition of soft law.[10] C.M. Chinkin explained the importance of the concept of soft law in international law as follows:

> The use of soft law instruments has presented a challenge to the normative structure, the traditional sources, the subjects and subject matter of international law. The international legal order is an evolving into new subject areas . . . Labelling these instruments as law or non-law disguises the reality that both play a major role in the development of international law and both are needed for regulation of State's activities and for creation of expectations. Soft law instruments allow for the incorporation of conflicting standards and goals provide States with the room manoeuvre in the making of claims and counterclaims. While this process inevitably causes normative confusion and uncertainty in terms of the traditional sources of international law, it is probably the inevitable consequence of unresolved pressures for change in international law.[11]

Soft law does not create legally binding obligations, however it does have indirect impact on the development of international law.[12] It is vital to note that whereas soft law is not legally binding, "soft law indicates the direction in which the international community is interested in moving."[13] As Pierre Marie Dupuy emphasizes, soft law "creates and delineates goals to be achieved in the future rather than actual duties, programs rather than prescriptions, guidelines rather than strict obligations."[14] I agree with this statement that the draft treaties, in our case the MAI draft treaty, shows which

---

[10] UNCTAD, TRENDS IN INTERNATIONAL INVESTMENT AGREEMENTS: AN OVERVIEW, 47-49 (1999); Joseph Gold, *Strengthening The Soft International Law of Exchange Arrangements*, 77 AM. J. INT'L L. 443, 443-444 (1983).

[11] C.M. Chinkin, *The Challenge of Soft Law: Development and Change in International Law*, 38 Int'l & Comp. L. Q. 850, 866 (1989) ; (Luis E. Rodriguez-Rivera, *Is The Human Right to Environment Recognized under International Law? It Depends on the Source*, 12 COLO. J. INT'L ENVTL. L & POL'Y 1, 42-43 (2001).

[12] Kenneth W. Abbott, *The Many Faces of International Legalization*, 92 American Society of International Law Proceedings. 57 (1998).

[13] Tinker, *supra* note 9, at 804.

[14] Dupuy, *supra* note 9, at 428.

law ought to be in the future. Thus, it is vital to analyze the MAI draft provisions and learn some lessons from its failure.

III. General Provisions of the MAI Draft Treaty

As stated in a report by the MAI Negotiating Group delivered to the OECD Council Meeting, the MAI was intended to: "provide a comprehensive framework for investment with high standards of liberalization and investment protection, and with effective dispute settlement."[15] Furthermore, the MAI was a free standing treaty, opened to access by non-members who were willing and able to meet its obligations and was to be a comprehensive, high standards agreement establishing a legally binding multilateral framework for investment liberalization and investor protection.

The MAI was based on many existing BITs between developed and developing countries.[16] The MAI was also based on the investment provisions of the North American Free Trade Agreement (NAFTA).[17] On the other hand, the MAI expanded these provisions, and unlike NAFTA, which only applies to the U.S., Mexico and Canada, would apply them worldwide (at least 30 OECD member countries).

Most BITs in their preambles refer simply to the promotion of the flow of capital, and the creation of favourable conditions for investment on the basis of sovereign

---

[15] OECD, *Report on the MAI*, OECD/GD (95) 65, 1995.

[16] *Id.*

[17] NAFTA contains the most comprehensive investment rules in its Chapter 11. Canada, United States and Mexico are the parties of the Agreement. Wesley Scholz, *International Regulation of Foreign Direct Investment, Symposium,* 31 CORNELL INT'L L. J. 485, 486 (1998)

equality, non-discrimination and mutual benefit.[18] There are also some variations from the general language of the preamble. For example, a number of BITs concluded between Central and Eastern European countries made references to the Final Act of the Helsinki Conference which is related to human rights.[19]

On the other hand, preamble of the MAI contains references not only to the flow of capital, and the enhancement of economic cooperation, but also to appropriate environmental policies, the Rio Declaration on Environment and Development and Agenda 21, and internationally recognized core labour standards.[20] The reason stipulating this issue in the preamble is to avoid criticism from civil society. Especially Non-Governmental Organizations (NGOs) criticized the MAI due to the fact that the MAI did not contain any provisions regarding environmental concern and labor issues.

After heavy criticism of these issues, negotiators of the MAI tried to insert some provisions that address environmental and labor concerns of the civil society.[21] I contend that in order to achieve sustainable development (the balancing of economic, social and environmental objectives), international agreements should recognize the integration of

---

[18] RUDOLF DOLZER& MARGRETE STEVENS, BILATERAL INVESTMENT TREATIES (1995).

[19] *Id.* at 23.

[20] Preamble of the MAI states that "...Recognizing that appropriate environmental policies can play a key role in ensuring that economic development, to which investment contributes, is sustainable, and resolving to desiring to implement this agreement (in accordance with international environmental law and) in a manner consistent with sustainable development, as reflected in the Rio Declaration on Environment and Development and Agenda 21,......
Renewing their commitment to the Copenhagen Declaration of the World Summit on Social Development and to observance of internationally recognized core labour standards, i.e. freedom of association, the right to organize and bargain collectively, prohibition of forced labour, the elimination of exploitative forms of child labour, and non-discrimination in employment, and noting that the International Labour Organization is the competent body to set and deal with core labour standards world wide." OECD, *The MAI Negotiating Text*, as of 24 April 1998, at 7.

[21] John Wickham, *Toward A Green Multilateral Investment Framework: NAFTA and The Search for Models,* 12 GEO. INT'L ENVTL. L. REV 617, 618 (2000).

economic and environmental policies. The MAI should provide a general exception for environmental measures based on Article XX of the GATT. I also argue that there should be a provision in the MAI for not to lower environmental and labor standards in order to attract investment. The MAI should not undermine government authority to regulate for the protection of the environment, health, and safety. However, some countries claimed that labor and environmental standards should not be included in the MAI, since there are other international forums, such as the ILO, specifically established to address these issues[22]. The final draft text of the MAI had references to these issues in brackets, that is to say that, negotiators had not been able to agree on how to respond to these criticisms.[23] Even though the MAI Preamble provides some language with respect to environmental and labor issues, this Preamble still lacked legal implications, since the Vienna Convention on the Law of Treaties precisely states that preambular language is not binding on parties to a treaty[24]. On the other hand, the preamble is relevant to the interpretation of the treaty since it reflects the treaty's object and purpose.[25]

---

[22] OECD, *The MAI Negotiating Text, as of 24 April 1998*, at 7-10.

[23] *Id.*

[24] Samrat Ganguly, *The Investor-State Dispute Mechanism (ISDM) and a Sovereign's Power to Public Health,* 38 COLUM. J. TRANSNAT'L L 113, 129 (1999).

[25] UNCTAD, BILATERAL INVESTMENT TREATIES IN THE MID 1990s 29 (1998).

IV. Scope and Application Of the MAI Draft Treaty

A. Definitions

The scope of investment agreements is determined mainly through definitions of key terms, such as "investment" and "investor". In other words, these two definitions have two significant roles in an agreement: they determinate those assets to which the treaty applies, and they may determine the nature of the obligations created by the treaty. These terms have an important role in determining the normative content of an instrument. Therefore, the definition of these terms is based on the purpose of the international investment agreement.[26]

An international investment agreement applies only to certain types of investment. One important character of such investment is that it must be foreign, namely, investment by investors from one country in the territory of another. Thus, the definition of the term "investor" complements the definition of "investment".[27]

As UNCTAD Publication, entitled "Scope and Definition", states that "there is no single, static conception of what constitutes foreign investment. Rather, the conception has changed over time as the nature of international economic relations has changed."[28] This publication analyses the terms "investment" and "investor" very deeply. Many countries have different investment policies. These differences are result of using various terms of investment in international investment agreements. If signatories seek to only

---

[26] UNCTAD, SCOPE AND DEFINITION 32 (1999).

[27] *Id.* at 6.

[28] See more information regarding historical development of the definition of investment and investor in a detail concept at the UNCTAD, Scope and Definition *supra* note at 26, at 7.

liberalize investment regulations, they will generally accept a narrow based definition of investment. For example, the OECD Code of Liberalization of Capital Movements utilized narrow definition of investment.[29] On the other hand, if signatories seek to protect foreign investment, they will generally accept a broad definition of investment. For example Most BITs and MIGA used broad definitions of investment.[30]

Recently, most international investment agreements seek both to liberalize investment regulations and to protect foreign investment. A broad definition of investment is utilized in recent agreements. In many cases, the definition is a broad one that contains all assets in the territory of one party owned by investors of another party.[31] However, some investment agreements limit the definition in various ways. For example, some BITs may exclude certain sectors of the economy from the definition.

The MAI defines the terms "investor" and "investment" very broadly.[32] Most BITS have very broad definitions of the terms "investment" and "investor", which are not greatly different in substance from those in the MAI.[33] The MAI negotiators recognized that for greater certainty there was a need for an interpretative note to indicate that "in order to qualify as an investment under the MAI, an asset must have the characteristics of an investment, such as the commitment of capital or other resources, the expectation of

---

[29] *Id.* at 15.

[30] *Id.* at 15.

[31] *Id.* at 17.

[32] Mark Vallianatos, *De-Fanging the MAI*, 31 CORNELL INT'L L.J. 713, 714 (1998).

[33] Manfred Schekulin, *Scope of the MAI, Definition of Investor and Investments*, OECD, The Multilateral Agreement on Investment, State of Play as of February (1997), at 11.

gain or profit, or the assumption of risk."[34] This situation shows that the only asset based definition is not enough to determine the terms.

Investment agreements apply only to investment by investors. Therefore, the definition of term investor is an important in determining scope of an agreement as that of investment. The definition of "investor" generally includes natural persons and legal persons. With respect to natural persons, determination of the relevant link between the investor and the home state party to the agreement is the only important issue that will arise. On the other hand, with respect to legal entities, there are problems defining and excluding legal entities in the agreement.[35] According to the UNCTAD publications, Scope and Definitions, "Regarding investor, legal persons possessing such an effective link with a State contracting party. Certain exclusions may be introduced into the agreement based on either legal form of the entity, the purpose of the entity and the nature of ownership."[36].

Like in other international agreements, the terms investment and investor are central to the MAI. Under the MAI draft the terms has been given a very comprehensive coverage. Under the MAI, the definition of investor covered all natural persons who are nationals or permanent residents of a contracting party in accordance with its applicable laws, and legal persons or entities constituted under the applicable law of a contracting party, whether or not for profit, or whether private or government-owned or controlled.[37]

---

[34] OECD, *The MAI Negotiating Text, (as of 24 April 1998)*, at 11.

[35] UNCTAD, SCOPE AND DEFINITION, *supra* note 26, at 32.

[36] See for more information, UNCTAD, Scope and Definition, *supra* note 26, at 32-49.

[37] Article II, Scope and Definition, 1- (i) and (ii) explains what investor means, OECD, MAI Negotiating Text, as of 24 April 1998, at 1

The MAI has a single, broad asset based, and open-ended definition of investment.[38] Single meaning that the definition of investment would have application both before and after a foreign investor has established itself in the host country.[39] Broad meaning that the definition of investment covers not only tangible assets but also intangible assets and also portfolio investment.[40]

Even though, there was a broad support for an asset based definition of investment, a few delegations debated for the exclusion of portfolio investment from the MAI.[41] They argued that the inclusion of portfolio investment under the MAI could restrict the ability of governments to impose controls on "volatile" and "speculative" capital investment.[42] As Mark Vallianatos emphasizes their argument, portfolio investors "do not control or manage the companies they invest in…This lack of commitment to any economic activity makes portfolio investment more liquid and volatile than direct investment."[43] He also recommends that the MAI should cover portfolio investment in a way that requires "minimum time frame, of one or two years" duration for investment.[44] Some negotiators also disagreed about accepting an open ended based definition. In order to deal with these arguments, contracting parties agreed to rely on safeguard

---

[38] Schekulin, *supra* note 33, at 11.

[39] *Id*. at 11.

[40] *Id*. at 11.

[41] UNCTAD, *supra* note 2, at 11.

[42] Vallianatos, *supra* note 32, at 715-716.

[43] *Id.*

[44] *Id.*

provisions, such as balance of payments exceptions.[45] Furthermore, there were three specific areas they needed to resolve, namely; indirect investment, intellectual property, concessions.[46] With respect to indirect investment, it was agreed that indirect investment covered when they were made into an MAI country via a subsidiary established in the same MAI country. However, there were different views on whether an investment should be covered by the MAI if it were made in one MAI country to another MAI country in the case where the investment was made through a subsidiary located outside the MAI zone.[47] With respect to intellectual property, the definition of the intellectual property, the relationship between other intellectual property agreements, specifically TRIPS and the MAI were only few examples of questions that were unresolved in the MAI negotiations.[48] With respect to concessions, the remaining problem was to determine the term of concessions since many countries have different meanings for this term.[49]

B.   Geographical Application

The MAI would apply in relation to land territories, internal waters, the territorial seas and maritime zones beyond the territorial seas (in particular the exclusive economic

---

[45] UNCTAD, *supra* note 2, at 11.

[46] *Id.* at 11.

[47] Robert Ley, *The Scope of the MAI, Multilateral Agreement on Investment*, State of Play in April (1997), at 17.

[48] *Id*, at 17.

[49] *Id*, at 17.

zone (EEZ) and the continental shelf).[50] Most BITS have the same geographical application as the MAI, by virtue of the definition of "territory" in article 1.[51]

The aim of the definition of territory usually is not to describe the land territory of the parties, but to indicate that territory includes maritime zones over which the host country exercises jurisdiction.[52] Therefore, mineral exploration or extraction facilities in the host country's maritime jurisdiction will be covered by the agreement.

V. The Main Substantive Provisions of the MAI

A. Non-Discrimination Principle

The main provision of the MAI is non-discrimination principle. National Treatment (NT), and Most Favoured Nation (MFN) are core concepts of international trade law. They are included in the GATT, and other WTO agreements.[53] Like WTO agreements, NT combined with MFN are central to the MAI. The non-discrimination principles of national treatment is assured for the establishment of new investments by non-resident investors and for the operation and expansion of established investments under foreign control. Contacting parties tried to make a better definition for non-discrimination principles.

---

[50] OECD, The MAI Negotiating Text, (as of 24 April 1998), at 12.

[51] UNCTAD, BILATERAL INVESTMENT TREATIES, *supra* note 25, at 41-42

[52] *Id*, at 44.

[53] UNCTAD, MOST FAVOURED NATION TREATMENT (herein after MFN) 13 (1998).

Article III, Paragraph 1 of the MAI defines the NT as of requiring foreign investors to be given treatment no less favourable than the treatment accorded to domestic investors in relation to all phases of investment from establishment to disposition.[54] Paragraph 2 of Article 3 defines the MFN as of requiring foreign investors to be given equal treatment in relation to all phases of investment, regardless of whether or not the foreign investors concerned are from MAI contracting parties.[55] Paragraph 3 of the Article 3 stipulates that the best of two treatments would be granted if there is a difference between NT and the MFN.[56]

NT requires that foreign investors must be treated in the same manner as domestic investors. This means that a foreign investor is subject to the same laws, regulation and policies as a domestic investor. These laws, regulations or policies must not impose different standards of treatment or obligations or provide preferential treatment between nationals and foreigners in like circumstances.

In broad terms, MFN requires that a nation treat all other nations in the same way. Thus, if MFN were to apply and special privileges were accorded to the investors of

---

[54] Article III, paragraph 1 of the MAI states that: "Each Contracting Party shall accord to investors of another Contracting Party and to their investments, treatment no less favourable than the treatment it accords (in like circumstances) to its own investors and their investments with respect to the establishment, acquisition, expansion, operation, management, maintenance, use, enjoyment and sale or other disposition of investments." OECD, MAI Negotiating Text, as of 24 April 1998, at 13.

[55] Paragraph 2 of Article 3 states that: "Each Contracting Party shall accord to investors of another Contracting Party and to their investments, treatment no less favourable than the treatment it accords(in like circumstances) to investors of any other Contracting Party or of a non-Contracting Party, and to the investments of investors of any other Contracting Party or of a non-Contracting Party, with respect to the establishment, acquisition, expansion, operation, management, maintenance, use, enjoyment, and sale or other disposition of investments." Id, at 13.

[56] Paragraph 3 of the Article 3 states that: "Each Contracting Party shall accord to investors of another Contracting Party and to their investments the better of the treatment required by Articles 1.1 and 1.2, whichever is the more favorable those investors and investments." Id, at 13.

home nation by host nation, then the investors of every other nation would have to be treated no less favourably.

Under the MAI, MFN and NT are required to be provided to investors and their investments in relation to the establishment, acquisition, expansion, operation, management, maintenance, use, enjoyment and sale or other disposition of investments, that is from the time an investment is proposed, through to the time when the investment is disposed of. Namely, the contracting parties extend MFN to the pre-establishment stage. However, under most BITs, NT and MFN treatment are required to be accorded only in relation to investments admitted after the proposal for investment is examined in accordance with the national law.[57] In other words, most BITs provide post-establishment NT and MFN treatment to foreign investment. Thus, the standards of treatment contained in the MAI are more extensive than that provided for in most existing BITs. Nevertheless, Part IX of the draft MAI provides for country specific exceptions and exemptions to National Treatment and MFN treatment. These exemptions will be examined at the below. One may argue that the draft schedule of exceptions to the MAI tried to make its application much closer to the type of system which exists under most BITs.

The aim of the MAI is to ban any discrimination against foreign investors. Its aim is not to ban countries from pursuing their own foreign investment policies if they are not discriminatory. Robin Morgan stated that: "The purpose of the MAI is to promote non-discrimination; it is not intended to harmonize individual countries' investment

---

[57] UNCTAD, MFN, *supra* note 53, at 14.

policies."[58] NT and MFN clauses' aim is to make sure that foreign investors receive similar treatment to national investors, not to establish an absolute standard on investment policy. Furthermore, there were no agreements whether or not to insert comparative terminology for the NT and MFN clauses. Some negotiators agreed to insert the words "in like circumstances" which added in the brackets at the Negotiating text of 24 April 1998.[59] However some negotiators claimed that there was no need to insert these words to the Negotiating text, since the comparative nature of NT and MFN clause is evident.[60]

B. Transparency of Laws

The MAI requires each Contracting Party to promptly publish, or otherwise make publicly available its laws, regulations, procedures and administrative rulings and judicial decisions of general application as well as international agreements which may affect the operation of the MAI.[61]

---

[58] Robin Morgan, *Treatment and Protection of Investors and Investments, OECD, Multilateral Agreement on Investment*, State of Play in April (1997), at 21.

[59] Valerie Charolles, *National Treatment, Most Favoured Nation Treatment and Transparency, OECD, Multilateral Agreement on Investment*, State of Play as of February (1997), at 20.

[60] *Id.* at 20.

[61] Article III, Transparency, Paragraph 1 states that: "Each Contracting Party shall promptly publish, or otherwise make publicly available, its laws, regulations, procedures and administrative rulings and judicial decisions of general application as well as international agreements which may affect the operation of the Agreement...." Id. The MAI Negotiating Text, at 13.

The MAI provisions states that nothing in the agreement is to be taken to limit the power of a party to collect information for information or statistical purposes, or to require it to reveal confidential or proprietary information about foreign investors.[62]

Most BITs do not explicitly require each contracting party to make its laws pertaining to investment public and readily accessible.[63] In addition, most BITs have no provisions relating to gathering statistical information and to revealing confidential information about foreign investors.[64] This is by all means less specific than the requirement under the MAI.

C. Investment Protection Obligations

1. General Treatment

Pursuant to the MAI provision, investments shall receive fair and equitable treatment and full and constant protection and security.[65] Contracting parties are obliged under the MAI to accord fair and equitable treatment and full and constant protection to

---

[62] Article III, Transparency, Paragraph 3 states that: "Nothing in this Agreement shall prevent a Contracting Party from requiring an investor of another Contracting Party, or its investment, to provide routine information concerning that investment solely for information or statistical purposes. Nothing in this Agreement requires a Contracting Party to furnish or allow access to:
a) information related to the financial affairs and accounts of individual customers of particular investors or investments, or
b) any confidential or proprietary information, including information concerning particular investors or investments, the disclosure of which would impede law enforcement or be contrary to its laws protecting confidentiality or prejudice legitimate commercial interests of particular enterprises." Id, at 14.

[63] UNCTAD, BILATERAL INVESTMENT TREATIES, *supra* note 25, at 85.

[64] *Id.*

[65] Article IV, Investment Protection, 1-General Treatment, 1.1, The MAI Negotiating Text, as of 24 April 1998, at 57.

the investments of foreign investors. Treatment shall in no case be less favourable that what is required by international law.[66] Contracting parties undertake not to impair the operation, management, maintenance, use, enjoyment or disposal of investments in its territory of the investors of other contracting parties.[67] However, the test of impairment could not be resolved in the MAI negotiations. Thus, MAI provision contains "unreasonableness" and "discrimination" for the test of the impairment in two different brackets.[68] Some argued that it would go too far to prohibit measures that only are "unreasonable" since the term is so ambiguous. Others argued that it would be too narrow to insert only "discriminatory" measures since there may be some non-discriminatory measures which badly affect the investors' activities.[69]

Overall, the MAI guarantees the investor and investment fair and equitable treatment and full protection and security in a general treatment provision that is usually supplemented by national treatment which applies to all matters of investment protection. Most BITS provisions with respect to general treatment are not significantly different.[70] Indeed most BITs provide for investments which have been admitted under domestic law to be accorded fair and equitable treatment.

---

[66] Article IV, Investment Protection, 1-General Treatment, 1.1 states that: "Each contracting Part shall accord to investments in its territory of investors of another Contracting Party fair and equitable and full and constant protection and security...", The MAI Negotiating Text, as of 24 April 1998, at 57.

[67] Article IV, Investment Protection, 1-General Treatment, 1.2 states that: "A Contracting Party shall not impair by [unreasonable or discriminatory] [unreasonable and discriminatory] measures the operation, management, maintenance, use, enjoyment or disposal of investments in its territory of investors of another Contracting Party.", The MAI Negotiating Text, as of 24 April 1998, at 57.

[68] *Id.* at 57.

[69] Joachim Karl, *Investment Protection, The Multilateral Agreement of Investment*, State of Play as of February (1997), OECD, at 14.

[70] *Id.*

2. Expropriation and Compensation

The MAI grants foreign investors a right to compensation when a host government directly or indirectly expropriates their investments or profits or takes an action that has the "equivalent effect" of expropriation. Chapter IV. 2.1 of the MAI states:

> A Contracting Party shall not expropriate or nationalize directly or indirectly an investment in its territory of an investor of another Contracting Party or take any measure or measures having equivalent effect except for a purpose which is in the public interest, on a non- discriminatory basis, in accordance with due process of law, and accompanied by payment of prompt, adequate and effective compensation.[71]

Pursuant to the MAI, an expropriation, or other measure having the equivalent effect, is only permitted if it is in the public interest, non-discriminatory, subject to prompt, adequate and effective compensation, and in accordance with the due process of law.[72] Article IV, 2, Expropriation continued by specifying in more detail what the terms "prompt, adequate, and effective and due process" mean. There were agreements among the contracting parties that compensation shall be paid without delay, that is to say, prompt, and shall be equivalent to the fair market value of the investment, that is to say, adequate, and shall be paid according to a convertible currency, that is to say effective.[73] Furthermore, the MAI provides that the investor has the right to have its case reviewed by

---

[71] Article IV, 2. Expropriation and Compensation, MAI Negotiating Text, as of 24 April 1998, at 57.

[72] *Id.*

[73] Article IV, 2. Expropriation and Compensation states that: "
2.2 Compensation shall be paid without delay.
2.3 Compensation shall be equivalent to the fair market value of the expropriated investment immediately before the expropriation occurred. The Fair market value shall not reflect any change in value occurring because the expropriation had become publicly known earlier.
2.4 Compensation shall be fully realisable and freely transferable. . .." *Id.*

a judicial authority or another component and independent authority in the host country, that is to say, due process of law.[74]

Under the MAI, the term "expropriation" is not defined, but it is clear form the language of the expropriation provision that its meaning is very broad. According to this provision, "expropriation" is defined not just as the outright seizure of a property, but also includes governmental actions tantamount to expropriation which could include some regulatory laws. Problems arose from the inclusion of indirect expropriation and measures having the equivalent effect of expropriation, such as tax or zoning measures. By broadening expropriation to include indirect expropriations, the MAI offered a new opportunity for foreign investors to extend their legal rights with respect to investment protection.[75] The MAI's broad definition of expropriation includes so-called "regulatory takings" imposing obligations on governments not to implement regulatory measures that may reduce the value of an investment. This definition could grant investors the ability to demand compensation for land-use, zoning and environmental protection laws.[76]

NGOs claimed that the investor protection provisions, when used in conjunction with investor-state dispute settlement process, could inhibit the exercise of normal regulatory powers of governments to protect environment and public health.[77] Their

---

[74] Article IV, 2. Expropriation and Compensation states that: "
2.6 Due Process of law includes, in particular, the right of an investor of Contracting Party which claims to be affected by expropriation by another Contracting party to prompt review of its case, including the valuation of its investment and the payment of compensation in accordance with the provisions of this article, by a judicial authority or another competent and independent authority of the latter Contracting Party." *Id.*

[75] Vallianatos, *supra* note 32, at 722.

[76] Edward M. Graham, *Regulatory Takings, Supernational Treatment, And the Multilateral Agreement on Investment: Issues Raised By Nongovernmental Organizations,* 31 CORNELL INT'L L. J. 599, 603 (1998).

[77] *Id.*

claim was based on arbitration cases under the NAFTA dispute settlement process. The following two arbitration cases will show their concern regarding broad expropriation provision and investor-state dispute settlement process.

a.   **Ethyl Corp. V. Government of Canada**[78]

Ethyl Corporation, a Virginia-based corporation, was the manufacturer of Methylcylopentadienyl Manganese Tricarbonyl (MMT), a gasoline additive, filed a US$ 251 million suit against the Canadian government under the arbitration provisions of NAFTA, asserting that the Bill C-29, which banned the international and inter-provincial trade in MMT, was an expropriation of its products in violation of the NAFTA investment provisions.[79]

On 9 April 1997, the Canadian Parliament approved a Bill C- 29, prohibiting the use of the additive MMT in gasoline produced in Canadian refineries, citing evidence that MMC was dangerous to human health and harmed the environment by damaging emissions control equipment in automobiles.[80] Arbitration claim was failed on 14 April 1997.[81]

---

[78] NAFTA CHAPTER 11 ARBITRAL TRIBUNAL: ETHYL CORPORATION v. THE GOVERNMENT OF CANADA (AWARD ON JURISDICTION) June 24, 1998, (Herein after Ethyl Award) International Legal Materials, Judicial and Similar Proceedings, May (1999).

[79] Ethyl Award, *supra* note 78, at 713.

[80] The Bill C-29 passed by the House, on 2 December 1996, and on 16-17 December Bill c-29 submitted to reading and referred to Committee. *Id.* Ethyl Award, at 714; Chris Baumgartner, *The Demise of the Multilateral Agreement on Investment*, 1998 COLO J. INT'L ENVTL. L. & POL'Y. 40 , 44 (1998).

[81] Ethyl Corporation has submitted its claim under the UNCITRAL Arbitration Rules, which govern this arbitration under the Article 1120 of the NAFTA, Ethyl Award, *supra* note 78, at 711.

Ethyl claimed that the Bill C-29 breached three provisions of Chapter 11 of NAFTA: a) Article 1102-National Treatment; b) Article 1106- Performance Requirements; and c) Article 1110-Expropriation and Compensation.[82] Canada argued that the tribunal does not have jurisdiction to adjudicate Ethyl's claim.[83] In particular, Canada's objections was based on the following "extensive jurisdictional" claim:

> As to the scope of Chapter 11, Canada urges (paraphrasing Paragraphs 6(a) of its Memorial on Jurisdiction):
> i) at the time the Claimant submitted its Notice of Arbitration there was no measure adopted or maintained by Canada within the meaning of that phrase in NAFTA Article 1101 (1);
> ii) the alleged measures of which Ethyl complains do not relate to an investment or an investor within the meaning of Article 1100 (1); and
>
> iii) the Claimant's claim in respect of expropriation and loss or damage outside Canada is not contemplated by Chapter 11.
>
> As regards the requirements of Section B of Chapter 11, Canada asserts (paraphrasing Paragraph 6(b) of its Memorial on Jurisdiction):
> i) the claimant failed to comply with the six month waiting period from the date of the alleged events giving rise to a claim before submitting a claim to arbitration, as required by article 1120;
> ii) the claimant did not deliver written consent and waivers required as conditions precedent to submission of a claim to arbitration under Article 1121; and
> iii)the claimant introduced new claims in its Statement of Claim not contained in its Notice of Arbitration (or in the Notice of Intent that preceded it under Article 1119.[84]

The Tribunal rejected these jurisdictional objections.[85] After interpreting relevant NAFTA articles in good faith and object and purpose of the NAFTA agreement, the tribunal found that the parties of NAFTA did not intend that procedural requirement

---

[82] *Id.* Ethyl Award, at 710.

[83] *Id.* Ethyl Award, at 712.

[84] *Id.* Ethyl Award, at 712.

[85] Andrea K. Bjorklund, *Contract Without Privity: Sovereign Offer and Investor Acceptance*, Chicago Journal of International Law, Spring 188 (2001).

provisions must be strictly fulfilled.[86] Furthermore, the tribunal found that even the Bill C-29 has received royal assent on 25 April 1977, just eleven days following claimant's Notice of Arbitration, The Bill C-29 constituted a "measure" subject to arbitration under Chapter 11 of the NAFTA. The Tribunal found what constitute a "measure" pursuant to Canada's statement on implementation of NAFTA which basically stated that "clearly something other than a "law" even something in the nature of a "practice" which may not even amount to a legal structure, may qualify."[87] That is to say that, the court broadly construed what constitute "measure".

The dispute was settled in July 1998.[88] Under the settlement terms, the Canadian government agreed to lift its prohibitions on MMT. Furthermore, government also agreed to pay almost CAN $19 million in damages, and provided a written letter of apology to Ethyl Corporation.[89] Some may argue that Canada opted to settle the dispute since it believed that it would be unable to prevail in NAFTA Tribunal. This case precisely indicates that government's regulatory power to protect environment and health of its people may be challenged by the foreign investor.[90]

---

[86] The court concludes that " this results from interpreting those articles in good faith in accordance with the ordinary meaning to be given to the terms thereof in their context and in the light of the object and purpose of NAFTA, as prescribed by Article 31 of the Vienna Convention, and that, considering particularly the circumstances of NAFTA's conclusion, any different interpretation would lead to a result which is manifestly absurd or unreasonable within the meaning of Article 32 of the Vienna Convention." Ethyl Award, *supra* note 78, at 728.

[87] *Id*. Ethyl Award, at 725.

[88] NAFTA; *Canadian Government Withdraws MMT Ban; Ethyl Drops Suit in Exchange For $13 Million*, International Trade Reporter, Americas/NAFTA, July 22, (1998).

[89] *Id*. at 44.

[90] Ruper Schlegelmilch, *WTO, Why still not Multilateral Rules for Foreign Direct Investment*, International Trade Law & Regulation 81 (2000).

b.   **Metalclad Corp. v United Mexican States** [91]

This case was the first case to be brought forth under Chapter 11 of NAFTA to the ICSID tribunal. Under NAFTA's broad expropriation provision, the Metalclad Corporation, a hazardous waste disposal company based in Newport Beach, California, sued the government of Mexico on the grounds that the Mexican State of San Luis Potosi, by declaring that a waste disposal facility acquired by Metalclad was part of a protected ecological zone, effectively expropriated its investment. Metalclad claimed that, even though it had bean ready since 1995 to open the landfill, it has been prevented from going forward by Mexican authorities of the state government of San Luis Potosi. In particular, the state government denied Metalclad's application for a construction permit.[92] However the government refused to allow opening this facility since the site was on an ecologically sensitive underground alluvial stream. Metalclad asserted that this action effectively expropriated its future expected profits and seeks $90 million in damages.[93] Ironically, according to the Washington-based Preamble Collective, the amount that Metalclad sought was more than the combined annual income of every family in the San Luis Potosi where Metalclad's facility is located.[94] Mexico denied the Metalclad's

---

[91] Metalclad Corp v United Mexican States, ICSID Case No ARB(AF)/97/1, Award (Aug 30, 2000) (Herein after the Award), 40 ILM 36, January 2001.

[92] Ganguly, *supra* note 24, at 146.

[93] Elizabeth May, *Fighting the MAI, in* DISMANTLING DEMOCRACY 39 (Andrew Jackson & Matthew Sanger, eds., 1998).

[94] *Id.*

claims. Mexico's argument was based on jurisdictional issues. In particular, "Mexico argues that a claimant must ensure its claim is ripe at the time it is filed".[95]

The Tribunal met July 15, 1997, and Metalclad filed its memorial October 14, 1997. The Mexico filed its response on February 17, 1998.[96] The fact of the case shows that Metalclad had taken over the facility with the obligation that it clean up preexisting contaminants.[97] However, local residents and environmental groups were not satisfied with the arrangement since this place had a history of contaminated local ground water.[98]

The ICSID tribunal issued its award on behalf of Metalclad corp. on August 30, 2000.[99] According to the Award, the Mexican government has to pay $16.685.000.000 to the Metalclad Corp. The tribunal concluded that the actions of the Mexican state and municipal authorities violated the investment treatment provision of NAFTA which is obliged member countries to accord investment treatment "in accordance with international law, including fair and equitable treatment and full protection and

---

[95] The Award, *supra* note 91, Paragraph 63-64.

[96] The Award states, "On January 2, 1997, and pursuant to the NAFTA, Article 1120, Metalclad filed its Notice of Claim with the International Centere of Settlement of Investment Disputes (hereinafter "ICSID"), [FN1] and requested the Secretary- General of ICSID to approve and register its application and to permit access to the ICSID Additional Facility." Id, the Award, at paragraph 8. The tribunal chosen by Metalclad and Mexico includes: Benjamin R. Civiletti, former Attorney General of the United States; Jose Luis Siqueiros, an international lawyer and Mexican law professor, and Elihu Lauterpacht, a British law professor at Cambridge University, who served as president of the tribunal.

[97] *Id.* at 146.

[98] According to the study done by environmental groups, the waste disposal plant was an alluvial stream. The waste disposal facility could contaminate the local water supply for toxic chemicals. Thus, San Luis Potosi's Governer turned down the Metalclad Plant and announced that the area part of a 300,000 hectare ecological area. *Id.*

[99] The Award, *supra* note 91.

security."[100] The tribunal held that Mexico "failed to ensure a transparent and predictable framework for Metalclad's business planning and investment. The totality of these circumstances demonstrates that a lack of orderly process and timely disposition in relation to an investor of a party acting in the expectation that it would be treated fairly and justly in accordance with the NAFTA."[101] Alejandro A. Escobar spells out that this award "one of the first rulings every to apply to standard of fair and equitable treatment under a treaty governing matters."[102]

Furthermore, the tribunal found that the actions of the Mexican state and municipal authorities constituted expropriation under NAFTA Article 1110.[103] The tribunal acknowledged that:

> Expropriation under NAFTA includes not only open, deliberate and acknowledged takings of property, such as outright seizure or formal or obligatory transfer of title in favour of the host State, but also covert or incidental interference with the use of property which has the effect of depriving the owner, in whole or in significant part, of the use or reasonably- to-be-expected economic benefit of property even if not necessarily to the obvious benefit of the host State.[104]

The tribunal also found that the actions of the Mexican government constituted an indirect expropriation of Metalclad's investment. The court stated, "the exclusive

---

[100] NAFTA Agreement, article 1105 (1), Lucien J. Dhooge, *The North American Free Trade Agreement And The Environment: The Lessons of Metalclad Corporation v. United Mexican States*, 10 MINN. J. GLOBAL TRADE. 209, 249-250 (2001).

[101] The Award, *supra* note 91, at. Paragraph 99.

[102] Alejandro A. Escobar, Senior Counsel, ICSID, *Introductory Note*, the Award, at 2.

[103] NAFTA, Article 1110, which provides that "no Party to NAFTA may directly or indirectly nationalize or expropriate an investment of an investor of another Party in its territory or take a measure tantamount to nationalization or expropriation of such an investment ('expropriation'), except: (a) for a public purpose; (b) on a non-discriminatory basis; (c) in accordance with due process of law and Article 1105(1); and (d) on payment of compensation in accordance with paragraphs 2 through 6".

[104] The Award, *supra* note 91, at. Paragraph 103.

authority for siting and permitting a hazardous waste landfill resides with the Mexican federal government."[105]

After losing the case, Mexico filed an application to the Supreme Court of British Columbia to set aside the Metalclad award on the grounds that the ICSID tribunal acted outside its jurisdiction by deciding matters of Mexican law that should have been referred to Mexican Courts.[106] The British Columbia Supreme Court has set aside the interest portion of a $16.7 million North American Free Trade Agreement (NAFTA) award in favor of the Metalclad Corp.[107]

It should be noted that the MAI's expropriation provision is the expanded version of the NAFTA expropriation provision. The MAI's expropriation provision did not distinguish between compensable and noncompensable takings; if a law were ruled expropriatory, governments would have to compensate investors regardless of whether the planned use of the investment would threaten the environment or public health and safety.

Pursuant to Edward M. Graham, the main problem with the expropriation provision in the MAI is that it supplied investment dispute settlement and awards of compensation to foreign investors who would not have right to sue a government for regulatory takings in the national law.[108] Indeed, foreign investors would have an

---

[105] The Award, *supra* note 91, at. Paragraph 105.

[106] Supreme Court of British Columbia, Reasons for Judgement, of May 2, 2001, The United Mexican States v. Metalclad Corporation, 2001 BCSC 664. Mealey's International Arbitration Reports, May 2001, NAFTA, Portion of $16.7 Million METALCLAD Award Set Aside.

[107] *Id.*

[108] Graham, *supra* note 76.

discriminatory advantage in that they could challenge a measure under the MAI, while domestic investors can not have right to sue for regulatory takings of the government in national court or under the dispute settlement system of the MAI.[109] This is so called "supernational treatment" of foreign investment.[110] In addition, Michelle Swenarchuk argues that expropriation provision extends the principle of national treatment, because even measures applied to both foreign and domestic investors could give rise to claim for compensation by the foreign investors.[111] I agree with this opinion and this situation also nullified the purpose of the MAI which is the non-discrimination principle. Because most domestic laws such as the US, Canadian, and Mexican laws do not require government to compensate a domestic investor for loss of asset value resulting from a regulatory taking. For example, the regulatory taking issue is unclear in the US laws. Takings under US law are based on the Fifth Amendment to the US Constitution which states that "nor shall private property be taken for public use, without just compensation."[112] Under the case law on regulatory takings, regulation as opposed to physical taking of private land generally has not been considered takings.[113] Justice Holmes defined the concept of regulatory takings in Pennsylvania Coal v Mahon case, "the general rule at least is that while property may be regulated to a certain extent, if

---

[109] *Id.* at 613.

[110] *Id.* at 613.

[111] Michelle Swearchuk, *The MAI and The Environment*, in DISMANTLING DEMOCRACY 122 (Andrew Jackson & Matthew Sanger, eds., 1998).

[112] U.S Constitution, Amend. V.

[113] Ganguly, *supra* note 24, 141.

regulation goes too far it will be recognized as a taking."[114] This case created "too far" test in regulatory takings' case. However, the court did not determine the "too far" test. It means that "too far" test can be applied "into the circumstances of each particular case" by the courts.[115] This analysis shows that the content of the regulatory takings is not clear in the US laws, and the US courts generally rejected the compensation claims for regulatory takings.[116] Moreover, the US government argued in the MAI negotiation "normal regulatory action, even when it affects the value of investment, should not be considered an expropriation or "taking" requiring compensation."[117]

Most BITs provisions with respect to expropriation are not materially different from the proposed MAI provisions dealing with expropriation. As was pointed out earlier in the first chapter, these provisions may represent customary international law, at least insofar as they provide for compensation. Articles of this kind are to be found in many international agreements dealing with investment. On the other hand, the MAI's provision on expropriation went much further than that of the BITs, and customary international law as well. Especially inserting clauses on "indirect taking" into the

---

[114] Pennsylvania Coal v Mahon, 260 U.S 393, 415 (1922), Don Wallace, Jr & David B. Bailey, *The Inevitability of National Treatment of Foreign Direct Investment With Increasingly Few and Narrow Exceptions*, 31 CORNELL INT'L L. J. 615, 626 (1998).

[115] *Id.*

[116] For example, in Concrete Pipe ad Prods of Cal., Inc. V. Construction Laborers Pension Trust for S. Cal., case the court held that, " cases have long established that mere diminution in the value of property, however serious, is insufficient to demonstrate a taking." (508 U.S. 602, 645 91993). Id. Samrat Ganguly at 141. In addition, Lower courts of the United States have rejected compensation claims arising out of a wide range of laws protecting the environment or human health, including, among many others, laws requiring the clean-up of harmful commercial by products or other hazardous materials; limiting harmful commercial restricting the sale and transport of endangered species; restricting the right to hunt particular animals on private land; requiring the destruction of abandoned buildings; and prohibiting the exploitation of natural resources on private property for reasons of public health, safety and welfare.

[117] Stuart Eizenstat, Under Secretary for Economic, Business and Agricultural Affairs, and Jeffrey Lang, Deputy U.S. Trade Representative, *Remarks following the OECD meeting on MAI*, Paris, France, February 17, (1998). http://www.state.gov/www/policy_remarks/1998/980217_eizen_mai.html (visited 11/22/00).

expropriation provision was one of the vital criticisms by the NGOs and developing countries of the MAI.

3. Protection from strife

Like most BITs, the MAI provision on protection from strife has two types of broad coverage. The first one is that with or without the host government involvement in the case of civil strife and other similar events; host government is liable only non – discriminatory bases. The protection from strife clause deals with a situation where investors suffer losses in the host country as a consequence of war, other armed conflict, state of emergency, revolution, insurrection, civil disturbance or similar events.[118] Most BITs have same kind of provision with respect to protection from strife.[119] Like most BITS, according to the MAI, the host country shall not be obliged to pay compensation in such situations and the host country has a discretionary power with regard to the decision to compensate.[120] The MAI provision provides that if the host country decides to compensate, then the non-discriminatory principle, namely national treatment and most favored national treatment shall apply.[121] In other words, it provides for restitution, indemnification or compensation for the investor on the same basis as it would be

---

[118] Article IV. 3, Protection From Strife, MAI Negotiating Text, as of 24 April 1998, at 58.

[119] Report by OECD Working Group C, *Investment Protection*, in TOWARDS MULTILATERAL INVESTMENT RULES 148 (OECD, ed., 1996).

[120] *Id.* at 148.

[121] Joachim Karl, *Investment Protection, The Multilateral Agreement on Investment*, State of Play as of February (1997), OECD, at 15.

accorded to domestic investors or investors from third states, whichever is the more favourable.[122]

The second coverage is regarding direct involvement of host country's arm forces in specified circumstances. The host country shall compensate the investor in two situations: a) in the case that the armed forces of the host country requisition the property of the investor; and b) in the case where the property is destroyed by the armed forces of the host country where this demolition was not required by the necessity of the situation.[123] Furthermore, compensation in both cases must be prompt, adequate and effective.[124]

It should be noted that the first category of the MAI provision on protection from strife is very broad and could be invoked by foreign investors to seek protection from and compensation for events like armed forces were an act of rebellion. According the first category of the MAI provision, the host state is still liable to foreign investor on the basis of non-discrimination principle since the MAI provision on protection from strife has some vague terms such as " other similar events" which could apply for events like armed forces were act of rebellion, and could create dispute in the practice. The MAI provision might also be interpreted broadly by international Tribunals. For example, the ICSID Tribunal in Asian Agricultural Products Ltd (AAPL) v Republic of Sri Lanka

---

[122] Article IV, 3. Protection From Strife provision states that: ".... Contracting Party, shall be accorded by the latter Contracting Party, as regards restitution, indemnification, compensation or any other settlement, treatment no less favourable than that which it accords to its own investors or to investors of any third State, whichever is most favourable to the investor." Protection From Strife, MAI Negotiating Text, as of 24 April 1998, at 58.

[123] Article IV, 3.2 Protection From Strife, at 58.

[124] *Id*. at 58.

Case construed broadly "the standards of diligence owed by government forces to foreign investors under general international law."[125]

4. Transfer of Funds

Another investment protection provision is a transfer of funds in which all payments into and out of a host county related to an investment may be freely transferred without delay.[126] In this provision, the MAI prohibits countries from putting restrictions on excessive flows of currency into or out of their economies.

The provision has a non-exhaustive list of what kind of payments are included. According to the transfer of fund provision, such transfers shall include: "a) the initial capital and additional amounts to maintain or increase an investment; b) returns; c) payments made under a contract including a loan agreement; d) proceeds from the sale or liquidation of all or any part of an investment; e) payments of compensation under Article

---

[125] Summary of the facts of the case are as follows "On January 28, 1987, Sri Lanka security forces destroyed AAPL's installation (Serendib Seafoods Ltd.) after receiving reports that it was being used by local rebels. The Sri Lanka government did not respond to AAPL's claim for compensation, so AAPL initiated this arbitration pursuant to the Sri Lanka- UK Bilateral Investment Treaty (BIT), seeking US$8,067,368. Sri Lanka argues in response that AAPL's venture was not profitable; that the destruction was caused by combat between the Tamil rebels and the Security Forces; and that the BIT requires Sri Lanka to exercise due diligence and does not impose strict liability for damages sustained by AAPL. AAPL alleges that there was no combat, only unilateral destruction by the Security Forces". The Court rejected of AAPL's interpretation of "full protection and security", and MFN argument (vis-a-vis the Sri Lanka-Switzerland BIT). According to the court "AAPL did not meet its burden of proving that government troops caused the destruction or that the destruction caused was avoidable; the counter-insurgency guerrilla warfare constituted "combat action"; AAPL is nonetheless entitled to compensation vis-a-vis the renvoi provision in Art. 4.(1). of the Sri Lanka-UK BIT" The court discussed state responsibility with respect to insurrections and found that Sri Lanka had duty to exercise due diligence to prevent damages to AAPL and the court concluded that "government responsible because it failed to engage in less-violent precautionary actions to prevent damages" ICSID: Final Award in Asian Agricultural Products Ltd. (AAPL) v Republic of Sri Lanka, (Bilateral Investment Treaty Interpretation, State Responsibility; Compensation Liability, June 21, 1999, International Legal Materials, Judicial and Similar Proceedings, May, 1991.

[126] Article IV, 4. Transfers, MAI Negotiating Text, as of 24 April 1998, at 59.

2 and 3; f)payments arising out of the settlement of a dispute; g)earnings and other remuneration of personnel engaged from abroad in connection with an investment."[127]

There were some issues of debate on transfer of funds provisions among the negotiators of the MAI. The most important was the question of whether a balance of payments clause should be included. Some negotiators thought that the free transfer should be an absolute obligation and that even in a balance of payment crisis there was not really a need to restrict FDI.[128] However, other negotiators claimed that the host country has to maintain the possibility of controlling all kinds of payments in serious crises.[129]

The second issue debated and not resolved was with regard to the currency in which transfers may be made. The majority of negotiators supported that transfers may be made in a freely convertible currency. However, "freely convertible currency" could not be defined by the negotiators. Under the MAI draft, there were two meanings for this term. One is that "freely convertible currency means a currency which is widely traded in international foreign exchange markets and widely used in international transactions".[130] The other one is that " freely convertible currency means a currency which is, in fact, widely used to make payments for international transactions and is widely traded in the principal exchange markets".[131]

---

[127] Article IV, 4. Transfers, MAI Negotiating Text, as of 24 April 1998, at 59.

[128] Karl, *supra* note 121, at 16.

[129] *Id.* at 16.

[130] *Id. MAI Negotiation Text*, at 59.

[131] *Id.* at. 59.

The third issue not decided was whether a clause is needed to deal with the situation where there is no market rate of exchange. The MAI draft stipulated in the brackets that in this situation the rate to be used shall be the most recent exchange rate for conversion of currencies into Special Drawing Rights.[132]

D. New Elements

The MAI negotiations also bring up new elements relating to the obligations that are seen as complementary to the key MAI principle of non-discrimination. These obligations are not commonly discussed in investment treaties. Additionally, OECD countries call them "special topics". These are five main elements: Key Personnel, Performance Requirements, Monopolies, Privatization, and Investment Incentives.

1. Key Personnel Provisions

Key personnel provisions address the desires of international firms to be able to transfer or hire personnel to perform vital functions. In other words, the investors would not be faced with restrictions regarding the temporary entry of individual investors, managers, executives and specialists in the MAI members. The business community sought to have some sort of guarantees for key personnel so as to such personnel could perform significant key functions in foreign investment.[133] On the other hand, a major

---

[132] *Id*. at 59

[133] Anders Ahnlid, *Special Topics, The Multilateral Agreement on Investment*, State of Play as of February (1997), at 27.

problem facing the key personnel provision was that of the political ramifications in OECD countries that have unemployment problems.[134]

The MAI requires parties to grant temporary entry, stay and authorization to work for an investor or an employee in the capacity of executive, manager or specialist and who is essential to an investment enterprise, often referred to as "key personnel", subject to the application of national law and regulations.[135] However, contacting parties do not allow to restrict the entry, stay and work of key personnel and investors for reasons relating to labour market or other economic needs tests or simple numerical restriction.[136] The MAI also provides for temporary entry permits to be given to the spouse and minor children of the investor and the key personnel of the investor.[137] Parties are also encouraged to grant work permits to spouses.[138]

The MAI stipulates that contracting parties would not be permitted to require an investor to appoint executives, managers and directors of a particular nationality.[139] The MAI also indicates that investors would be able to employ persons of any nationality or citizenship, provided that the person concerned holds a valid work permit, and the

---

[134] Michael Grau, *Temporary Stay and Work of Investors and Key Personnel, The Multilateral Agreement on Investment*, State of Play in April (1997), at 25.

[135] Article III, Treatment of Investments and Investors, Temporary Entry, Stay and work of Investors and Key Personnel, states that: "Subject to the application of Contracting Parties' national laws, regulations and procedures affecting the entry, stay and work of natural persons.....", The MAI Negotiating Text, as of 24 April 1998, at 14.

[136] *Id*. at 15.

[137] *Id*. Article III, Treatment of investors and investments, Temporary Entry, Stay and Work of Investors and Key Personnel, 1.(b) states that Spouses and dependent children are likely to be given the same right of entry and stay as key personnel.

[138] *Id*. at 15.

[139] Article III, Treatment of Investors and Investments, Nationality requirements for Executives, Managers and Members of Boards of Directors, MAI Negotiating Text, as of 24 April 1998, at 16.

employment of the person conforms to the requirement of the permit.[140] However, the extent to which immigration legislation might need to be amended to accommodate these requirements was not considered in the MAI negotiations.

It is worth noting that pursuant to MAI, there is a distinction between the investor and key personnel.[141] Most BITs provisions, dealing with entry and sojourn of personnel are fairly simple provisions by comparison with the MAI provisions.[142] The obligations are subject to the law and regulations of the host country relating to entry and sojourn of non-citizens. Investors and their personnel are to be permitted to enter and remain in the territory of the host country to enable the conduct of activities connected with their investments. Parties can also employ key technical and managerial personnel of their choice.

2. Performance Requirements

Performance requirements are requirements that governments impose on the performance of investors so as to secure perceived economic benefits for the country as a whole, or for a certain region. These requirements have been designed to achieve minimum levels of local employment, investment exports and proportions of locally-source materials, or to insist on joint ventures and technology transfers. Some countries argued that the MAI rules on non-discrimination were not sufficient to stop the distortions and inefficiencies created by performance requirements. Thus, there should

---

[140] *Id.* at 17.

[141] *Id.* at 14.

[142] UNCTAD, BILATERAL INVESTMENT TREATIES, *supra* note 25, at 83.

be performance requirement provisions in the MAI that should prohibit a number of such requirements.[143] However, developing countries claimed that these requirements could not be banned since they are important economic and social development instruments for developed and developing countries.[144] It should be noted that apart from USA BITs, most BITs do not contain provisions prohibiting performance requirements of the kind set out in the MAI.[145]

Even though the negotiating countries expected to pursue quickly the negotiation on the performance requirements, due to the its complexity and its possible adverse effects on a host country's development policy, it took time and some relevant issues did remained unresolved in the final draft of the MAI.[146]

The MAI contains a number of provisions relating to "performance requirements", which would be applicable to foreign investment. In particular, Contracting Parties would not be able to:

> impose enforce or maintain any of the following requirements, or enforce any commitment or undertaking:
> (a) to export a given level or percentage of goods or services;
>
> (b) to achieve a given level or percentage of domestic content;

---

[143] Anders Ahnlid, *Performance Requirements and Investment Incentives, The Multilateral Agreement on Investment*, State of Play 28 (1997),

[144] Martin Khor states that: "Many developing countries have regulations or policies obliging foreign investors to follow many or most of the performance requirements that are banned by the MAI. These requirements are felt necessary to ensure that foreign investors help host countries fulfill their national goal, such as upgrading technology, stimulating local economies, creating jobs for local citizens, and earning or saving foreign exchange so as to enhance the balance of payments. Without these policies, desired development might not take place or be sustainable.", Martin Khor, *the MAI and Developing Countries, in* DISMANTLING DEMOCRACY (Andrew Jackson &Matthew Sanger, eds.) 279 (1999).

[145] UNCTAD, BILATERAL INVESTMENT TREATIES, *supra* note 25, at 81.

[146] UNCTAD, *supra* note 2, at 16.

(c) to purchase, use or accord a preference to goods produced, or services provided in its territory or to purchase goods or services from persons in its territory;

(d) to relate in any way the volume or value of imports to the volume or value of exports or to the amount of foreign exchange inflows associated with such investment;

(e) to restrict sales of goods or services in its territory that such investment produces or provides by relating such sales to the volume or value of its exports or foreign exchange earnings;"[147]

All requirements are not likely to be banned in all circumstances. Thus, the MAI stipulates that certain performance requirements are allowed if voluntary and linked to advantages, often in the form of investment incentives.[148] These certain requirements were:

f) to transfer technology, a production process or other proprietary knowledge to a natural or legal person in its territory, except when the requirement
-is imposed or the commitment or undertaking is enforced by a court, administrative tribunal or competition authority to remedy an alleged violations of competition laws, or
-concerns the transfer of intellectual property and is undertaken in a manner not inconsistent with the TRIPS agreement;

(g) to locate its headquarters for a specific region or the world market in the territory of that Contracting Party;

(h) to supply one or more of the goods that it produces or the services that it provides to a specific region or the world market exclusively from the territory of that Contracting Party;

(i) to achieve a given level or value of research or development in its territory;

(j) to hire a given level of nationals;

(k) to establish a joint venture with domestic participation;

---

[147] Performance Requirements, MAI Negotiating Text, as of 24 April 1998, at 18-21.

[148] UNCTAD, *supra* note 2, at 16.

(l) to achieve a minimum level of domestic equity participation other than nominal qualifying shares for directors or incorporators of corporations.".[149]

The performance requirement provisions of the MAI are subject to some exceptions. Paragraph 4 of the performance requirement provision provides that contracting parties are not precluded from taking measures, including environmental measures necessary to secure compliance with laws and regulations that are not inconsistent with the MAI, that are necessary to protect human, animal or plant life or health or that are necessary for the conservation of living or non living exhaustible natural resources.[150] Furthermore, the MAI provision includes an exception for some relevant performance requirements in the context of export promotion, foreign aid programmes, preferential tariffs or preferential quotas, and government procurement.[151]

The MAI expands the provisions on performance requirements found in the WTO TRIMS Agreement, based on trade related requirements, and NAFTA, which does not stipulate requirements in the fields of services.[152] The MAI is based on investment related measures and included both goods and services. On the other hand, it is worth noting that developing countries try to ensure that the obligations do not go beyond the existing TRIMS agreement.[153]

Although the negotiators of the MAI were developed countries, they had many controversial arguments and disagreements when they were negotiating performance

---

[149] Performance Requirements, MAI Negotiating Text, as of 24 April 1998, at 18-21.

[150] *Id*. at 23.

[151] See Performance Requirements Provision for detail exceptions. Id at 23-26.

[152] Ahnlid, *supra* note 133, at 28.

[153] A. V. Genesan, *Strategic Options Available to Developing Countries with Regard to a Multilateral Agreement on Investment*, UNCTAD Discussion Papers, UNCTAD/OSG/DP/134, April (1998).

requirement provisions. Developing countries have more and stronger disagreements on this issue than developed countries have. This illustrates that performance requirement provision should not be gone beyond the existing TRIMS agreement.

Many NGOs opposed the performance requirement provision, since the list of prohibitions relating to performance were very comprehensive, and in effect provided for unconditional freedom for foreign investors to carry out their investment activities in host countries. In addition, many NGOs contended that these requirements have an adverse effect on the regulatory capacity of host countries.[154] This provision also nullified the main purpose of the MAI, so called non-discrimination principle. Since even host countries have right to impose requirements on domestic investors, they cannot impose same requirements to the foreign investor.[155] Ovide Mercredi criticized performance requirement provision and suggested that: " The so called performance requirements of the proposed MAI should be more accurately called "non-performance" requirements, since they severely restrict the ability of nation states to better provide for the redistribution of wealth and social benefits in society."[156]

3. Privatization and Monopolies

Privatization and Monopolies are complex and politically sensitive new disciplines that are related to national treatment and most favoured nation principles. Even though privatization has been a common phenomenon in the world economy, there

---

[154] UNCTAD, *supra* note 2, at 16.

[155] Vallianatos, supra note 32, at 719.

[156] Ovide Mercredi, *The MAI and The First Nations, in* DISMANTLING DEMOCRACY 70 (*Andrew Jackson &Matthew Sanger*, eds., 1999).

are no special international investment agreements to cover such privatization.[157]. One may argue that the inclusion of the privatization provisions in the MAI is necessary, since the definition of investment is so broad in the MAI, and the acquisition of shares in a company to be privatized is considered as investment.[158] Some negotiators were against the separate article confirming the application of the NT and MFN obligations to privatization process and monopolies.[159] Therefore, privatization and monopolies fall outside the scope of interference resulting from international treaty law.[160]

The clause dealing with privatization expands the scope and operation of the general national treatment and most favoured nation provisions of the MAI. Paragraph 1 in the draft states that:

"The obligation of a Contracting Party to accord National Treatment and MFN Treatment as defined in Paragraph XX(NT/MFN) applies to:

(a) all kinds of privatization, irrespective of the method of privatization (whether by public offering, direct sale or other method); and
(b) subsequent transactions involving a privatized asset".[161]

The MAI acknowledges that each State has the right to privatize and that nothing in the agreement obliged a State to initiate a privatization of its economy. However, a State shall apply the principles of NT and MFN treatment in the privatization process. Hence, this would apply both initial sale and subsequent sales associated with the

---

[157] Ahnlid, *supra* note 133, at 29.

[158] Madalena Oliveira e Silva, *Privatization and Monopolies*, Multilateral Agreement on Investment, State of Play in April 1997, OECD, at 33.

[159] OECD Confidential DAFFE/MAI (97) 1/REV2.

[160] Oliveira, *supra* note 158, at 33.

[161] Privatization, MAI Negotiating Text, as of 24 April 1998, at 27.

privatization process.[162] The main problem in the negotiations was how to regulate special share arrangements, such as retention of "golden shares", management buy-outs, special schemes for the public, choice of particular category of buyers and other similar arrangements, which could involve a violation of non-discrimination treatment.[163] According to majority of delegations, such arrangements should not be considered inconsistent with non-discrimination treatment, unless they explicitly or intentionally discriminate against foreign investors.[164] Others hold the view that these arrangements would result in discrimination and, therefore, should be banned under the MAI.[165] The MAI also defines privatization and applies the transparency principle to it.[166] Under this principle, a contacting party must make publicly available all the conditions and the procedures with respect to privatization. Overall, the MAI tried to contain provisions regarding privatization. On the other hand, most BITs do not contain provisions dealing with privatization of assets.[167]

There is a connection between monopolies and privatization since state enterprises previously operated as monopolies are often privatized.[168] Like privatization

---

[162] Ahnlid, *supra* note 133, at 29.

[163] Olieveira, *supra* note 158, at 35.

[164] *Id*. at 35.

[165] *Id*. at 35.

[166] Privatization, Paragraph 5 (Definition) states that: " Privatization means the sale by a Contracting Party, in part or in full, of its equity interests in any entity or other disposal having substantially the same effect. This definition does not cover transactions between different levels or entities of the same Contracting Party; excludes transactions in the normal conduct of business.", OECD, The MAI Negotiating Text, as of 24 April 1998, at 31.

[167] UNCTAD, BILATERAL INVESTMENT TREATIES, *supra* note 25, at 138.

[168] OECD, Report by Working Group B, New Issues, OECD, TOWARD MULTILATERAL INVESTMENT RULES 125 (1996).

issues, monopoly issues have been not regulated in the international investment agreements.[169] Like privatization provisions, the MAI acknowledges that the discretionary competence of States on issues relating monopolies could not be challenged. In other words, the MAI provides that contracting parties are able to maintain, designate or eliminate monopolies, but must accord "non-discriminatory treatment" when doing so.[170] There was general agreement that any government monopoly should act in accord with NT and MFN treatment provisions.

Apart from the non-discriminatory principle, there were some subjects discussed regarding monopolies such as the subject of anti-competitive practices, the subject of demonopolisation, the subject of state companies and concessions. However most of these subjects remained unresolved. Overall, the draft text demonstrated that there is considerable disagreement within the negotiating group as to what the scope of the monopolies provision should be, and indeed whether there should be such a provision at all.[171] It is worth noting that most BITs do not have provisions relating to monopolies.

4. Investment Incentives

---

[169] Oliveira, *supra* note 158, at 36.

[170] Article on Monopolies states that: "1-Nothing in this Agreement shall be construed to prevent a Contracting Party from maintaining, designating or eliminating a Monopoly. 2-Each Contracting Party Shall (endeavor to) accord non-discriminatory treatment when designating a Monopoly." Monopolies, MAI Negotiating Text, as of 24 April 1998, at 32.

[171] Monopolies, MAI Negotiating Text, as of 24 April 1998, at 32-40.

To encourage FDI, countries offer investment incentives for potential investors, such as direct and indirect investment grants, tax credits, and export allowances.[172] This topic is the most difficult one in the new elements on the MAI since it involves technically and politically complex and sensitive issues.[173] The draft text explicitly acknowledges that the role of investment incentives with respect to the purposes of policies, such as regional, structural, social, environmental or R&D policies of the Contracting parties must be recognized in the MAI.[174]

There was a debate as to why the investment incentive was determined as an issue in the MAI. This question was answered in a different way by countries. Many countries were against specific rules on incentives in the MAI.[175] They asserted that the application of non-discrimination principle would be a sufficient outcome.[176] On the other hand, some countries claimed that disciplines on investment incentives would be an important element of the MAI.[177]

---

[172] A. V. Ganesan spell outs that: "Empirical evidence suggests that incentives are less often used now to attract FDI flows in general, but are used more to achieve specific purposes. However, international competition for FDI with fiscal, financial and other incentives is becoming pervasive, and is even more intense now than it as some ten years ago." Ganesan, *supra* note 153.

[173] Ahnlid, *supra* note 133, at 28.

[174] MAI Negotiating Text, as of 24 April 1998, at 48.

[175] *Id*. Investment Incentives, MAI Negotiating Text, as of 24 April 1998, at 46.
According to the Provision Alternative 1: "Several delegations believe that no additional text is necessary. They consider that the current draft articles in the MAI are sufficient to cover investment incentives at this time."

[176] Anders Ahnlid, Performance Requirements and Investment Incentives, *supra* note 143, at 30.

[177] Especially New Zealand and European Commission proposed the draft provision on investment incentives. OECD, Confidential DAFFE/ MAI (97) 1/ REV 2.

The MAI includes investment incentives indirectly as part of provisions on non-discrimination principle, performance requirements and transparency.[178] On the other hand, some negotiators tried to encourage others to have specific provision with respect to investment incentives.[179] Pursuant to uncompromising draft article regarding incentives, the MAI requires national treatment and MFN treatment in relation to giving investment incentives.

Investment incentives provisions were not accepted among negotiators. However, there was some sort of compromising in the negotiations that investment incentives provisions should be included in the built-in agenda of the MAI after its entry into force.[180] It is worth noting that the implication of the WTO Subsidies Agreement on incentives should be taken into account before negotiating investment agreements. This issue will be explained in the coming chapter.

VI. Procedural Provisions (Dispute Settlement) of the MAI

The MAI is a draft agreement with high standards for the treatment and protection of investments for foreign investors. Treaty can provide comprehensive rules regarding investment. However, it does not have power to apply these rules in practice, unless

---

[178] UNCTAD, *supra* note 2, at 16.

[179] According to the Draft treaty, Investment Incentives provision, Alternative 1 and 2: " Several delegations believe that no additional text is necessary. They consider that the current draft articles in the MAI are sufficient to cover investment incentives at this time. Many delegations, however, would favour specific provisions on incentives in the MAI although they hold different views as to their nature and scope. Some proposed a built-in agenda for future work. Discussion of possible provisions focused on the following draft article which is regarded as a compromise text by those who would still prefer more far-reaching disciplines." The MAI Negotiating Text, as of 24 April 1998 at 46.

[180] UNCTAD, *supra* note 2, at 16.

treaty has enforcement mechanism of these rules. That is to say, the need for the binding dispute settlement process is necessary for the credibility of the agreement. For this reason, the OECD countries had included dispute settlement provisions in the MAI so as to avoid and resolve the investment disputes.

The dispute settlement provisions of the MAI set out specific courses of action that may be taken in regard to disputes arising between contracting parties "State-State dispute settlement procedures" and between contracting parties and foreign investors "Investor-State dispute settlement procedures".[181] If a foreign investor believes that a country where it has invested is violating the MAI, the investor has a choice. It can complain to its own government, who can take the other country to binding international arbitration. Or the investor can directly challenge the host country. In other words, the MAI provides "State to State dispute settlement" that could involve international arbitration and, unlike the WTO, there is provision for an "investor to state the dispute settlement procedure". In either case, the panel can decide whether governments are violating the agreement, and if so, can advise them to change laws and then award damages.

It should be noted at the outset that there is very little in the proposed dispute settlement procedures which is novel. Indeed, the dispute settlement articles are a combination of provisions from the ICSID Convention and NAFTA Dispute Settlement Process.[182] Moreover, many of the provisions are similar to those contained in most

---

[181] David R. Adair, *Investors' Rights: The Evolutionary Process of Investment Treaties,* 6 Tulsa Journal of Comparative and International Law. 195, 216 (1999).

[182] Christopher N. Camponovo, *Dispute Settlement and the OECD Multilateral Agreement on Investment,* UCLA Journal of International Law and Foreign Affairs, 208-209 (1996).

BITS. The proposed dispute mechanism is thus a combination of well known and well accepted international commercial dispute resolution provisions which are already laid down in most BITs. As already evaluated in the third chapter of this study, most BITs have provisions for the settlement of disputes. This provisions deal respectively with the settlement of disputes between a Party and an investor of the other Party, disputes between the Parties as to the interpretation and application of the agreement, and disputes between investors of the Parties.

A. State-State Dispute Settlement Procedure

The dispute settlement procedures for disputes between States that are party to the MAI are dealt with in Article V, A-C.[183] Like the WTO, the "State-State dispute settlement procedure" provides for an amicable procedure which allows a contracting party to initiate consultations with another contracting party and if this fails to seek multilateral consultations in the Parties Group.[184] The Parties Group would be made up of all the contracting parties and would have power to make recommendations to the contracting parties that are in dispute. This is substantially the same mechanism provided for the in Article XXIII the GATT 1947, now supplemented by the DSU, and the Parties

---

[183] Dispute Settlement, MAI Negotiating Text, as of 24 April 1998, at 63-70.

[184] Adair, *supra* note 181, at 216.

Group was analogous to the Dispute Settlement Body, which comprises all the WTO members.

If the consultation process is failed, the Parties may recourse to good offices or to mediation or conciliation. If the amicable process is failed, disputes between contracting parties as to whether one of them has acted in contravention of the MAI may be referred to arbitration by any contracting party that is a party to dispute.[185] Furthermore, Article V. C.1b does not allow contracting parties to initiate "State-State dispute settlement process" if an investor of one of the contracting parties in dispute has already submitted or consented to submit the dispute under the investor-state dispute settlement provisions.[186] Moreover, under the same provisions, if the dispute could fall within the MAI or some other obligation in a bilateral agreement between the contracting parties that are in dispute, the complaining contracting party may choose which agreement to apply to the dispute.[187]

Arbitrational panels can consist of either three or five members.[188] Three members can be selected by the agreement of the parties to the claim, based on a proposal made by the Secretary -General of ICSID.[189] Either of the parties to the disputes can opt to the five member panel, in which case each can appoint one additional member.

---

[185] Article V, Dispute Settlement, C.1, states that: "Any dispute between Contracting Parties as to whether one of them has acted in contravention of this Agreement shall, at the request of any Contracting Party that is a party to the dispute and has complied with the consultations requirements of the Article B, be submitted to an arbitral tribunal for decision..." *Id.* MAI Negotiating Text, As of 24 April 1998, at 64.

[186] *Id.* at 65.

[187] *Id.* at 65.

[188] Article V, C.2 Formation of the Tribunal, MAI Negotiating Text, As of 24 April 1998, at 65.

[189] *Id.* at 65.

The MAI provides basic rules and procedures for "State-to State dispute settlement process". However, the MAI also allows the parties to a dispute to modify the rules.[190] Moreover, the applicable law for a dispute is the MAI substantive provisions.[191] Further, international law is also applicable. Article C, 2, 3 and 5 of the Dispute Settlement Provisions establishes procedures for the formation of the arbitral tribunal as well as providing for other procedural rules such as the calling of scientific or other technical evidence and the consolidation of proceedings and involvement of third parties.[192]

According to the article C.6, the tribunal may at the request of a Party, recommend provisional measures which either Party should take to avoid serious prejudice to the other Party.[193] Article 47 of the ICSID Convention is substantially similar, although the Tribunal under that article is bound to recommend any provisional measures either party should take, unless the parties agree that the tribunal should not do so.

With respect to remedies, the tribunal may declare an action of a Party is in contravention of its obligations and may recommend that a Party bring its actions into conformity with its obligations.[194] That is to say, a "State-State dispute tribunal" can call

---

[190] Article V, Dispute Settlement, A. General Provisions states that: "The rules and procedures set out in Articles A-C shall apply to the avoidance of conflicts and the resolution of disputes between Contracting Parties regarding the interpretation or application of the Agreement unless the disputing parties agree to apply other rules or procedures.....", MAI Negotiating Text, As of 24 April 1998, at 63.

[191] Article V, C6, Proceeding and Awards, states that: "The tribunal shall decide disputes in accordance with this Agreement, interpreted and applied in accordance with the applicable rules of international law...", MAI Negotiating Text, As of 24 April 1998, at 67.

[192] *Id.* at 66.

[193] *Id.* at 67.

[194] *Id.* at 67.

for a country to change its law to conform with MAI rules. This is substantially similar to the powers of WTO panels and the Appellate Body under article 19 of the DSU. Moreover, the tribunal may award pecuniary compensation for any loss or damage to the requesting Party's investor or its investment.[195] Further, the tribunal may award any other form or relief to which the Party against whom the award is made consent, including restitution in kind to an investor.[196]

Pursuant to the Article V.C. 6 of the "State-State dispute settlement procedure", the MAI specifies that the arbitral tribunal should issue a draft award to the parties on a confidential basis.[197] The parties would then have a period of 30 days in which to comment upon or make submissions about the award. The tribunal would then be required to finalize its award, and submit a copy to the Parties Group, which must make it publicly available.[198]

The award is final and binding between the parties to the dispute unless the award is annulled under paragraph 7.[199] The reasons for nullification includes that "the Tribunal was not properly constituted, the Tribunal has manifestly exceeded its powers, there was corruption on the part of a member of the Tribunal or on the part of a person providing decisive expertise or evidence, there has been a serious departure from a fundamental rule

---

[195] *Id*. at 67.

[196] *Id*. at 67.

[197] *Id*. at 67.

[198] *Id*. at 67.

[199] Article V. C.6.e states that: " Tribunal awards shall be final and binding between the parties to the dispute, subject to paragraph 7 below". *Id*. at 67.

of procedure, or the award has failed to state the reasons on which it is based."[200] A party may seek a nullification of an award in a new tribunal constitutes under the MAI or to any other available forum.[201] This is almost exactly the same, in substance, as is provided for in articles 51 and 52 of the ICSID Convention.

The MAI also deals with the situation where a party to an award refuses to comply with it. Article C.9 provides that if consultations have failed to move the other contracting party to comply with an award, the contracting party may take retaliatory measures or suspend application to the other contracting party of obligations under the MAI.[202] The framework provided for this is very similar to that provided for in article 22 of the DSU, where WTO members have failed to implement measures recommended by a dispute settlement panel or the Appellate Body.

B. Investor-State Dispute Settlement Procedures

One of the most controversial issues in the MAI is the settlement of investor to State procedures. The MAI grants foreign investors the right to directly take host State to international dispute process to sue for damages if they think that their rights under the agreement have been violated. Article V.D paragraphs 1-20 provides the mechanism for the resolution of disputes between investors and a host contracting party. It states that:

> "a. This articles applies to disputes between a Contracting Party and an investor of another Contracting party concerning an alleged breach of an obligation of the former under this Agreement which causes loss or damage to the investor or its investments.

---

[200] Article V. C .7, Nullification, Id, at 68.

[201] *Id.* at 68.

[202] Article C.9, Response to Non- Compliance, *Id.* at 69.

> b. An investor of another Contracting party may also submit to arbitration under this article any investment dispute concerning any obligation which the Contacting Party has entered into with regard to a specific investment of the investor through:
>
> i. An investment authorization granted by its competent authorities specifically to the investor or investment.
>
> ii. A written agreement granting rights with respect to (categories of subject matters) on which the investor has relied in established acquiring, or significantly expanding an investment.".[203]

Like the State to State dispute settlement provisions, these provisions covers both pre-and post-investment issues. Some negotiating countries did object to the extension of the investor -State dispute settlement process to the pre-establishment stage.[204] Furthermore, with regard to (b), it would appear that disputes may be brought under the MAI relating to agreements entered into before the MAI, as well as contractual arrangements that fall outside the MAI obligations. Both these aspects go beyond what is currently available for investors under most BITS.

According to this procedure, foreign investor has the right to decide directly to challenge laws of the Contracting parties. There is no governmental mechanism in place to screen foreign investor claims. Some negotiators asserted that there should be some mechanism.

The opponents of the MAI claimed that foreign investors will use their right to sue the host country in international dispute process to undermine environmental, public health, and labor regulations. Their claim was based on recent NAFTA cases. As

---

[203] Investor-State Procedures, Dispute Settlement, MAI Negotiating Text, as of 24 April 1998, at 70.

[204] Rainer Geiger, *Towards Multilateral Agreement on Investment*, 31 CORNELL INT'L L. J. 467, 471 (1998).

already mentioned, the MAI's provision have been explicitly modeled on those of the NAFTA. The cases being adjudicated under NAFTA's rules are the important examples where foreign investors have attacked environmental and public health regulations.[205] Many NGOs asserted that the results of the cases will set precedents for future law suits initiated under the MAI's similar provisions. They claimed that the MAI's "Investor-State dispute settlement process" was potentially threatening to domestic regulatory policies than that established in the NAFTA, since MAI's provisions were broad, vague and covered new issues. This illustrates that the "Investor-State dispute settlement process" have a great deal of uncertainty as to the MAI's implication for the host countries regulatory power.

Response to these criticisms, some MAI negotiators contended that MAI should provide a " Screening Mechanism" to minimize the number of claims and the related costs to governments of defending lawsuits. Pursuant to the annex of the MAI, entitled "Advisory Opinion: Suggestion for MAI Dispute Settlement or Institutional Matter Experts", Parties Group may set up a legal advisory body on "the interpretation and application of the Agreement." However this annex does not assure that any restrictions will be set in advance to screen claims, since it is so called "advisory opinion". Another response to these criticisms, some MAI negotiators gave a proposal for the establishment of an appellate process for dispute settlement process, however, this issue was not resolved in the MAI negotiation.[206]

---

[205] Ganguly, supra note 24, at 132.

[206] UNCTAD, *supra* note 2, at 19.

The main features of the investor-state dispute settlement mechanism are:

1-The first step to resolve disputes is amicable process, through negotiation or consultation.

2-Only the foreign investor has the right to choose which forum in which to settle the dispute. The foreign investor may submit it to the domestic courts or administrative tribunals of the Contracting Party, to previously agreed dispute settlement procedures.

3-Signatory countries give their unconditional consent to submit to dispute resolution process(Article V. D.3 (a)). On the other hand, some negotiators did not accept the idea of the prior consent at all. Thus, the MAI provided an exception for the prior consent arrangement. Pursuant to the Article V. D. 3b, contracting parties may not consent in cases where the investors has previously submitted the dispute either to a national court or to international arbitration in accordance with any other dispute settlement procedure.

4-The MAI lists three institutions at which foreign investors can choose to file a claim against the host country. The first, ICSID, is part of World Bank. The host country must be a member of the ICSID convention to use the facility. If the host country is not a ICSID Member, foreign investors could opt to use either UNCITRAL or the arbitration facility of the International Chamber of Commerce (ICC). There were some disagreements among negotiators with respect to these arbitration institutions. For example, ICC is not a neutral institution regarding the MAI since it was playing a leading role in the MAI negotiations. The ICC lobbied not only to have multilateral regulation for international investors, but also to have an official role in the MAI.[207] Thus, the ICC's role in the dispute settlement process is highly controversial.

---

[207] Vallianatos, supra note 32, at 727.

5-There is a five-year limitation period on the investor's ability to bring a claim.

6-The remedies available on the "Investor-State dispute settlement process" are specified in the MAI. These remedies include: a declaration that the contracting party has failed to comply with its obligations under the MAI, pecuniary compensation, restitution in kind, and with the consent of the all parties to the dispute, any other form of relief.[208]

7-Pursuant to the "Written Agreement of the Parties" provision, Article V. D5, MAI requires that MAI signatories consent to Article II of the New York Convention, which requires domestic standing in domestic courts for the enforcement of the rulings of the international dispute settlement process. This provision is new in kind since neither NAFTA nor WTO has provided for the enforcement of the international arbitration rulings according to the New York Convention.

VII. Exceptions to the MAI

The issues of exceptions became controversial in the MAI negotiations. It is unimaginable that the MAI will be free of exception. However, the exceptions had been kept minimum and narrow. The MAI text provides three types of exceptions: general, temporary and country specific; by the end of the negotiation, this text was still under consideration.

A. General Exceptions

---

[208] Adair, *supra* note 181, at 217.

MAI negotiators agreed with only three general exceptions to the MAI: national security, public order, and international peace and security. Article VI-(2) of the MAI provides a general exception for national security concerns:

"Nothing in this Agreement shall be construed:

a. to prevent any Contracting Party from taking any action which it considers necessary for the protection of its essential security interest....;[209]

b. to require any Contracting Party to furnish or allow access to any information the disclosure of which it considers contrary to its essential security interest;

c. to prevent any Contracting Party from taking any action in pursuance of its obligations under the United Nations Charter for the maintenance of international peace and security."[210]

Article VI (3) provides the public order exceptions narrowly: "Subject to the requirement that such measures are not applied in a manner which would constitute a means of arbitrary or unjustifiable discrimination between Contracting Parties, or a disguised investment restriction, nothing in this Agreement shall be construed to prevent any contracting Party from taking any measure necessary for the maintenance of public order."[211] Interpretive note states that this exception may be invoked only where a genuine and sufficiently serious threat is posed one of the fundamental interests of

---

[209] Article VI, Exceptions and Safeguards, General Exceptions, 2 continued that: " (i) taken in time of war, r armed conflict, or other emergency in international relations; (ii) relating to the implementation of national policies or international agreements respecting the non-proliferation of weapons of mass destruction; (iii) relating to the production of arms and ammunition...", MAI Negotiating Text, as of 24 April 1998, at 77.

[210] Article VI, Exceptions and Safeguards, General Exceptions, MAI Negotiating Text, as of 24 April 1998, at 77.

[211] *Id.* at 77.

society.[212] Interpretive note illustrates that this exemption apply narrowly. Further, there was a discussion among negotiators as to whether or not the public order exception should be inserted in the MAI; and, if it would be, what would be the scope of this exception.[213]

The general exceptions provision does not apply to Article IV, 2 and 3 which deals with expropriation and compensation and protection form strife.[214] If a contracting party believes that actions or measures are taken solely for economic reasons or are not proportionate to the interest being protected, it may challenge these under the "State-State Consultation Procedures".[215] That is to say, under the MAI, general exceptions cannot be taken 'Solely for economic reasons" and must be "in proportion to the interest being protected".

The General exceptions provision is different than the WTO and the NAFTA agreements. The WTO general exceptions cover many more categories such as public health and environmental issues. The NAFTA inserted the WTO general exception to its investment chapter.

Canada and France proposed the "cultural exceptions" to the MAI.[216] These countries were concerned with preserving the integrity of their cultural heritage. Proposed exception would protect the movie and publication industries, etc., from foreign

---

[212] *Id.* at 77.

[213] Don Wallace & Jr, David B. Bailey, *supra* note 114, at 626.

[214] Article VI, Exceptions and Safeguards, General Exceptions, MAI Negotiating Text, as of 24 April 1998, at 77.

[215] *Id.* at 77.

[216] Stephen J. Canner, *The Multilateral Agreement on Investment*, 31 CORNELL INT'L L. J. 657, 671 (1998).

competition. However, some negotiators did not agree with general cultural exception clause. There were two possible solutions proposed by UNCTAD studies, one was that the inserting the cultural exceptions in the List B of the exceptions, the other was that adopting the "bottom up" approach for the cultural industries.[217] I think that cultural exceptions should have been carefully determined in the MAI.

A regional economic integration organization (REIO) exception was another disagreement with respect to exceptions among the negotiating countries.[218] The EU proposed this exception in order to supply preferential treatment to its member nations. Some negotiators, specifically US opposed the REIO exception clause that would violate non-discrimination principle of the MAI.[219] There were several problems with this exception, since it would violate the non-discrimination principle, and it would create lack of transparency and uncertainty in investment rules.[220] This issue remained as an unresolved one in the final negotiations of the MAI.

B. Temporary Safeguard

MAI provides for an exception depending on balance of payments or exceptional circumstances whereby capital movements give rise or threaten to cause serious difficulties in the macro economic management, particularly monetary and exchange rate

---

[217] UNCTAD, *supra* note 2, at 15.

[218] UNCTAD, *supra* note 2, at 14.

[219] Jeffrey Lang, Keynote Address, Symposium, *The International Regulation of Foreign Direct Investment: Obstacles & Evolution*, 31 CORNELL INT'L L. J. 455, 462 (1998).

[220] Canner, *supra* note 216, at 671.

policies.[221] Namely, under this provision, contracting party will be able to take measures necessary to respond to a balance of payments crisis. These measures must be consistent with the Articles of the International Monetary Fund (IMF).[222] Further these measures must be temporary.

Some negotiators wanted to review further relationship between this temporary safeguard clause and the IMF articles since an extension of the IMF's jurisdiction is under consideration.[223] For example, Belgium reserved its position to deny the role of the IMF with respect to some provisions of this exception.[224]

C. Country Specific Exceptions[225]

Article IX of the MAI provides for country specific exceptions to the non-discrimination principle. This article states that: "(a) any existing non-conforming measure as set out by a Contracting Party in its schedule to Annex A of the Agreement, to

---

[221] Article VI, Exceptions and Safeguards, Temporary Safeguard, MAI Negotiating Text, as of 24 April 1998, at 79.

[222] Temporary Safeguard, paragraph 2 states that: " Measures referred to in paragraph 1:
(a) shall be consistent with the Articles of Agreement of the International Monetary Fund;
(b) shall not exceed those necessary to deal with the circumstances described in paragraph 1;
(c) shall be temporary and shall be eliminated as soon as conditions permit." *Id*. at 79.

[223] OECD, Multilateral Agreement on Investment: *Consolidated Text and Commentary*, DAFFE/MAI (97) 1/REV 2.

[224] *Id.*

[225] Interpretative Note states that: "It was generally agreed to replace the term "reservations" by the term "exceptions". Under treaty law, "reservations" normally have reciprocal effect unless otherwise specified. This is clearly not intended to be the case with respect to Country Schedules. The use of the term "exception" would not prevent the listing of a measure with a reciprocity requirement. It would help avoid confusion in the case of any genuine "reservations" in the treaty law sense were to be made and called as such.", Article IX. Country Specific Exceptions, MAI Negotiation Text, as of 24 April 1998, at 90.

the extent that the measure is maintained, continued or promptly renewed its legal system;..."[226]

There was an intensive disagreement as to the scope and type of exceptions each nation can take from the MAI. Unlike WTO, the MAI is the "top down" meaning that all economic sectors are covered and that individual contracting parties must negotiate limited exceptions to the agreement.[227] The WTO, on the other hand, is 'bottom up" meaning that each country opts to the sectors that will be covered. Because of this "top down" approach, contracting parties should carefully submit their reservations. It is worth noting that the final draft of the MAI did not impose rollback obligation.[228]

The contracting parties are allowed to lodge two kinds of country specific exceptions to the application of the non-discrimination principle and other provisions of the MAI to be determined.[229] List A of the exceptions would enable a contracting party to maintain any existing non-conforming measures and to make an amendment to them provides these do not increase the non-conforming of the measure.[230] The MAI provides for list A exceptions that each listed exception must set out a number of elements to assure the certainty and transparency of the exception.[231]

---

[226] Article IX, Country Specific Exceptions, MAI Negotiating Text, as of 24 April 1998, at 90.

[227] Lang, *supra* note 219, at 462.

[228] UNCTAD, supra note 2, at 12.

[229] Article IX. Country Specific Exceptions, MAI Negotiating Text, as of 24 April 1998, at 90.

[230] *Id.* at 90-91.

[231] Each exception sets out the following elements:(a) sector refers to the general sector in which the exception is taken; (b) Sub- sector refers to the specific sector in which exception is taken; (c) Obligation specifies the MAI provision referred to in paragraph 1 for which an exception is taken; (d),Level of government indicates the level of government maintaining the measure for which an exception is taken;....." Introduction to Annex A of the Agreement listing Country-Specific exceptions, Id. at 93.

The proposal with respect to list B of the exceptions had been placed in brackets, indicating that negotiating countries addressed it, but agreement had not been drafted.[232] Indeed, there were different views regarding to list B of the exceptions, which would allow new non-conforming measures to be introduced after the Agreement came into force.[233] One view was that the unspecified and potentially open-ended nature of the exceptions allowed in such a provision might undermine the MAI disciplines.[234] The opposite view was that such provision would allow for flexibility and thus make it easier to preserve the high standard in the MAI.[235]. By the end of the negotiations, Contracting Parties had lodged 600 exceptions and amendments.[235] This illustrated that even developed countries did not have confidence in the liberalization process determined by the MAI.

VIII. Financial Services

The MAI embraces special provisions relating to investment in the financial services sector. These provisions would enable prudential measures with respect to financial services, and measures to ensure the integrity and stability of a country's

---

[232] Article IX. Country Specific Exceptions, B was in bracket : "{3 Article X; Y {Article Z....., and Article....} do not apply to any measure that a Contracting Party {adopts}or {maintains} with respect to sectors, subsectors or activities, as set out in its Schedule to Annex B of the Agreement.}, MAI Negotiating Text, as of 24 April 1998, at 92.

[233] Article IX. Country Specific Exceptions, Interpretative Note 9, MAI Negotiating Text. as of 24 April 1998, at 92.

[234] *Id.*

[235] *Id.*

[236] William Crane, *Corporations Swallowing Nations: The OECD and The Multilateral Agreement on Investment*, 9 COLO. J. INT'L ENVTL. L & POL'Y. 429, 458 (1998).

financial system.[237] According to the Article VII/2: "Where such measures do not conform with the provisions of the Agreement, they shall not be used as a means of avoiding the Contracting Party's commitments or obligations under the Agreement."[238] In other words, such measures could be inconsistent with the non-discriminatory provisions of the Agreement, and the other provisions of the Agreement. However, they must not be utilized as a means of avoiding a contracting party's commitments and obligations under the MAI.

There was some disagreement as to whether there is a need for specific provisions dealing with financial services, since the financial services sector tends to be highly regulated for prudential reasons. Some delegations took the view that no specific provisions are necessary.[239]

The Negotiation Group discussed the issues pertaining to the financial services and agreed to insert specific financial service provision in the MAI. It can be observed from the final draft of the MAI, the Negotiation Group had an agreement on the definition of financial services and the proposed text on the prudential measures and the proposed text on the additional transparency provision.[240] However, the proposed text on payments and clearing system, lender of last resort and specially dispute settlement

---

[237] Financial Services, MAI Negotiating Text, as of 24 April 1998, at 81.

[238] *Id.*

[239] Footnote 1 of the VII Financial Services provisions: "EG5 has agreed that the financial sector, which is highly regulated for prudential reasons, is unique in some respects and to some extent calls for specific treatment. However, a number of delegations consider that the general provisions of the MAI are sufficient to meet the needs of the financial services sector in a number of potential areas.".

[240] *Id.* 81-83

remained to be unresolved.[241] Indeed, the Negotiation group was divided as to the need for specific provisions for "Investor-State dispute settlement process" in certain financial issues.[242]

IX. Taxation

There were some disagreements as to whether taxation should be included in the MAI or not.[243] The majority of the negotiators was opposed to including any provision for taxes with respect to the principle of non-discriminatory treatment.[244] These negotiators acknowledged that the need to see tax measures affecting the principle of non-discriminatory treatment in the context of international treaty obligations and tax policy as a whole, and the need of governments to preserve the freedom to introduce new measures for their economic, social and technological developments.[245] Furthermore, more importantly these negotiators underscored that double taxation agreements cover most OECD countries, provide comprehensive non-discriminatory obligations and have a long and successful history resolving tax disputes among the OECD countries.[246]

---

[241] *Id.* 84.

[242] Pursuant to the Consolidated Text and Commentary of the MAI, some delegations believe that the decision of a Contracting Party to invoke prudential measures, and perhaps some other kinds of measures, should not be the subject to the dispute settlement provisions of the MAI. However, some delegations believed that an investor to state panel should be free to decide all financial services issues. These delegations are concerned that a special provision dealing with certain financial services matters could lead to a call for special provisions in other areas. The Majority of the delegations believed that MAI parties should have a voice in the question of whether a prudential measure and perhaps a temporary safeguard or action by a monetary authority, is consistent with the MAI. These delegations took the view that there must be a balance between the interest of an investor in pursuing its remedies under the MAI and the need for stability in financial markets, OECD, Confidential DAFFE/MAI (97) 1/REV2.

[243] UNCTAD, *supra* note 2, at 20-21.

[244] *Id.*

[245] OECD, Confidential DAFFE/MAI (97) 1/REV 2.

[246] *Id.*

On the other hand, five negotiators (Germany, Italy, Belgium, Switzerland, and the European Commission) argued to insert taxation with respect to the non-discriminatory principle in the MAI negotiations.[247] They claimed that even though the taxation agreements are extensive among the OECD countries, some of these agreements do not include adequately comprehensive non-discrimination provisions.[248] On the basis of the foregoing arguments, the majority of the negotiators agreed to carve taxation out of the MAI negotiations, apart from the expropriation and transparency provisions. It seems that majority opinion is strong. The Most BITs do not state provision regarding taxation since double taxation treaties exist in the international investment law. Like the most BITs, the MAI should not include taxation provisions so as to avoid problems with the double taxation treaties.

Part VIII of the draft MAI states that nothing in the agreement shall apply to taxation measures, other than the articles dealing with expropriation, transparency and dispute settlement, to the extend that the dispute relates to matters concerning expropriation or transparency.[249] The Negotiation Group agreed to carve in taxation for expropriation. It should be noted that all taxation measures do not constitute expropriation. Thus, the MAI has an interpretative note providing elements for determining whether a specific measure should be considered expropriation or not.[250]

---

[247] *Id.*

[248] *Id.*

[249] Taxation, MAI Negotiating Text, as of 24 April 1998, at 87.

[250] See for details in interpretative note 3 of the Article VIII, for Paragraph 2. Interpretative Note states that: "When considering the issue of whether a taxation measure effects an expropriation, the following elements should be borne in mind: a) The imposition of taxes does not generally constitute expropriation. The introduction of a new taxation measure, taxation by more than one jurisdiction in respect to an investment, or a claim of excessive burden imposed by a taxation measure are not in themselves indicative

Taxation must be taken to include direct and indirect taxation, and social security contributions.[251] Most negotiators agreed for defining taxes so as to provide certainty for foreign investors by clarifying the dividing line between those measures that are carved out or back into the MAI.[252] However, with respect to social security measures, there was a disagreement among the negotiators. Some negotiators argued that social security benefits be carved out of the Agreement and they proposed the following separate article: "Nothing in this Agreement shall apply to social security."[253]

Transparency must not extend to requiring a contracting party to reveal information protected by secrecy laws or administrative practices protecting confidentiality in domestic law or under international agreements.[254] In particular, information:

> "(a) contained in or exchanged pursuant to any agreement or arrangement relating to taxation between government and investors;
>
> (b) pursuant to any agreement with a foreign government concerning the application or interpretation of an international agreement relating to taxation in the case of an investor, including exchange of information between governments;
>
> (c) concerning the identity of an investor or other information which would disclose any trade, business, industrial, commercial or professional secret or trade process;

---

of an expropriation. . .d) Taxation measures may constitute an outright expropriation, or while not directly expropriatory they may have the equivalent effect of an expropriation (so called "creeping expropriation"). Where a taxation measure by itself does not constitute expropriation it would be extremely unlikely to be an element of a creeping expropriation". *Id* at 87.

[251] Article VIII, Paragraph 5 states that: "... Taxes shall be taken for this purpose to include direct taxes, indirect taxes and social security contributions." *Id*. at 88.

[252] OECD, Confidential DAFFE/MAI (97) 1/REV 2.

[253] Interpretative Note to the taxation provision, Paragraph 5. *Id*. at 89.

[254] *Id*. at 87.

(d) pertaining to the negotiation of tax treaties or any other international agreement relating wholly or partly to taxation or participation by a government in the work of international organizations; or

(e) the disclosure of which would affect the assessment or collection of, the enforcement or prosecution in respect of, or the determination of appeals in relation to, taxation, or any information the disclosure of which would aid or assist in the avoidance or evasion of taxes."[255]

must not be required to be disclosed under the MAI.

X. Concluding Remarks on the Substance of the MAI

One may claim that the MAI draft treaty was expected to make an effective contribution to the liberalization and protection of international investment. Indeed, the MAI contains substantive and procedural rules that provide "investment security", "investment neutrality" and "market facilitation". As already analyzed in this chapter, even though the MAI is based on most BITs concluded between developed and developing countries, the MAI differs substantially from traditional norms found in most BITs. The following summary findings set forth comparison and contrast between the MAI draft treaty and most BITs and relevant international instruments:

- The scope of the MAI is much broader than that of most BITs. The definition of investment is broader in that it encompasses every kind of asset owned or controlled directly or indirectly by an investor.
- Like most BITs, the non-discrimination principle (NT and MFN) is the main substantive provision of the MAI.

---

[255] *Id.* at 87-88.

- As already mentioned, the standards of treatment provided in the MAI are broader than that contained in most existing BITs. This is because most BITs rarely extend national treatment (NT) principle to the pre-establishment phase.

- Most BITs provisions with regard to the general treatment principle are not considerably different.

- Traditional investment protection rules, including expropriations and compensation, and protection from strife, have been incorporated into the MAI.

- A few BITs, mainly those concluded by the US, contain provisions on investment restrictions such as performance requirements. Compared to the WTO TRIMs agreement, the MAI extends rules governing performance requirements.

- Like most BITs, the MAI has legally binding procedures for the settlement of investment disputes that include an investor-state dispute settlement provision.

- Unlike most BITs, the MAI contains a transparency provision that grants market facilitation to international investment.

- The MAI addresses new elements on international investment agreements such as privatization, monopolies, and key personnel.

CHAPTER SIX. THE FAILURE OF THE OECD MULTILATERAL AGREEMENT ON INVESTMENT

I. Reasons of the Failure of the MAI

There are three main factors that contributed to the failure of the MAI negotiations. These factors are: A-The impact of the non-governmental organizations, B-Lost of interest by business community, C-Political changes in some negotiating countries. One may argue that all these reasons are mainly political.[1]

A. The Impact of the NGOs on the MAI

NGOs activities involved almost every area in international law. Recently, NGOs have played important roles in the development of areas of international law such as human rights and environment.[2] For example, in order to promote peaceful society in Sierra Leone, NGO worked together with the UN and its agencies under the Joint Code of Conduct agreed by UN agencies and NGOs operating in Sierra Leone in 1998.[3]

The impact of the NGOs on the MAI negotiations is the main factor for the failure of the MAI. The "process of globalization" can be deemed as a reason for the proliferation of the NGO activities on trade and investment. NGOs started their intensive

---

[1] DAVID HENDERSON, THE MAI AFFAIR, A STORY AND ITS LESSONS 61 (1999); UNCTAD, LESSONS FROM THE MAI 23-24 (1999).

[2] See the detail history of NGOs activities in international law at Karsten Nowrot, *Legal Consequences of Globalization: The Status of Non-Governmental Organizations Under International Law*, 6 Indiana Journal of Global Legal Studies 579 (1999).

[3] Joint code of conduct agreed upon by UN Agencies and NGOs operating in Sierra Leone (1998), www.db.idpproject.org (visited 10/25/2001).

opposition campaign against the MAI at the beginning of 1997.[4] Some individuals played a main role in this campaign. For example, after obtaining a document issued for the OECD Ministerial meeting of May 1995, Martin Khor, Director of the Third World Network, realized that his organizations' main opposition on multilateral investment negotiations at the WTO would be replaced in the OECD.[5] He contacted with some NGOs. Tony Clark is one of the person that informed by him. Tony Clarke was able to get a copy of the MAI draft. After analyzing the draft, he sent it to an international email list called "le forum international sur la globalization."[6] The NGO Public Citizen Global Watch placed the draft on its homepage.[7]. Massive and intensive NGOs work against the MAI started.

NGOs such as Council of Canadians, Sierra Club, World Development Movement, Worldwide Fund for Nature, Third World Network and Friends of Earth, had fundamental concerns with the MAI with respect to its substantive provision and process.[8] Indeed, nearly 600 organizations working in over 70 countries issued a statement on the MAI to publicize their concern on it.[9] For example, according to the this statement, NGOs had following substantive concern on the MAI: "(the NGOs call on the OECD and National Governments to) 1) Undertake an independent and comprehensive

---

[4] Katia Tieleman, *The Failure of The Multilateral Agreement on Investment (MAI) and The Absence of a Global Public Policy Network*, UN Vision Project on Global Public Policy Networks, at 12.

[5] *Id.*

[6] *Id.* at 13.

[7] *Id.*

[8] Joint NGO Statement on the MAI, NGO/ OECD Consultation on the MAI, Paris: 27 October, 1997, In DISMANTLING DEMOCRACY, (Andrew Jackson & Matthew Sanger eds., 1998).

[9] *Id.* at 319.

assessment of the social, environmental, and development impact of the MAI with public participation. The negotiations should be suspended during this assessment. 2) Require multinational investors to observe binding agreements incorporating environment, labour, health, safety and human rights standards to ensure that they do not use the MAI to exploit weak regulatory regimes...."[10] Furthermore, NGOs argued that the developing countries and the public did not involve the negotiation process of the MAI.[11]

It is vital to note at that majority of the NGOs acknowledge that international investment can provide substantial benefits, and promote social and economic development for developing countries.[12] However, they claimed that this positive impact of the FDI would occur only with a balance approach agreement which promotes sustainable development and environmental protections. Most NGOs claimed that the MAI undermined government authority to regulate for the protection of health, safety and the environment.

Even though NGOs were not involved officially in the negotiation process of the MAI, they had direct impact on some substantive issues that were negotiated in the MAI. NGOs arguments that caused failure of the MAI can be divided into two categories.

---

[10] *Id.* at 322.

[11] This statement included following process concern of the MAI : "1) Suspend the MAI negotiations and extend the 1998 deadline to allow sufficient time for meaningful public input and participation in all countries. 2) Increase transparency in the negotiations by publicly releasing the draft texts and individual reservations and by scheduling a series of on going public meetings and hearings in both member and non member countries, open to the media, parliamentarians and the general public. 3) Broaden the active participation of government departments in the official negotiations beyond state, commerce and finance to a broader range of government agencies, ministries and parliamentary committees. 4) Renegotiate the terms of withdrawal to enable countries to more easily and rapidly withdraw from the agreement when they deem it in the interest of their citizens. Developing countries and countries in transitions which have not been a party to the negotiations must not be pressurized to join the MAI." Id. at 323.

[12] Nick Mubey, *International Investment Agreements and their Implications for Arab countries*, WWF Presentation to the UNCTAD/League of Arab States Regional Symposium, May (1999).

First, the MAI includes provisions such as expropriation and investor v state dispute settlement provisions that harm the environment and violate sovereignty principles. Second, the MAI does not provide issues that control the behavior of foreign investor. In addition, as mentioned earlier, the environmental and labour issues had been inserted in the MAI after the criticism of the NGOs. The NGO had impact also to stop the negotiations after recognizing that their concern on substantive and procedural issues could not be carried out by the negotiators. They influence public and especially participant countries' parliament members.

The NGOs challenged the MAI negotiations through utilizing the Internet.[13] Many NGOs established home pages relating to the MAI so as to create public awareness and criticism as well. It is interesting that they had a Web Television, with respect to MAI on the Internet.[14] They criticized MAI negotiations through not only using the Internet but also arranging some symposiums and making public protest. After the official announcement of the OECD ending the negotiations of the MAI, they celebrated as a victories party, but they were still worried about the future development of the multilateral agreement on investment.

B. Lost of Interest by Business Community to the MAI

The business community lost its interest in the MAI since some of the expected MAI provisions had not been inserted in the draft treaty. For example taxation would be

---

[13] Katie Tieleman states that: "The larger network took shape mainly in the form of email distribution lists, ranging sometimes from local to national levels and often form capital to capital. No doubt the internet played a crucial role in the anti-MAI campaign. In part, existing networks like the NAFTA opposition movement, were revitalized. The network also grew fast, to include, in the end, (mainly green) members of the national and European Parliaments, TUAC and the Unions.", Tieleman, *supra* note 4, at 13.

[14] See at the " http://www.workingtv.com/focus/mai.html" (visited 05/20/1998)

carved out from the Agreement. Even though the business community was one of the initiative forces to commence the negotiation process of the MAI, it lost interest in the negotiation progress.[15] The most important reason for losing its interest is that taxation provisions would be carved out of the MAI.[16] The business community favored a taxation provision which provide additional national treatment principle. It also argued that subjecting tax disputes arising in connection with NT to binding disputes settlement procedures under the MAI, particularly "Investor-State dispute settlement procedure", should be addressed in the MAI.[17]

One of the concerns of the business community was the providing environment and labour issues in the MAI. After major criticism from the NGOs, the MAI negotiators agreed to insert some provisions for the environment and labor issues.. However, the business community did not approve this development in the negotiation process.

C. Political Changes in the MAI Negotiating Countries

Political changes in some negotiating countries had an immense effect on the failure of the MAI negotiations. The OECD governments could not live up to their commitments and due to the inability of the negotiating countries to resolve discrepancies between them caused the failure of the MAI.

---

[15] UNCTAD, *supra* note 1, at 24.

[16] *Id.* at 24.

[17] OECD, Confidential DAFFE/MAI (97) 1/ REV 2.

The new center/left governments in many OECD countries criticized MAI negotiations and gave new priorities in their political issues.[18] These governments needed to carry out economic reforms, particularly in the fields of pensions and labour market deregulation. Indeed, "Social justice" is one of the main objectives of the center/leftist parties' policy. That is to say "social democrats want to keep welfare spending high and they reject the libertarian position to privatize large parts of the welfare states."[19] For example, the socialist-led coalition government in France had prior economic policies such as reducing unemployment and halting privatization.[20] In Germany, the Social Democratic Part (SDP) won the election in September 1998 and had a coalition government with the Green Party.[21] Like the French government, the German government had the prior policy to reduce unemployment. In addition, the coalition governments, particularly in Germany and France like other EU members, had to prepare for their participation in European Economic and Monetary Union (EMU).[22] Thus, the new governments are not interested in negotiation on the MAI

---

[18] For example, after the election, French had a coalition government encompasses Socialists, four other leftist movements (including the Greens and the Communist). Thomas Sanction, *Losing Bet*, Time Europe, http://www.time.com/time/europe/timetrails/france/france970616.html (visited 05/20/2002).

[19] Christian Watrin, *Europe's "New" Third Way, Heritage Lectures*, No.634, May 11, (1999).

[20] Thomas Sanction explains new French government's promises in the election in 1997. He emphasizes "Jospin and his allies had promised to fight France's stubborn 12.8% unemployment rate by creating some 700,000 government backed jobs, reducing the work week from 39 to 35 hours with no reduction in pay, suspending planned privatization, cutting the sales tax and raising the minimum wage." Sanction, *supra* note 18.

[21] Watrin, *supra* note 19.

[22] Euro-Focus, *The Center for Strategic and International Studies, Hello Jospin! Bye Bye EMU?* Volume 2 Number 3 June 9, (1997).

Socialist led coalition governments opposed the MAI in order to maintain socialist parties' value with its rival party, and rightist president of Jacques Chirac.[23] Indeed, for example, leftist government, French Prime Minister Lionel Jospin states, "when you see the impact of recent upheavals in world markets and the hasty and often thoughtless movement of capital it would appear wiser not to allow excessive private interests to bite into the sphere of state sovereignty."[24] After the withdrawal of France from the Negotiation of the MAI, the United Kingdom and Australia supported French opinion and withdrew from the MAI as well.[25]

David Henderson argues in his book, " The MAI Affair; A Story and its Lessons" that "government failure" brought about the failure of the MAI negotiations.[26] Moreover, Professor Moran agrees with this opinion and he asserts that negotiating countries' unwillingness to commit their own MAI objectives set down in the Agenda is the fundamental reason for the failure of the MAI. He further rightly claims that refusing the regulation on the investment incentives, carving out the taxation from the agreement and making priority for investment protection in the negotiation, show the negotiation countries' own doubts about the MAI.

---

[23] Edward Graham, *Regulatory Takings, Supernational Treatment, and the Multilateral Agreement on Investment: Issues Raised By Nongovernmental Organizations*, 31 CORNELL INT'L L. J. 599, 613 (1998).

[24] Larry Elliot et al., *French Scupper " Charter for Multinationals"; Investment Pact in Tatters*, Guardian (London), October 15, (1998).

[25] Marc Selinger, *Nations Drop Efforts on Global Investment Deal*, Washington Times, December 5, (1998).

[26] David Robertson, *The Role of Foreign Investors in Developing Countries, OECD Conference on the Role of International Investment in Development, Corporate Responsibilities and the OECD Guidelines for Multinational Enterprises*, Paris, 20-21 September (1999).

II. Lessons From the MAI

The MAI was only recent effort to regulate multilateral investment rules. Although every investment treaty negotiation will depend on individual circumstances, and has its own aims and procedures, there is an opportunity to learn some general lessons from these negotiations.[27] The lessons to be learnt from the MAI are helpful to avoid same kinds of problems in the future negotiations of the FDI, whether these negotiations will be bilateral, regional, plurilateral and multilateral negotiations. The statement by Professor David Henderson is expressed as to why the need to draw some lessons from the MAI. He stated that: "Historians are apt to view the past in terms of two contrasting elements, continuity and change. In assessing the significance of the MAI episode, there is a place for both."[28] The followings are some key lessons from the MAI.

A. The Need for Procedural Changes in the Negotiation of the Agreement
1. General Arguments

The negotiating process should be transparent at both the intergovernmental and national level. One may argue that the MAI negotiation process is not transparent. Even in OECD countries, the public has not been informed about the agreement. The draft text was leaked and posted on the Internet by the NGOs and after that public opposition grew fast. The Internet thus supplied the transparency that was lacking in the MAI.

A criticism of the MAI negotiations with respect to negotiation process was that developing countries were excluded from the negotiations. Professor David Henderson

---

[27] UNCTAD, *supra* note 1, at 27.

[28] HENDERSON, *supra* note 1, at 48.

responded to this criticism stating that the MAI was conceived from its inauguration that would be designed by the OECD members and non-members could accede later. Further he stated that even countries that did not join the negotiation process of any international agreement, they would accede later.[29] For instance, China wanted to become a member of the WTO even it did not attend the establishment negotiations of this organization.

One may argue that the choice of principal negotiators was one of the failures of the MAI. Indeed, different bodies of government representation took place in the MAI negotiations.[30] For example the United States representation was shared by the State Department, the Office of the US Special Trade Representative and the Treasury, For New Zealand, the responsible department was the Ministry of Foreign Affairs and Trade, In Germany the Ministry of Economics.[31]

The involvement of all interested parties in from the inauguration stages of negotiations, through the future process, may have a substantial effect for the success of the negotiations.[32] Rubens Ricupero, the Secretary General of UNCTAD, argued that the MAI negotiations: " ...have demonstrated that a meaningful international agreement in this area requires that international investment discussion and negotiations involve all those affected by such an agreement. Not only representatives of governments should be heard, but also those from civil society who have a real stake in the outcome. This is the

---

[29] *Id.* at 20.

[30] *Id.*

[31] *Id.* at 21.

[32] John Gara, *Trends in International Investment Agreements*, Sub Regional Workshop for South Asia on Recent Development in International Investment Agreements, The United Nations Conference on Trade and Development and the Government of Sri Lanka, 15-16 December (1996).

logical consequence of the internationalization of the domestic agenda"[33] I agree with his opinion; however, it is important to define what should be the legal status and role of the NGOs in the negotiation process.

2. The Legal Status of NGOs in International Law

a. Civil society and the UN

NGOs have attended some symposiums, discussions, and consultations in various international organizations such as the UN and the World Bank and the WTO. The question will be raised in many minds as to whether or not they are really representatives of the civil society and what kind of legal status will they have. Professor David Henderson explains that: "the whole notion of a civil society which has claims of its own to represent and speak for the people of a country is misguided when that country has a democratically elected and responsible government: persons who are not elected, and not accountable to a duly elected and generally representative legislature, can have no such status." [34] He further points out that: "This is not to argue that democracy is only a matter of elections, nor that the notion of civil society is without meaning or value, despite the questionable use that is often now made of it. The point at issues is one of defining admissible roles and claims, and not accepting at face value pretensions that have little or no basis." [35] Indeed, even though NGOs can effectively carry out many activities, they are not serving as representative of the people. For example, Maude

---

[33] Rubens Ricupero, opening remarks at the Regional Symposium for Asia on " *International Investment Arrangements and their Implications for Developing Countries*", held in New Delhi in July (1998).

[34] HENDERSON, *supra* note 1, at 58.

[35] *Id*. at 58.

Barlow, head of the Council of Canadians, worked in the frontline against the MAI, but she did not have broad support in Canada.[36]

UNCTAD studies on investment take different approach with respect to what civil society means. UNCTAD World Investment Report stated that: *"While civil society can be seen as a counterbalance to the state, both are inextricably linked. Civil Society is a "work in progress" which, while existing throughout much of the world in different shapes and forms, at different levels of organization, capacity and strength, is a sociopolitical reality whose continuing expansion demands active support if the goals of development, democracy, and human rights are to be realized. In this sense, the building of civil society can be seen as an objective whose achievement must be purposefully and actively sought, in order to achieve wider economic, political and social goals."*[37] I agree with UNCTAD studies that civil society is a living process, including not just elected government, but also various organizations whose aim is to protect and promote social, economic and political development of their states. However, it is necessary to draw a line in which NGOs are the representatives of civil society.

Internet has negative implications in daily life. For example two or three people will come together and establish an NGO, without having any institutions, they will create home pages on the Internet and they will publicize and criticize negatively any international event. Do NGOs which do not have any agendas or enough executive members have legitimate claim that they are the representatives of the civil society and want to attend the negotiation of the MAI? The answer should be no for that kind of

---

[36] John King Gamble, Charlotte Ku, *International Law-New Actors and New Technologies: Center Stage For NGOS?*, 31 LAW & POL'Y INT'L BUS. 221, 257-258 (2000).

[37] UNCTAD, WORLD INVESTMENT REPORT 60 (1998).

NGOs. How about the other NGOs, who will decide that they have the legal capacity to represent civil society in which stage of international negotiations. These questions are unresolved.

The growing influence of NGOs in international law, particularly in international environment and human rights law, let the discussion of their legal status in international law. NGOs such as Greenpeace and Amnesty International are increasingly participating in decision-making and enforcement of international law activities. In addition "the question of legitimacy" provides another reason for the regulation of NGOs activities in international law. Before starting to analyze their existing legal status under international law, I contend that there is a need to establish the international legal guidelines for NGOs for not only to allow them active participation in international decision-making process, but also to grant accountability for their action.

There have been many initiatives on regulations of NGOs status in international law since 1923. The Institut de Droit International drafted the first treaty on the legal status of international associations in 1923.[38] International association is defined as non-profit private association having an international purpose and permitting membership from different countries. The draft treaty also provided "central international registration" of these associations.

Many international agreements and resolutions have addressed the legal position of NGOs in international law. The UN experiences with the NGOs need to be mentioned in order to designate their legal position in international law. Article 71 of the UN Charter provides that the Economic and Social Council (ECOSOC) can arrange

---

[38] Steve Charnovitz, *Two Centuries of Participation: NGOs and International Governance*, 18 MICH. J. INT'L L. 183 (1997).

consultation with NGOs concerned with related issues within the competence of ECOSOC. Article 71 of the UN Charter states that the "Economic and Social Council may make suitable arrangements for consultation with non-governmental organizations which are concerned with matters within its competence." Karsten Nowrot rightly argues that this article grants discretionary power to the ECOSOC on arrangements for consultations with NGOs.[39]

In order to implement Article 71 of the UN Charter, the ECOSOC adopted a resolution called "Consultative relationship between the United Nations and non-governmental organizations" in 1996.[40] This resolution recognized that national, subregional, regional and international NGOs may seek consultative status.[41] This resolution establishes three main categories of NGOs depending on the their involvement with the activities of ECOSOC. The first category organizations have "general consultative status", and they are concerned with most of ECOSOC's activities. For example the World Federation of Trade Unions (WFTU) and the ICC were admitted as a "general consultative status."[42] The second category organizations have "special

---

[39] Nowrot, *supra* note 2, at 624.

[40] Economic and Social Council Resolution 1996/31, 49 U.N., ESCOR supp. (No.1), U.N. Doc. E/1996/96 (1996).

[41] *Id.* E.S.C. Res. 1996/31, at para.4.

[42] Paragraph 22 of the Resolution states that "Organizations that are concerned with most of the activities of the Council and its subsidiary bodies and can demonstrate to the satisfaction of the Council that they have substantive and sustained contributions to make to the achievement of the objectives of the United Nations in fields set out in paragraph 1 above, and are closely involved with the economic and social life of the peoples of the areas they represent and whose membership, which should be considerable, is broadly representative of major segments of society in a large number of countries in different regions of the world shall be known as organizations in general consultative status." *Id.* E.S.C. Res. 1996/31. at para. 22.

consultative status", and they are concerned with a few ECOSOC's activities.[43] Organizations in the third category have do not have either general or specific consultative bodies, but they can have "roster status".[44]

This resolution grants rights to NGOs in particularly the first and second categories of NGOs. For example, the NGOs in the "General consultative status" can submit proposals for consideration on the provisional agenda, and NGOs in "general consultative status and special consultative status" may be represent by authorized person as an observer status at public meetings of the ECOSOC and its subsidiary bodies.[45] It can be argued that the UN experiences with NGOs shows that international community recognizes NGOs activities and thus they have legal personality under the international law.[46]

It is essential to note that UNCTAD has been working closely with civil society groups. The integration of civil society groups in its activities is one of the objectives of

---

[43] Paragraph 23 of the Resolution states that "Organizations that have a special competence in, and are concerned specifically with, only a few of the fields of activity covered by the Council and its subsidiary bodies, and that are known within the fields for which they have or seek consultative status shall be known as organizations in special consultative status." *Id*. E.S.C. Res. 1996/31. at para. 23.

[44] Paragraph 24 of the Resolution states that "Other organizations that do not have general or special consultative status but that the Council, or the Secretary-General of the United Nations in consultation with the Council or its Committee on Non-Governmental Organizations, considers can make occasional and useful contributions to the work of the Council or its subsidiary bodies or other United Nations bodies within their competence shall be included in a list (to be known as the Roster). This list may also include organizations in consultative status or a similar relationship with a specialized agency or a United Nations body. These organizations shall be available for consultation at the request of the Council or its subsidiary bodies. The fact that an organization is on the Roster shall not in itself be regarded as a qualification for general or special consultative status should an organization seek such status." *Id*. E.S.C. Res. 1996/31. at para. 24.

[45] *Id*. E.S.C. Res. 1996/31. at para. 27-32.

[46] Karsten Nowrot states that "These participatory rights, granted to NGOs under the international law of the UN, can be viewed as some form of entitlement recognized by State practice within the UN that is an indication of an at least indirect legal personality for NGOs under international law." Nowrot, *supra* note 2, at 625.

the UNCTAD. Indeed, this integration produces proposals and reports.[47] For example, one may assert that the Doha Declaration on the TRIPS Agreement and on Public Health is the result of the UNCTAD and civil societies' cooperative works on trade areas. UNCTAD pursued to further collaboration with civil society groups.[48] . The declaration adopted UNCTAD X Conference at Bangkok reflects the role of the NGOs on development,

> UNCTAD's work can serve to address the challenges and opportunities of globalization and inform an open and systematic debate on diverse development-related issues of global interest among partners in the development process, including the private sector, NGOs, academia and parliamentarians. It should pursue this dialogue to help shape international economic relations in the twenty-first century.[49]

After the Bangkok meeting, the UNCTAD established the Civil Society Outreach (CSO) in order to strengthen further cooperation with NGOs.[50]

b. Code of Conduct For NGOs

One may wonder even though NGOs activities' have an important impact in international law area, why NGOs do not have legal accountability and whom they are represent. Most NGOs criticized the MAI since it did not provide a balance approach that is to say that the MAI did not provide legal obligations for transnational corporations. However, one may argue that NGOs themselves do not have any legal

---

[47] Tony Hill, UNCTAD and NGOs: An Evolving Cooperation, *in* UNCTAD-CIVIL SOCIETY DIALOGUE, 55-56 (UNCTAD ed., 2002).

[48] Rubens Ricupero, Secretary General of UNCTAD, Foreword *in* UNCTAD-CIVIL SOCIETY DIALOGUE 8 (UNCTAD ed., 2002).

[49] UNCTAD, Report of UNCTAD on its Tenth Session, TD/390, 21 Sep. (2000).

[50] Amel Haffouz, *Institutional Framework for Civil Society Cooperation with UNCTAD and Suggestions for its Further Evolution*, *in* UNCTAD-CIVIL SOCIETY DIALOGUE, 47 (UNCTAD, ed., 2002).

responsibility specified by the international community. In order to provide legal status for NGOs, the international community should adopt code of conduct for NGOs.

Regulations of the rights and the duties of non-state actors in international law such as transnational corporations have already taken place in various multinational and regional arrangements.[51] As we already mentioned in Chapter 2, the code of conduct for transnational corporations drafted under the UN is legally non-binding. The international community should negotiate and adopt a code of conduct not only for transnational corporations but also for NGOs since NGOs also have played an important role as non-state actors in international law.

It is vital to note at the outset that there is no "universal" code that applies to all NGOs. The NGOs are in the process of adopting their own voluntary Codes of Conduct. That is to say that they have a "self regulation"[52] For example, the International Red Cross and Red Crescent Societies adopted code of conduct in 1994.[53] Due to the fact that this regulation is voluntary, there is need to have binding laws that sets out minimum standards of conduct. Indeed, many governments can impose by special NGO law that in order to be an NGO, one entity has to adopt its code of conduct and submit it to the government. For instance, Kenya has imposed "compulsory self regulation" to NGOs

---

[51] Nowrot, *supra* note 2, at 635.

[52] According to the World Bank publication, "self regulation is an ambiguous term. Although it most clearly and literally refers to the efforts of an NGO to regulate itself, it is in fact used most often to refer to efforts of groups of NGOs to set and enforce standards for all members in the group. Both kinds of self regulation are valuable and should be encouraged." World Bank, HANDBOOK ON GOOD PRACTICES FOR LAWS RELATING TO NON_GOVERNMENTAL ORGANIZATIONS (Discussion Draft) Prepared for the World Bank by The International Center for Not for Profit Law on May 1997, at Chapter M: Self Regulation.

[53] International Federation of Red Cross and Red Crescent Societies, *Code of Conduct*. http://www.ifrc.org/publivat/conduct/index.asp (visited 10/25/2001).

under the NGO Act of 1990.[54] Gambia, and South Africa have special legislations that set outs standards of behavior and accountability for NGOs.[55]

The code of conduct should include following issues that are rightly pointed out by Anthony Adair:

> a) An obligation to be legally constituted, with full disclosure of financial information, including sources of funding, application of funds and audited accounts;
> b) Clearly identified aims and objectives together with a commitment to operate within the law in pursuit of those objectives;
> c) Open democratic process, including the election of officers, and the participation of members in decision making such as the establishment of broad policy;
> d) A commitment to avoid becoming involved in party politics while still being free to pursue legitimate public policy objectives;
> e) A code of ethics for all staff and members who engage in activities on behalf of the NGOs.[56]

The code of conduct should require democratic process for NGOs' internal mechanisms. One may argue that NGOs do not have democratic bodies in their organizations since most NGOs' presidents and executive body are not elected by their members.[57] If the NGOs have their own code of conduct that provides standards of ethical behavior, democratic governance and transparency of their financial situations, they will have legal credibility and "legitimacy" to pursue their claim at the international decision making process.

---

[54] *Id.* According to the Act, the first 100 NGOs which registered under the law created NGO Council in order to adopt compulsory code of conduct for NGO.

[55] Anthony Adair, *A Code of Conduct For NGOs- A Necessary Reform*, October (1999). http://www.iea.org.uk/wpapers/NGO.htm, (visited 10/25/2001)

[56] *Id.* at 10.

[57] Peter J. Spiro, *New Global Potentates: Non-Governmental Organizations and the "Unregulated" Marketplace*, 18 CARDOZO L. REV. 957, 962 (1996).

It is possible to argue that the best way to grant legal status of NGOs under international law is to adopt a "universal" international code of conduct for NGOs. The UN is the appropriate organization to adopt this code. The international organizations such as the World Bank and the WTO should work together with the UN to adopt certain standards for NGOs. In addition, NGO must participate in the drafting this code since it will govern NGOs' activities.[58]

3. Concluding Remarks on Negotiation Process

To sum up, future negotiations on investment should be democratic, transparent and ensure public participation in some level. OECD should have worked closely with other international organizations such as UNCTAD and WTO. Internal transparency should be provided through involving more national delegates. Moreover, considering the complexity of negotiations on the multilateral investment agreement, determining the pre-negotiation process is important. Kobrin spells out that "The days of negotiating treaties behind closed doors are over. Future negotiations will require a balance between public involvement and the need for effective global governance." In order to ensure a democratic and transparent negotiation process, the number of representatives participating in the negotiations on behalf of the negotiating countries should be

---

[58] Karsten Nowrot points out "the advantage of an international treaty regulating the duties and rights of NGOs would be its precision compared to be often uncertain and inexact legal positions under customary international law. Furthermore it would be dispel any given doubts concerning legal personality of NGOs under international law, since these entities could be, at least toward the contracting parties, regarded as derivative subjects of international law." Nowrot, *supra* note 2, at 635.

increased in a way that representatives can work in coherence with government and at the same time let public and especially opposition parties know the negotiation process.[59]

One may rightly argue that negotiators of the MAI did not know how to inform the public.[60] Participant countries should establish special working group that will encompass parties in the government and opposition parties.[61] The creation of a network under the international organizations that negotiated agreements is vital to exchange information among civil society groups and representatives of government. Furthermore, developing countries should participate actively in the negotiation process. In order to provide their active involvement, the international organizations such as UNCTAD should technically help them.[62] NGOs should attend discussion and consultations process of the negotiation. However, they should not participate in the formal substantive discussions and negotiations since they are not legally responsible from the outcome of the negotiations.[63] I agree with Peter T. Muchlinski's opinion that civil society's

---

[59] Peter T. Muchlinski, The Rise and Fall of the Multilateral Agreement on Investment: Where Now?, 34 INT'L LAW. 1033, 1050 (2000).

[60] Jan Huner, assistant to the Dutch chair states, "The main problem with the MAI is that its negotiators did not expect to have to sell it politically. Most of the MAI negotiators are investment specialist not used to viewing from a political perspective the concepts that they consider logical and essential parts of an investment discipline....They were thus wholly unprepared to defend these concepts vis-à-vis opponents that were distorting them to portray the MAI as a threat."

[61] For example, Peter T. Muchlinski argued that "it may be necessary to establish improved systems of policy development, building on the informal networks already existence, and accounting for not only the views of civil society, but the views of local and regional interests in relations to inward investment. This is given greater weight in the light of the establishment of Regional Development Agencies and of the devolution of inward investment issues to the Scottish Parliament and Welsh Assembly>" Id, at 1052.

[62] Muchlinksi, *supra* note 59, at 1050.

[63] HENDERSON, *supra* note 1, at 60.

representatives should be officially involved in the negotiations as "advisers" and not "merely as observers".[64]

I contend that the international organizations should create a framework for criteria how to select which NGOs should join the international decision-making process, in particular (in our case) if any international organizations initiate the future multilateral agreement on investment negotiations, they should draft a legal guideline for the participation of NGOs in the "preparatory work". The World Bank Operational Manual can be utilized as an example for the creation of the framework. Article 15 of the Manual provides "selection criteria" for the NGOs:

> NGO partners should be selected according to the specific skills and expertise required for the task at hand as it relates to the development goals being pursued. The following are some of the qualities that should be considered in selecting individual NGO partners (depending on the nature and purpose of a particular task):
> (a) credibility: acceptability to both stakeholders and government;
> (b) competence: relevant skills and experience, proven track record;
> (c) local knowledge
> (d) representation: community ties, accountability to members/beneficiaries, gender sensitivity;
> (e) governance: sound internal management, transparency, financial accountability, efficiency;
> (f) legal status; and
> (g) institutional capacity: sufficient scale of operations, facilities, and equipment.[65]

---

[64] Muchlinksi, *supra* note 59, at 1050.

[65] The World Bank, *The World Bank Operational Manual, Good Practices, Involving Nongovernmental Organizations in Bank Supported Activities*. GP 14.70, February 2000.

B. **The Content of the Agreement**

The success of the negotiation of the agreement depends on its content.[66] In the light of what has been analyzed above, the MAI is very broad agreement. The scope of the terms "investor" and "investment" are central to the MAI and these terms have been defined very broadly. Further, the MAI has a top-down approach whereby parties accept the obligations of the agreement unless they lodge reservations. That is to say that, all sectors of economy are subject to the general provisions unless they are specifically excluded in a way that the MAI provided. Even the developing countries could not agree on broaden liberal investment agreement. Therefore, the lesson should be drawn that future agreements on investment should not be on "full liberalization", like GATS agreement "selective liberalization" should be aimed from the outset.[67]

An UNCTAD study on the MAI asserts that for the multinational negotiations, it is advisable to take a "modest and incremental approach". Further, this study states that: "Too ambitious investment negotiating agendas at the international level may have a lesser likelihood of success than more modest and incremental proposition."[68]

One may argue that one of the reasons for the failure of the MAI is that agreement was based on the "pure" investor and investment protection principle.[69] This failure however shows that future agreements should not only provide "pure" investment and investor protection, but also include investor rights and obligations on issues that highly demanded from the people of the world such as protecting environment, preventing and

---

[66] UNCTAD, *supra* note 1, at 28.

[67] Muchlinski, *supra* note 59, at 1051.

[68] UNCTAD, *supra* note 1, at 28.

[69] Muchlinski, *supra* note 59, at 1049.

punishing corrupt practices of officials.[70] Therefore, these contemporary issues should be addressed in future agreements.

One of the criticisms of the MAI was that MAI did not have a balance approach in terms of the rights and responsibilities of the foreign investors. The failure of the MAI demonstrates that responsibilities of foreign investors must be determined within the same agreement or be established in collaboration with other binding or non-binding agreements that provides balance between rights and obligations of the foreign investor.[71]

One of the other criticism of the MAI was that it would prevent host countries from using investment policy to promote their economic policy aims such as new job creation, export promotion, technology transfer. This occurs due to the restrictions placed on performance requirements. In responding this criticism MAI at least should have provided to contracting countries to lodge some reservations with respect to existing policies. Moreover, social and environmental policies should be taken into consideration in the negotiation of the future investment treaties. Investment treaties should not undermine the impact of their provisions on social and environmental goals.[72]

C. The Flexibility for Negotiating on Investment Treaties

Not only developing countries but also developed countries need to some sort of certain flexibility in any agreement that they signed in order to pursue their social, economic and cultural development. Indeed, the negotiation on the exceptions of the

---

[70] *Id.* at 1050.

[71] *Id.*

[72] Oxfam GB *Update on the MAI (Multilateral Agreement on Investment)*, December (1998), <http://www.oxfam.org.uk> (visited 1/15/1999)

MAI demonstrates that even developed countries lodged various exceptions to protect their social, economic and cultural development. One of the reason for the failure of the MAI was the countries could not agree some areas on the exceptions issues. For example the REIO exception clause and the cultural exceptions are the most controversial issues among the USA, Canada and European Union.

Suppose the Developing countries negotiated this agreement, it seems that many issues in terms of exceptions or carved out from agreement will be raised from them. As UNTAD study points out that the main objective for the developing countries to sign investment agreement is just to pursue as strongly as possible their development objectives.[73] Overall, the failure of the MAI teaches us that the more broad and inflexible negotiation on multilateral investment agreement will cause inevitable result of the collapse of that negotiation.

D. The Ripeness of the Multinationalization of the Investment Regime

One of the main reason to commence negotiations on multilateral investment agreement was the proliferation of the BITs in the international law on foreign investment. However, the collapse of the negotiations of the MAI illustrates that the constantly increased number of bilateral investment treaties cannot be taken as evidence in the readiness of the world community to sign multilateral investment agreement.[74] Indeed, the signing bilateral, or regional treaties is different than multilateral one in terms of not only the number of the parties involved but also the nature of the agreements

---

[73] *Id.*

[74] UNCTAD, *supra* note 1, at 28.

involved.[75] Especially, as we analyzed in the third chapter that BITs are lex specialis between the parties, that is to say they create special law between the parties. Multilateral investment treaties, on the other hand, have more broad international legislative character among the world community.[76]

---

[75] Gara, *supra* note 32.

[76] UNCTAD, *supra* note 1, at 28.

CHAPTER SEVEN. THE WORLD TRADE ORGANIZATION (WTO) AGREEMENTS RELATED TO INVESTMENT

I. Historical Background for Investment within the GATT Framework

The General Agreement on Tariffs and Trade (GATT) derives from the attempt to establish the International Trade Organization (ITO) within the United Nations.[1] The ITO Charter covered trade issues, restrictive business practices, commodity agreements and foreign investment. That is to say that its scope was broader than the GATT Agreement since initially the GATT agreement only provided issues on trade in goods until the Uruguay Round negotiations in 1994. Nevertheless the ITO Charter was not ratified. So, an attempt to create an international organization for trade, in the form of the ITO, failed.[2] Even though the establishment of the ITO was unsuccessful, the GATT remained as an agreement for trade until 1995.[3] The GATT (1947) was a legally binding agreement on tariff and trade between signatory states.

Over the years the GATT have developed through several rounds of negotiations. The main reason for the trade rounds was and continues to be the process of reducing tariffs. Furthermore, they have created new aspects of trade. For example, the Tokyo Round (1973-1979) concluded many agreements on non- tariff barriers; "Subsidies and countervailing measures", "Technical barriers to trade",

---

[1] Paul Bryan Christy III, *Negotiating Investment In the GATT: A Call for Functionalism*, 12 MICH. J. INT'L L. 773 (1991).

[2] *Id*. at 775.

[3] Eric. M. Burt, *Developing Countries and the Framework for Negotiations on Foreign Direct Investment in the World Trade Organization*, 12 AM. U. J. INT'L L. & POL'Y. 1015, 1029 (1997).

"Government procurement" are some of the examples of such agreements so -called "codes" since they were binding only subscribed GATT members.[4] The latest round was the Uruguay round which lasted from 1986-1994 and established the WTO.[5]

A.   The Havana Charter

Due to the fact that the Uruguay round brought about new agreements directly dealing with investment issues, it is vital to mention the previous attempt to regulate investment issues in the GATT framework. The United States did not propose any investment provisions at the beginning of the first negotiation round since the US thought that the FCN was enough to provide investment security.[6] Nonetheless, at the London Conference, less developed countries accomplished adding a new chapter within the Agreement for their "economic development" needs. Pursuant to this new chapter, members were obliged to "impose no unreasonable impediments that would prevent other members from obtaining access to facilities required for their economic development."[7] After this outcome at the London Conference, the US brought up the investment issues so as to protect American investor' rights. Thus, members agreed to "take no unreasonable action injurious to the interest of other Members, business

---

[4] WORL TRADE ORGANIZATION, TRADING INTO THE FUTURE 10 (1998).

[5] *Id.* at 12-13.

[6] Christy, *supra* note 1, at 773.

[7] Report of the First Session of the Property Committee of the United Nations Conference on Trade and Employment, art 12, paragraph 2, at 28, U.N. Doc. E/PC/T/33 (Oct. 1946) (London Conference).

enterprises or persons."[8] It was the first recognition of rights for transnational corporations within the ITO and GATT negotiation round.

It should be noted that there were many debates between developed and developing countries with respect to the regulation of international investment within the ITO and GATT framework.[9] These debates still are taking place in the WTO working groups. Developing countries advanced their interest concerning international investment in the Havana Charter. Under this Charter, members acknowledged that "international investment, both public and private, can be of great value in promoting economic development and reconstruction, and consequent social progress." Moreover, pursuant to Article 12 of the Charter, a member is allowed to "take any appropriate safeguards necessary to ensure that foreign investment not used as a basis for interference in its internal affairs or national policies."[10] In order to promote foreign investment a member is obliged to: "to provide reasonable opportunities for investment acceptable to them and adequate security for existing and future investments...and to give due regard to the desirability of avoiding discrimination as between foreign investment."[11] One may argue that this regulation is "considerably short of the minimum standard of international customary law on the protection of foreign property."[12], since it has vague terms such as "adequate", and "due regard".

---

[8] *Id*. art. 12, paragraph 4.

[9] Christy, *supra* note 1, at 774-775.

[10] See *supra* note 7, art. 12, paragraph 1(c).

[11] *Id*. art. 12, paragraph 2(a).

[12] Christy, *supra* note 1, at 775.

The Havana Charter recognized the importance of investment to economic development. However, due to the fact that developing countries' interests were incorporated in the Havana Charter, developed countries did not ratify the Charter. As a result not only the Havana Charter, but also the establishment of the ITO failed.[13]

After the failure to establish the ITO, the GATT contracting parties passed a resolution on "International Investment for Economic Development" in 1955.[14] This resolution recognized that in order to facilitate the objectives of the GATT, the countries should promote their investment flow.[15] Further, the Resolution urged countries to conclude bilateral agreements with respect to investment issues.[16]

Prior to the Uruguay Round, the US proposed to place investment issues within the GATT framework in 1982 at the Tokyo Round. However, this attempt by

---

[13] Todd S, Shenkin explains why the establishment of the ITO failed in the following: "{in the US} many members of the business sector were dissatisfied with the ITO Charter, particularly its foreign investment provisions. As a result, there was probably no chance that the Senate would approve the ITO. Another important reason was that, in 1951, Truman needed to persuade Congress to renew the Trade Agreements Act, which was due to expire in 1950, so that the US could continue to negotiate item by item tariff reductions in the GATT. Consequently, Truman decided in November 1950 to focus on the GATT negotiations at the expense of resubmitting the ITO Charter to Congress. Truman's decision effectively thwarted the creation of the ITO because the participation of the United States in the organization was a precondition by most other nations.", Todd S. Shenkin, *Trade Related Investment Measures in Bilateral Investment Treaties and the GATT: Moving Toward A Multilateral Investment Treaty*, 55 U. PITT. L. REV.541, 557-558 (1994)

[14] International Investment for Economic Development Resolution, March 4, 1955, GATT B.I.S.D. (3d Supp.) at 49-51 (1955).

[15] The Resolution on International Investment for Economic Development recommended that "the contracting parties who are in a position to provide capital for international investment and the contracting parties who desire to obtain such capital use their best endeavors to create conditions calculated to stimulate the international flow of capital having regard in particular to importance for this purpose of providing by appropriate methods for security for existing and future investment, the avoidance of double taxation, and facilities for the transfer of earning upon foreign investment."

[16] WTO,TRIMS: Background, http://www.wto.org/english/thewto_e/whatis_e/eol/e/wto05/wto5_3.htm, (visited 2/3/2001)

the US was unsuccessful since other contracting parties argued that investment decision-making was within their sovereignty so that GATT's scope should not be extended. It is worthy to note that the issue of investment in the WTO is still debated in the same manner.

B.   The FIRA Case

One may argue that prior to the Uruguay Round negotiations, the most vital development regarding the issue of investment within the GATT framework was the decision of the GATT Panel with respect to disputes between the US and Canada.[17] The US filed a complaint that the written undertakings required by the government of Canada under the FIRA violated GATT Articles III:4, III:5, and XVII: 1 (c).[18] The US argued that the written undertakings, which compel investors to purchase goods of Canadian origin in preference to imported goods or in specified amounts or proportions, or to purchase goods from Canadian sources, violated Article III. 4 of the GATT Agreement since they provide requirements giving less favourable treatment to imported products than to like products of national origin.[19] Canada opposed that these requirements were voluntary and there was no specific provision or regulation in the FIRA.

---

[17] Riyaz Dattu, *A Journey From Havana to Paris: The Fifty- Year Quest For The Elusive Multilateral Investment Agreement on Investment*, 24 FORDHAM INT'L L. J. 275, 289 (2000).

[18] Canada Administration of the Foreign Investment Review Act, Feb. 7, 1984, 30 B.I.S.D. 157 (1984) (hereinafter FIRA Panel Report)

[19] GATT Article III: 4 states that: "The products of the territory of any contracting party imported into the territory of any other contracting party shall be accorded treatment no less favourable than that accorded to like products of national origin in respect of all laws, regulations and requirements affecting their internal sale, offering for sale, purchase, transportation, distribution or use."

The Canada enacted its investment law called Foreign Investment Review Act of Canada (hereinafter FIRA) on December 12, 1973.[20] Under the FIRA, a foreign investor can make investment in Canada, if investment is of "significant benefit to Canada."[21] Further, the FIRA stipulates five factors that can be considered as conditions for the approval of investment projects by the Canadian investment authorities.[22] Even though the FIRA did not require foreign investors to submit "written undertakings", the submitting "written undertakings" became ordinary in the practice, and when they approved by the Canadian investment authority they become legally binding.[23] The written undertakings were in the form of purchase undertakings, manufacturing undertakings, and export undertakings.[24] For example purchasing goods of Canadian origin was one of the purchase undertakings.

The GATT Panel, overseeing this dispute, held that the undertakings as local content requirements were inconsistent with the national treatment obligation of GATT Article III.4.[25] However, the Panel concluded that the purchase undertakings did not infringe Article XI:1 since this article applies to the importation of goods.[26]

---

[20] Foreign Investment Review Act, S.C., ch. 46 (1973-1974)

[21] *Id.*

[22] See for more detail, Paul Civello, *The TRIMS Agreement: A Failed Attempt At Investment Liberalization*, 8 MINN. J. GLOBAL TRADE. 97, 103, (1999)

[23] *Id.*

[24] *Id.*

[25] FIRA Panel Report, at 158-162.

[26] *Id.* at 162-163.

The Panel also concluded that the export performance requirements were not inconsistent with Article XVII: 1(c).[27]

The FIRA case was important because the linkage between trade and investment came up for the first time in this case within the GATT framework. The panel underlines that its decision was intended only to ensure that the national treatment principle applies for trade-related investment measures.[28] In particular, the Panel stated that: "the purpose of the article III (4) is not to protect the interests of the foreign investor but to ensure that goods originating in any other contracting party benefit from treatment no less favorable than domestic goods, in respect of the requirement that affect their purchase."[29] Further, the Panel ruled that "the national treatment obligations of article III of the General Agreement do not apply to foreign persons or firms but to imported products and serve to protect the interests of producers and exporters established on the territory of any contracting party."[30] Therefore, the GATT provisions only apply to the extent that trade related investment measures, which distorts trade. Namely, if investment measures do not have trade distorting effects, the GATT provisions will not be applied to them.

Another important issue regarding this case was the consideration of the developing countries. Although this case was between two developed countries, Argentina made submission to the Panel in order to protect developing countries interests asking that developing countries' national investment laws should be exempt

---

[27] *Id.* at 163.

[28] Christy, *supra* note 1, at 790.

[29] FIRA Panel Report, at 160.

[30] *Id.* at 167.

from the GATT provisions.[31] The Panel concludes that there is a special provisions in the GATT for developing countries such as Article XVIII:c.

This case influenced the US to resubmit a proposal dealing with investment measures for negotiation at the Uruguay Round. Like in previous attempts, the US proposal did not get sufficient support.[32] However, this attempt was successful to launch a negotiation on trade-related investment measures.[33]

II. Investment Issues Within the WTO

As noted above that the Uruguay round expanded disciplines of the GATT (1947) and established the WTO. One wonders how the WTO is different from GATT. The WTO-published book, The WTO, Trading into the Future, clearly states as follows: "They are different-the WTO is GATT plus a lot more."[34] Indeed, the WTO completely replaces its predecessor (GATT 1947), with strict dispute settlement process and more comprehensive trade stipulations and has a very different feature. (For more detailed analysis, see footnote bellow)[35] The GATT still exist as

---

[31] Civello, *supra* note 22, at 105.

[32] Dattu, *supra* note 17, at 290.

[33] Pursuant to the Ministerial Declaration of Punta Del Este: "Following an examination of the operation of GATT Articles related to the trade-restrictive and trade-distorting effects of investment measures, negotiations should elaborate, as appropriate, further provisions that may be necessary to avoid such adverse effects on trade.", The Ministerial Declaration of Punta Del Este, GATT Doc. 86-1572, B.I.S.D. (30th Supp.) at 9 (1986).

[34] WTO, *supra* note 4, at 14.

[35] The main differences between the GATT and the WTO are the following: "1-) The GATT was a set of rules, a multilateral agreement, with no institutional foundation, only a small associated secretariat which had its origins in the attempt to establish an International Trade Organization in the 1940s. 2-) The WTO is a permanent institution with its own secretariat. The GATT was applied on a "provisional basis" even if, after more than forty years, governments chose to treat it as a permanent commitment. The WTO commitments are full and permanent. 3-) The GATT rules applied to trade in merchandise goods. In addition to goods, the WTO covers trade in services and trade related aspects of intellectual

an integral part of the WTO Agreement called "GATT 1994", the amended and updated version of GATT 1947.[36]

Even though there is no single multilateral agreement on FDI, there are some agreements that include provisions dealing with specific aspects of FDI within the WTO. Within the WTO, investment-related provisions can be found in the following agreements:

A. Agreement on Trade-Related Investment Measures (TRIMS)

B. General Agreement on Trade in Services (GATS)

C. Agreement on Trade-Related Aspects of Intellectual Property Rights (TRIPS)

D. Agreement on Subsidies and Countervailing Measures (SCM)

A. Agreement on Trade-Related Investment Measures (TRIMs)

The TRIMs Agreement intends to eliminate restrictions on investment, which it seeks distort trade. The objectives of the Agreement, as stated in the preamble, are "desiring to promote the expansion and progressive liberalization of world trade and to facilitate investment across international frontiers so as to increase the economic growth of all trading partners, particularly developing country members, while

---

property. 4-)While GATT was a multilateral instrument, by the 1980s many new agreements had been added of a plurilateral, and therefore selective nature. The Agreements which constitute the WTO are almost all multilateral and thus, involve commitments for the entire membership. 5-) The WTO dispute settlement System is faster, more automatic, and thus much less susceptible to blockages, than the old GATT system. The implementation of WTO dispute findings will also be more easily assured.", (visited 01/19/1997) <http://www.wto.org>

[36] WTO, *supra* note 4, at 14.

ensuring free competition."[37] Article 1 of the TRIMs Agreement defines the scope of its application stating that the Agreement applies to investment measures related to trade in goods only.[38] That is to say that Agreement's scope of application is limited since it applies its non-discriminatory principle to investment measures related to trade in goods, but not services.[39]

It should be noted at the outset that the Agreement does not explicitly define the term "trade related investment measures" (TRIMs). However, the TRIMs Agreement lists local content requirements, trade balancing requirements, foreign exchange restrictions and export restrictions (domestic sales requirements) that would violate Article III:4 or XI:1 of the GATT.[40]

The TRIMs Agreement prohibits any TRIMs that are inconsistent with the GATT Article III (national treatment of imported products) and GATT Article XI (general elimination of quantitative restrictions on imports and exports), since such violations are considered directly detrimental to trade in goods.[41]

TRIMS listed under the Article 1 of the Annex of the Agreement are incompatible with the national treatment provision of the GATS agreement. They are

---

[37] Agreement on Trade Related Investment Measures (herein after TRIMs Agreement), preamble, Second paragraph.

[38] *Id*. TRIMs Agreement, Article 1.

[39] Alexander Lehmann, *Liberalizing Investment Policies, Prospects After the Uruguay Round*, Royal Institute of International Affairs, 34 (1995).

[40] Annex to the TRIMs Agreement.

[41] Robert H. Edwards, Jr. & Simon N. Lester, *Towards a More Comprehensive World trade Organization Agreement on Trade Related Investment Measures*, 33 STAN. J. INT'L L. 169, 195 (1997).

prohibited whether mandatory or linked to advantages.[42] Paragraph 1 (a) of the Illustrative List includes local content requirements, which require "the purchase or use by an enterprise of products of domestic origin or from any domestic source, whether specified in terms of particular products, in terms of volume or value of products, or in terms of a proportion of volume of values of its local production".[43] Paragraph 1(b) covers trade-balancing requirements, which require "an enterprise's purchase or use of imported products be limited to an amount related to the volume or value of local products that is exports."[44]

TRIMS listed under the Article 2 of the Annex of the Agreement are incompatible with the obligation on elimination of quantitative restrictions provision of the GATS agreement. They are prohibited whether mandatory or linked to advantages. Paragraph 2 (a) of the Illustrative List contains trade-balancing measures which limit "the importation by an enterprise of products used in or related to its local production, generally or to an amount relates to the volume or value of local production that it exports."[45] This Article bans the host countries use of TRIMS so as to quantitatively restrict foreign investors' use of imported products. This provision grants the freedom to foreign investors to import products of whatever volume or value required for their investments.

Further, Paragraph 2 (b) of the Illustrative List covers the foreign investment exchange-balancing requirement. It defines as follows: "the importation by an

---

[42] Annex to the TRIMs Agreement.

[43] *Id.* Annex to the TRIMs Agreement.

[44] *Id.*

[45] *Id.*

enterprise of product used in or related to its local production by restricting its access to foreign exchange to an amount related to the foreign exchange inflows attributable to the enterprise".[46] In other words, the host country cannot restrict the use of foreign exchange for the imported products used in or related to local production. Paragraph 3 (c) includes the exportation of or sale restriction for export by an enterprise. It defines as follows: "the exportation or sale for export by an enterprise of product, whether specified in terms of particular products, in terms of volume or value of products, or in terms of a proportion of volume or value of its terms of a proportion of volume or value of its local production."[47] Namely, the host country cannot force the enterprise to export or to sell its product whether specified products, number or quantity, or proportion of its local production in the host country.

These restrictions are considered to be obstacles to free trade. Nevertheless, Article 3 of the TRIMs Agreement provides that all exception under GATT must apply, as appropriate, to the provisions of the TRIMs Agreement. Moreover, Article 4 of the Agreement grants temporary exceptions to the developing countries.[48]

The TRIMs Agreement requires contracting parties to notify the WTO of all non- confirming TRIMs they operate. Some contacting parties have notified the WTO of such measures, many of which are local content requirements in the automotive and agricultural sectors.[49] Moreover, Article 5.2 of the TRIMs

---

[46] *Id.*

[47] *Id.*

[48] Article 4 of the TRIMs Agreement.

[49] By 26 August 1998, notifications under Article 5.1 of the TRIMs Agreement have been submitted by Argentina, Barbados, Bolivia, Chile, Colombia, Costa Rica, Cyprus, Dominican Republic, Ecuador,

Agreement requires elimination of all-non confirming TRIMs within two years for developed countries, within five years for developing countries and within seven years for least developing countries. The Agreement also establishes a Committee on Trade Related Investment Measures which will monitor the implementation of the Agreement.

One may argue that the Agreement does not bring about new provision for foreign investment, but it does codify the GATT decision on FIRA Dispute.[50] Indeed, the Agreement is not intended to impose new obligations, but to clarify the pre-existing GATT obligations. The Agreement does not attempt to regulate foreign investment issues such as the establishment, and treatment of foreign investment. Further, there are no provisions for the transfer of funds or the free movement of personnel, or expropriation. However, it does prohibit only those measures that impose discriminatory treatment on imported and exported goods. Among the measures not covered by the Agreement are: local equity requirements, technology transfer and licensing requirements, export performance requirement, etc.[51]

B. General Agreement on Trade in Services (GATS)

The GATS is the first legally binding multilateral agreement covering trade and investment issues in the services.[52] The GATS covers governmental measures

---

Egypt, India, Indonesia, Mexico, Malaysia, Nigeria, Pakistan, Peru, Philippines, Poland, Romania, South Africa, Thailand, Uganda, Uruguay, and Venezuela. <http://www.wto.org> (visited 2/3/2001)

[50] Burt, *supra* note 3, at 1037

[51] *Id.*

[52] Stephen J. Canner, *The Multilateral Agreement on Investment*, 31 CORNELL INT'L L. J.657, 663 (1998).

that would influence trade in all services (apart from services supplied in the exercise of governmental authority). The GATS defines 155 service sectors based on categories developed by the GATT Secretariat, and specifies four modes of trade in services:

(a) "Cross-border supply" (supply of services from the territory of one Member into the territory of another Member);

(b) "Consumption abroad" (supply of services in the territory of one Member to a service consumer of another Member);

(c) "Commercial presence" (supply of services by a service supplier of one Member through commercial presence in the territory of another Member); and

(d) "Presence of natural persons" (supply of services by a service supplier of one Member through the presence of natural persons of that Member in the territory of another Member.)[53]

Although the GATS does not specify the term of FDI, it is evident that the GATS covers FDI in services through the establishment of "commercial presence" in the territory of any other member.[54] It defines "commercial presence" as all kinds of commercial or professional establishments, through such means as: " i) the constitution, acquisition or maintenance of a juridical person, or ii) the creation or

---

[53] Article 1 of the General Agreement on Trade in Services.
J. Steven Jarreau states that: "Much like prior agreements, the GATS does not define the words "Service" and "services". The GATS does define "trade in services" as the "supply of a service". The "supply of a service" includes, but is not limited to "the production, distribution, marketing, sale and delivery of a service". See detail information concerning definition of services at the GATS framework at, J. Steven Jarreau, *Interpreting the General Agreement on Trade in Services and the WTO Instruments Relevant to the International Trade of Financial Services*: *The Lawyer's Perspective*, 25 N. C. J. INT'L L. & COM. REG.1, 54-55 (1999).

[54] Vanessa P. Sciarra, *The World Trade Organization: Services, Investment, and Dispute Resolution*, 32 INT'L LAW. 923, 924 (1998).

maintenance of a branch pr a representative office within the territory of a Member for the purpose of supplying service."[55] Thus, FDI in services sectors is regulated as one of the four modes of trade in services within the GATS agreement.[56] Moreover, the presence of natural persons method is also related to the FDI.[57] The GATS agreement becomes the first multilateral investment treaty containing a standard of admission and treatment of foreign investors who provide services.

It should be noted that the GATS agreement categorizes obligations of the Members into three types: (1) General principle and obligations. The main text applies to all sectors regardless of whether or not a commitment has been made by the Members. (2) Specific sectors. Some provisions apply to specific sectors in which commitments have been made by the Members. (3) Specific Commitments.[58] The GATS provisions apply according to the specific commitment undertaken by the Members.[59] Thus, in order to find out the applicability of the GATS rules to any sector which involves the issue of foreign investment, one must scrutinize whether the commitments under the "commercial presence" mode have been made.[60]

The GATS includes several provisions relevant to the FDI. The GATS extends the GATT's principles of most-favored nation and transparency to trade in

---

[55] Annex to the GATS, Article XXVIII-Definitions.

[56] Sciarra, *supra* note 54.

[57] The WTO, Working Group on the Relationship between Trade and Investment, Communication from Hong Kong- China, Identification of Differences, Possible Conflicts and Gaps in Existing International Investment Instruments, WT/WGTI/33, 8 April 1998.

[58] WTO, *supra* note 4, at 21.

[59] *Id.*

[60] Sciarra, *supra* note 54, at 925.

services. In addition, it includes the provisions of general application in areas of disclosure of confidential information, increasing participation of developing countries, economic integration, labour markets integration agreements. The GATS prohibits members from maintaining or introducing limits on market access and national treatment that are more restrictive or discriminatory than their specific commitments for the 155 areas contained in the Schedule of Commitments attached to the GATS.[61]

The GATS provides that the MFN treatment and transparency principle apply to all services.[62] Pursuant to the Article II of the GATS, members must accord equal treatment (MFN treatment) to all other members.[63] Unlike the agreements on goods (GATT), the GATS grants temporary exemptions from the obligation of MFN treatment. Article III of the GATS provides a general obligation to publish all relevant laws and regulations since the lack of transparency of laws, and legal measures related to trade in services may constitute a barrier to trade in services.[64]

Unlike MFN provided in the GATS Agreement, the National Treatment provision is an obligation to be determined through specific commitments.[65] In other words, the national treatment principle is specifically confined by the Agreement to

---

[61] Matthias Vocke, *Investment Implications of Selected WTO Agreements and the Proposed Multilateral Agreement on Investment*, International Monetary Fund, IMF Working Paper, 1997, WP/97/60, at 12.

[62] JOHN H. JACKSON & WILLIAM J. DAVEY & ALAN O SYKES, LEGAL PROBLEMS OF INTERNATIONAL ECONOMIC RELATIONS, CASES, MATERIALS AND TEXT 922 (1996).

[63] Article 2 of the GATS, Most Favored Nation Treatment Provision.

[64] Article 3 of the GATS, Transparency Provision.

[65] Vocke, *supra* note 61, at 12.

the services and service suppliers listed in the national schedules of commitments. Pursuant to the Article XVII, national treatment is a discriminatory principle that requires each Member to accord services and service suppliers of any other Member no less favourable treatment than that accorded to its own like services and service suppliers.[66] Each Member has the right to decide whether to undertake national treatment commitments in services and service suppliers. In undertaking a national treatment commitment, a Member may still maintain some discriminatory measures by making reservations. For example, in undertaking a national treatment commitment in the construction services, a Member can accord national treatment in all sectors of construction except engineering services.

Market access is also another obligation whose scope and application is determined through specific commitments.[67] Each Member has the right to undertake a market access commitment which is not to maintain or adopt certain measures contained in an exhaustive list in Article XVI in services and service suppliers.[68] For

---

[66] Article XVII of the GATS, National Treatment Provision.

[67] JACKSON, *supra* note 62, at 923.

[68] Article XVI of the GATS, Market Access, states that: "2. In sectors where market access commitments are undertaken, the measures which a Member shall not maintain or adopt either on the basis of a regional subdivision or on the basis of its entire territory, unless otherwise specified in its schedule, are defined as:
(a) limitations on the number of service suppliers whether in the form of numerical quotas, monopolies, exclusive service suppliers or the requirements of an economic needs test;
(b) limitations on the total value of service transactions or assets in the form of numerical quotas or the requirement of an economic needs test;
(c) limitations on the total number of service operations or on the total quantity of service output expressed in terms of designated numerical units in the form of quotas or the requirement of an economic needs test;
(d) limitations on the total number of natural persons that may be employed in particular service sector or that a service supplier may employ and who are necessary for, and directly related to, the supply of a specific service in the form of numerical quotas or the requirement of an economic needs test;
(e) measures which restrict or require specific types of legal entity or joint venture through which a service supplier may supply a service; and

example, the host-state cannot put pressure on foreign investors for entering the market only through a joint venture with a local corporation. Members may maintain or adopt some or all of these restrictions, which must then be specified in the Schedule of Commitments.

The GATS also includes provision on payments and transfers which is relevant to the FDI. Pursuant to Article XI, a member must not restrict international payments and transfers for current transactions covered by specific commitments undertaken in the GATS.[69] The same article also refers to Article XII (Restrictions to Safeguard the Balance of Payments) as an exemption for the restriction on international payments and transfers for current transactions. However, nothing in the GATS affects the rights and obligations of the Members of the International Monetary Fund.[70]

The GATS provides for a process of progressive liberalization.[71] In particular, special rules and continuing negotiations for specific sectors, such as financial services and telecommunications, are determined in the annexes of the GATS. Pursuant to these annexes, many negotiations have been concluded since the Uruguay Round in various sectors. For example, the Telecommunications Agreement

---

(f) limitations on the participation of foreign capital in terms of maximum percentage limit on foreign shareholding or the total value of individual or aggregate foreign investment."

[69] Article XI of the GATS, Payment and Transfers provision.

[70] *Id.*

[71] Thomas L. Brewer, *International Investment Dispute Settlement Procedure: The evolving regime for Foreign Direct Investment*, 26 LAW & POL'Y INT'L BUS. 633, 644 (1995).

was signed on February 15, 1997 by sixty-nine WTO members. The Financial Services Agreement also was signed on December 13, 1997.[72]

C. Agreement on Trade-Related Aspects of Intellectual Property Rights (TRIPs)

The importance of the protection of intellectual property for the world economy has been recognized by the bilateral and multilateral agreements on trade and investment since lack of protection of intellectual property can distort free trade. There are some international treaties that already establish a common legal framework for the protection of intellectual property, including the Paris Convention which entered into force in 1883 and covers patents, trademarks and other industrial property rights; and the Bern Convention, which entered into force in 1886 and covers copyrights.[73] Due to the development of the trade involving intellectual property, the world community has recognized that there is a need to have more comprehensive international agreement establishing standards for the trade aspects protecting intellectual property. As a result, GATT negotiators inaugurated negotiations on the Trade-Related Aspects of Intellectual Property Rights (TRIPS), one of the most important new areas included in the Uruguay Round negotiations.[74] A final consensus on the TRIPS Agreement was reached in Marrakesh in April 1994 and entered into force on 1 January 1995.

---

[72] The WTO Homepage.

[73] JACKSON, *supra* note 62, at 884.

[74] *Id.* at 885-889.

The TRIPs Agreement recognizes the importance of the protection of intellectual property in the multilateral trading system. However, the TRIPs Agreement does not address directly investment disciplines, although intellectual property is considered as an investment in many BITs, and the MAI draft.[75] Thus, this Agreement is relevant to investment disciplines.

With respect to scope of coverage, the TRIPs Agreement contains provisions for the following intellectual property rights: copyright and related rights, industrial designs, trademarks (including service marks), patents, geographical indications, layout-designs of integrated circuits and undisclosed information (including trade secrets).[76]

The TRIPS Agreement incorporates and improves the principles established in some international agreements pertaining to intellectual property rights such as the aforementioned Paris Convention for the Protection of Industrial Property Rights and the Bern Convention for the Protection of Literary and Artistic Works.[77] WTO Members who are not parties to the Paris or Berne Conventions will thereby be obligated to meet the standards of these conventions. Moreover, the TRIPs Agreement specifies significant levels of protection and rights for every specific intellectual property since some areas are not covered by these agreements.

The TRIPS Agreement requires Members to provide most-favoured-nation (MFN) treatment and national treatment (NT) to the nationals of other WTO

---

[75] See Chapter 3 and 5.

[76] United Nations Conference on Trade and Development, THE TRIPS AGREEMENT AND DEVELOPING COUNTRIES 8 (1998).

[77] Article 1, Paragraph 3 and Article 2 of the Agreement on Trade Related Aspects of Intellectual Property Rights, Including Trade in Counterfeit Goods (hereinafter TRIPs).

Members.[78] The TRIPS Agreement applies the national treatment exceptions laid down in Berne and Paris and MFN exceptions laid down in existing international agreement and multilateral agreements.[79] It should be noted that the Agreement provides not only the MFN and NT, but also provides the "minimum standard of protection".[80]

In order to enforce the intellectual property rights specified in the TRIPs Agreement, the TRIPs Agreement requires domestic procedures for enforcement to be fair and equitable.[81] It provides for enforcement through civil judicial process, through administrative procedures including border measures and administrative remedies, and through criminal judicial process. In addition, the Agreement is subject to the WTO dispute settlement process.

Like other WTO agreements, the TRIPs Agreement stipulates transitional arrangements for countries regardless of their development. Pursuant to Article 65 and 66 of the Agreement, developed countries have a transition period of one year from the date of entry into force of the WTO Agreement; developing countries and transformation countries have five years (until January 2000); and least-developed countries have 11 years (until January 2006).[82]

---

[78] Article 3 (National Treatment), and Article 4 (Most Favored Nation Treatment) of the TRIPs Agreement.

[79] *Id.*

[80] Vocke, *supra* note 61, at 6.

[81] WTO, *supra* note 4, at 28.

[82] Article 65 and 66 of the TRIPs Agreement, Transitional Arrangements.

In order to monitor the implementation of the Agreement, the WTO TRIPs Council is established by the Agreement. The Council has discussed notifications by WTO Members of changes to their national laws and regulations as required under the TRIPS Agreement, exchange of information on technical cooperation, and reviews of the implementation of the TRIPS Agreement. The Council is working closely with another international organization called World Intellectual Property Organization (WIPO) which provides technical assistance for the implementation of the Agreement.

D. Agreement on Subsidies and Countervailing Measures (ASCM)

As mentioned in the Chapter 3, investment incentives issues have proven difficult to deal with in MAI negotiations, since not only developing countries but also developed countries use investment incentives to attract FDI. Financial and indirect investment incentives which are utilized to attract FDI could fall under the definition of a "subsidy" under the Agreement on Subsidies and Countervailing Measures (ASCM).[83] Thus, it is vital to briefly articulate the ASCM agreement. The Agreement was negotiated during the Uruguay Round to provide new disciplines in place of the Agreement on the Interpretation and Application of Articles VI, XVI, and XXIII of the General Agreement on Tariffs and Trade adopted during the Tokyo Round.[84] Compared to the old Subsidies Code, the Agreement provides more explicit definitions of subsidies and stronger, clearer disciplines on countervailing duty.[85]

---

[83] Rupert Schlegelmilch, *International Rules on Foreign Direct Investment: A New Challenge For the World Trade Organization*, International Trade Law & Regulation, 216 (1996).

[84] JACKSON, *supra* note 62, at 769.

The Agreement addresses two separate, but related issues. Firstly, it provides multilateral disciplines with respect to the use of subsidies by the WTO members and enforcement of such disciplines through the WTO dispute settlement mechanism. Secondly, it provides the use of countervailing measures which can be unilaterally imposed by a member state.

The Agreement provides a definition of subsidies. Pursuant to Article 1 of the ASCM, a subsidy must be considered to exist if: "there is a financial contribution (i.e., a fiscal burden) by a government or any public body within the territory of a Member" or "there is any form of income or price support in the sense of Article XVI of GATT 1994," and "a benefit is thereby conferred." Furthermore, the same article defines which actions constitute financial contribution.[86] For example, government grants and loans are given as examples of direct transfer of funds which constitute financial contribution.

The Subsidies Agreement defines three categories of subsidies in terms of purpose and specificity: 1) subsidies that are prohibited. ("red-light subsidies"), 2) subsidies that are not prohibited but which may be subject to countervailing measures

---

[85] *Id.* at 769-770.

[86] Pursuant to the Article 1 of the ASCM, these actions constitute financial contribution:
(i) Government practice involves a direct transfers of funds (e.g., grants, loans and equity infusions) potential direct transfers of funds or liabilities (e.g., loan guarantees);
(ii) government revenue that is otherwise due, is foregone or not collected (e.g., fiscal incentives such as tax credits);
(iii) a government provides goods or services other than general infrastructure, or purchases of goods;
a government makes payments to a funding mechanism, or entrusts or directs a private body to carry out one or more of the type of functions illustrated in (i) to (iii) above which would normally be vested in the government and the practice, in no real sense, differs from practices normally followed by governments.

("yellow-light subsidies"), and 3) subsidies that are neither prohibited nor subject to countervailing measures ("green-light subsidies").[87]

Red-light subsidies mean prohibited subsidies. Pursuant to the Article 3 of the ASCM, with certain exceptions, such as preferential treatment for developing countries and transitional economies, all red-light subsidies must be eliminated.[88] If a red-light subsidy is granted, it will be subject to the remedies for red-light subsidies.[89] Moreover, the remedies for red-light subsidies will be invoked in parallel with countervailing measures; however, with regard to the effects of a particular subsidy in the domestic market of the importing member, only one form of relief (either a countervailing duty or the defined remedies) shall be available. There are two categories of red light subsidies: export subsidies and subsidies contingent upon the use of domestic over imported goods. Annex I of the Agreement illustrates list of measures as export subsidies: for example, measures which provide direct subsidies contingent upon export performance are deemed as export subsidies.[90]

Pursuant to the Article 7 of the ASCM, yellow-light subsidies are not prohibited per se but may be subject to the remedies if they cause adverse effects, such as serious injury ("serious prejudice") to other countries.[91] Furthermore, the remedies for yellow-light subsidies may be invoked in parallel with countervailing

---

[87] RALPH H FOLSOM, MICHAEL WALACE GORDON, JOHN A. SPANOGLE, INTERNATIONAL TRADE AND INVESTMENT 130 (1996).

[88] LEHMANN, *supra* note 39, at 37.

[89] Article 4 of the Agreement on Subsidies and Countervailing Measures.

[90] Annex I of the ASCM, Illustrative List of Export Subsidies (a) states that "The provision by governments of direct subsidies to a firm or an industry contingent upon export performance.".

[91] Article 7 of the ASCM.

measures; however, with regard to the effects of a particular subsidy in the domestic market of the importing member, only one form of relief (either a countervailing duty or the defined remedies) shall be available.

Article 8 states that Green-light subsidies are neither prohibited nor subject to countervailing measures.[92] Green-light subsidies include non-specific subsidies and those specific subsidies that meet certain conditions found in the Article 8.[93] Specific green-light subsidies include research and development subsidies, regional development subsidies, and environmental conservation subsidies that have been reported to the Committee before they take effect, reviewed by the WTO Secretariat, and approved by the Committee. Furthermore, pursuant to Article 9, specific green-light subsidies may be subject to the remedies for green-light subsidies if they cause damage which would be difficult to repair the domestic industry of a member.[94]

Part V (Article 10-24) of the Agreement provides the countervailing measures. Countervailing measures may be used for red-light and yellow-light subsidies when imports of subsidized goods harm a competing domestic industry. They are used to offset the effect of the subsidy by, for example, imposing a countervailing duty (limited to the amount of the subsidy) on the import of subsidized goods or securing quid pro quo commitments from the subsidizing country (that it will abolish or restrict the subsidy, or that exporters will raise prices).

---

[92] Edwards, *supra* note 41, at 208.

[93] Article 8 of the ASCM.

[94] Article 9 of the ASCM agreement.

Countervailing duties may only be applied after an investigation has been initiated and conducted according to procedures specified in the Agreement.[95] Furthermore, countries are obligated to explicitly articulate the method by which the amount of assistance will be calculated in either their national legislation or their implementing regulations. The Agreement provides guidelines for calculating the benefits of government equity infusions, loans, debt guarantees, and provisions or procurement of goods and services by governments.

The Agreement provides special and differential treatments for developing country members, and also provides transitional arrangements for members in the process of transformation from a centrally planned economy to a market economy.[96] In light of the fact that subsidies may play an important role in the economic development of developing country members, the Agreement contains preferential measures for developing countries, concerning red subsidies, remedies, dispute settlement, and countervailing measures.[97]

To ensure the transparency of subsidies, the Agreement contains detailed rules on members' obligation to provide notification of specific subsidies, Committee reviews of notified subsidies, etc. For countervailing measures, the Agreement also contains disciplines on reporting measures, furnishing semi-annual reports, notifications of domestic procedures, etc.

---

[95] WTO, *supra* note 4, at 31.

[96] JACKSON, *supra* note 62, at 771.

[97] *Id.*

III. Developments on Investment Issues After the Uruguay Round

A. The Establishment of Working Group on the Relationship between Trade and Investment: First Ministerial Conference in Singapore

The main development on investment issues within the WTO since the conclusion of the Uruguay Round is the establishment of the Working Group on the Relationship between Trade and Investment at the Singapore Ministerial Conference.[98] Pursuant to the mandate given by the Article IV:1 of the Marrakesh Agreement Establishing the World Trade Organization, Singapore Ministerial Conference was held in Singapore in December 9-13, 1996. Article IV:1 specifies that "there shall be a Ministerial Conference composed of representatives of all the Members, which shall meet at least once every two years."

The Singapore Ministerial Conference was the first Ministerial Conference following the conclusion of the Uruguay Round. The Ministerial Conference decided: a) to undertake a comprehensive study of the implementation of the WTO agreements, and b) to establish working groups to study new areas such as trade and investment, trade and competition.[99] The Working Group was to undertake only

---

[98] Mark Koulen, *The WTO Framework: From TRIMs to Treaty?*, Transatlantic and global Economic Integration: The Role of Investment, Report of The European Institute's Seventh Annual Transatlantic Seminar on Trade and Investment, November 17-18, (1997). Washington, DC, at 35.

[99] Paragraph 20 of the Singapore Ministerial Declaration (WT/MIN(96)DEC) states as follows:
Having regard to the existing WTO provisions on matters related to investment and competition policy and the built-in agenda in these areas, including under the TRIMs Agreement, and on the understanding that the work undertaken shall not prejudge whether negotiations will be initiated in the future, we also agree to:
Establish a working group to examine the relationship between trade and investment; and
Establish a working group to study issues raised by Members relating to the interaction between trade and competition policy, including anti-competitive practices, in order to identify any areas that may merit further consideration in the WTO framework.

educative process, without bias toward any one decision concerning initiation of multilateral investment agreement within the WTO. Future negotiations will take place only after an explicit consensus emerges among the WTO members. As already mentioned in the Chapter 2, the Working Group has been working on cooperation with UNCTAD.

The Working Group decided to study three substantive areas proposed by the Chairman, in the light of recommendations made by Members. Members have submitted written contributions and presented oral statements in the Working Group. Three main areas that specified for study as follows: "1) implications of the relationship between trade and investment for development and economic growth; 2) the economic relationship between trade and investment; and 3) stocktaking analysis of existing international instruments and activities regarding trade and investment."[100] Development issues must be considered in all the aspects of the Group's work program. The situation of the developing countries must also be taken into consideration.

There are many issues suggested for the study under three main subjects.[101] Macro- economic stability, balance of payments, technology transfer and management techniques are some of the issues which have been discussed under the consequences of the relationship between trade and investment for development. As regards to the economic relationship between trade and investment, the degree of

---

[100] WORLD TRADE ORGANIZATION, REPORT (1998) OF THE WORKING GROUP ON THE RELATIONSHIP BETWEEN TRADE AND INVESTMENT TO THE GENERAL COUNCIL, WT/WGTI/2.

[101] *Id.* at Annex 1, Checklist of issues suggested for study.

correlation between trade and investment, the effects of investment policies and measures on trade are the examples of the issues that have been discussed by the Group. As regards to the analysis of the existing international instruments, existing provisions in the WTO, and bilateral investment treaties are the two examples that have been examined by the Group.[102]

The Working Group has provided a forum to discuss and come up with better solutions for the differences, and to identify gaps and conflicts among existing international investment instruments. Many divergent opinions have been expressed on various investment issues at the Working Group. One of the findings of the Working Group is that international investment has a positive impact on growth and development. Despite the fact that possible multilateral investment agreement was not designed by the Ministerial decision, many negotiators have initiated discussion on the possibility of multilateral investment agreement at the WTO framework.[103] Indeed, the educative program should include the analysis of the future international investment instruments since many WTO members have already enough knowledge on the relationship between trade and investment.

The Working Group submitted a report to the General Council in December 1998, since it had a deadline.[104] After reviewing the report, the General Council

---

[102] *Id.*

[103] U.S. Bhatia, *Investment Issues at the Multilateral Level: issues in the WTO- Post Seattle, Sub-Regional Workshop for South Asia on Recent Developments in International Agreement*, The UNCDAT, and the Government of Sri Lanka, 15-16 December (1999).

[104] WORLD TRADE ORGANIZATION, ANNUAL REPORT 49 (2001).

decided to expand the Working Group's "educational" work program to further analyze and discuss investment.[105]

It should be noted that the Second Ministerial Conference was held at Geneva in May 1998.[106] Like the Singapore Conference, Ministers decided to implement the Agreement during the Uruguay Round, and to establish the future work program.[107] Furthermore, the EC with support of some countries like Japan, Canada, and Switzerland purposed an agreement on investment.

B. The Failure of Launching New Round: The Seattle Ministerial Conference

The Third Ministerial Conference was held in Seattle, Washington, from 30 November to 3 December 1999. The main goal of the Seattle Ministerial Conference was to launch a new round of multilateral trade negotiations focused on agriculture, services, investment, and intellectual property. However, no progress was made in these areas, the Ministerial Conference ended in failure. Indeed, the meeting did not even produce a Ministerial Declaration. Therefore, the initiation of the negotiation of multilateral investment rules under the WTO framework is also failed.

1. Reasons for the Failure of the Seattle Conference

---

[105] According to the Annual Report, The Working Group held meetings in March, June, and September 1999 and in June, October and November 2000. Id.

[106] WTO, Geneva WTO Ministerial 1998, *Ministerial Declaration*, adopted on 20 May 1998.

[107] Pursuant to the Ministerial Declaration "The General Council's work programme shall encompass the following: (a) recommendations concerning:
(i) the issues, including those brought forward by members relating to implementation of existing agreements and decisions;
(ii) the negotiations already mandated at Marrakesh, to ensure that such negotiations begin on schedule;
(iii) future work already provided for under other existing agreements and decisions taken at Marrakesh;

Robert M. Maclean states, "while success has many fathers, failure is sadly an orphan."[108] The failure of the launching new round at Seattle can be attributed to the fact that the WTO's negotiation structure and especially decision-making process does not work properly. According to Mike Moore, director general of the WTO, "We didn't need any help from the protestors to fail. We did it our own."[109] I agree with his opinion since the lack of complicity among member states on different issues is the primary reason for the failure to launch a new round of negotiations at the Seattle.

There are two important factors that contributed to the failure of the Seattle Ministerial Conference. First, there were important disagreements among member states regarding various issues. Second, the impact of NGO activities prior to the Conference and during Seattle Ministerial Conference also had an impact on the failure of the Conference.

a. **Disagreement among member states regarding various issues**

The main reason why the Seattle Ministerial Conference was unable to agree on the launching of a new round on investment was that it was unable to solve the problems among member states on framework of negotiation, investment, and implementation issues.[110] Member states could not have consensus on various issues at both the preparatory meeting and the Conference.

---

[108] Robert M. Maclean, *The Lessons of Seattle and the Need for WTO Institutional Reform*, International Trade Law & Regulation, 1 (2000).

[109] '*On Trade Protests Clinton: Legitimate Zedillo: Phobias*", Wall Street Journal, January 31, 2000.

[110] WTO, ANNUAL REPORT 2001, *supra* note 104, at 3.

With regard to the negotiation framework, the EC and Japan support the "comprehensive negotiations" framework including investment. On the other hand, the United States proposes a "built-in agenda framework" including agriculture, services, and labour. Some developing countries, led by India, oppose the launching of a new round of talks on these issues. Thus, it was impossible to form a broad-based negotiation at the Conference.

With regard to investment issues, India and Malaysia are the leading developing countries that are opposed to including investment issues at the WTO framework. However, the EC and Japan argued that investment should be included in the WTO framework.[111] Pursuant to them, increasing legal security and predictability for investors would promote both investment and trade. Therefore, the launching of multilateral rules for investment should be included the Conference.[112] The United States, on the other hand, was not willing to agree with the EC's and Japan's point of view at this time, since it wanted a more liberal investment regime than it thought could be achieved at the time of the Seattle Ministerial Conferences.

With regard to implementation issues, many developing countries rightly claimed that discussion of the implementation problems should have priority before launching any new round. Indeed, in the preparatory work for the Conference many developing countries supported views in favour of a review of the TRIMs Agreement, including the extension of its transitional periods. For example Mexico and

---

[111] World Trade Organization, PREPARATIONS FOR THE 1999 MINISTERIAL CONFERENCE, Proposal Regarding the Agreement on Trade-Related Investment Measures, Communication from the European Communities, 9 July 1999, WT/GC/W/245, Communication from Japan, 6 July 1999, WT/GC/W/239.

[112] *Id.*

Columbia purposed that the transitional periods for all the TRIMS which were notified to the Committee on TRIMs should be extended.[113] Brazil, for example, recommended that TRIMs should have more specific exceptions for the developing countries since developing countries need to have some sort of flexibility on the implementation of the Agreement for their social, and economic concerns.[114] However, there was no agreement on these issues at the end of the Conference.

b. **The Impact of NGO Activities on Seattle Ministerial Conference**

Like their impact on the failure of the MAI negotiations, NGOs challenged the launching new round at the Seattle Ministerial Conference. Massive demonstrations by NGOs, and labour unions were another important factors hampering the Conference. Their primary concern was that the WTO did not include sufficient, or any, provisions to labor rights and environmental problems.[115] Labour Unions protested the lack of international labour standards. Environmental NGOs claimed that the WTO has a lack of environmental issues and the WTO dispute settlement body ignores the environmental impact of its decisions. Many NGOs also protested the negotiation process of the WTO and its decision making because developing countries do not have direct power at the decision making process.

---

[113] World Trade Organization, PREPARATIONS FOR THE 1999 MINISTERIAL CONFERENCE, Proposal Regarding the Agreement on Trade-Related Investment Measures, Communication from Columbia, 14 September 199, WT/GC/W/311, Communication from Mexico, 11 October 1999, WT/GC/W/351.

[114] World Trade Organization, PREPARATIONS FOR THE 1999 MINISTERIAL CONFERENCE, Proposal Regarding the Agreement on Trade-Related Investment Measures, Communication from Brazil, 26 July 1999, WT/GC/W/271.

[115] Clyde Summers, *The Battle in Seattle: Free Trade, Labor Rights, and Societal Values*, 22 University of Pennsylvania Journal of International Economic Law 61 (2001).

Even though some of the NGOs' protest is based on the protection of the developing countries' social, and economic rights, most developing countries are willing to be a member of the WTO, and they object to the opinions of the protesters. For example, Ernesto Zedillo, president of Mexico, called these protesters "globophobics- a curious alliance of forces from extreme left, environmentalist and other self appointed critic in a common endeavor to save people of developing countries from development".[116]

2. Lessons From the Failure of the Seattle Conference

The failure of the Seattle Ministerial Conference has important implications for how a new round will be negotiated in the future. The lessons to be learnt from this failure are helpful to avoid same kinds of problems in the future negotiations of the any agreement issues including investment at the WTO framework. The followings are some important lessons from the failure of the Seattle Conference

a. The Need for Procedural Changes in the Negotiation of Any Agreement at the WTO Framework

Ironically enough the same lesson is also learned from the failure of the MAI negotiations. That is to say that the negotiation process should be well designed in order to conclude any substantive works. The involvement of all interested parties

---

[116] Ewell E. Murphy, Jr, *The Lessons of Seattle: Learning From the Failed Third WTO Ministerial Conference*, 13 TRANSNAT'L LAW. 273, 286 (2001).

from the preparation stages of negotiations, through the actual negotiation process, may have significant effect for the success of the negotiations.[117]

The WTO must provide internal transparency. All member states should participate in all negotiation process, especially in decision-making progress. Charlene Barshefsky, U.S Trade Representative, concluded the Seattle Ministerial Conference as follows: "The issues before us were diverse, complex and often novel. And together with this, we found that the WTO has outgrown the processes appropriate at an earlier time. An increased and necessary view, generally shared among the members, was that we needed a process which had a greater degree of internal transparency and inclusion to accommodate a larger and more diverse membership."[118] The WTO should recognize the developing countries involvement at the decision making process.[119] Developed countries are no longer the only factors to determine the international trade and investment policies within the WTO. Developing countries want to join participation of the WTO activities. However, some developing countries do not have enough human resources to participate in WTO activities.[120] In order to provide sufficient participation of the developing

---

[117] The European Community, Report to the European Parliament on European Community Activities in the WTO 1999, at 5.

[118] Ambassador Charlene Barshefsky, *"Remarks at the Closing Plenary of the WTO Ministerial Conference"*, December 3, 1999.

[119] David A. Gantz, *Failed Efforts to Initiate the "Millennium Round" in Seattle: Lessons for Future Global Trade Negotiations*, 17 Arizona Journal of International and Comparative Law 349, 351 (2000).

[120] Garcio Bercero, *Functioning of the WTO System: Elements for Possible Institutional Reform*, International Trade Law & Regulation, 105 (2000).

countries, the WTO Secretariat grants technical help to the developing countries, especially those who do not have any representatives in the WTO Center.[121]

After the failure of the Seattle Conference, the WTO has initiated consultation on the issue of "internal transparency and effective participation of all Members."[122] The following issues have been discussed: "a) means of ensuring an effective interaction between informal consultations and open-ended meetings; b) measures to improve the preparation and conduct of Ministerial Conferences; c) the possibility of establishing a limited-membership consultative body; d) measures to improve overseeing role of General Council."[123]

According to the WTO 2000 Annual Report, the WTO had completed the series of discussions to find a solution for the "fuller participation of all members" in the work of the WTO.[124] Even though the same report shows that there is no need for radical changes in the WTO decision making process, many observes rightly argues that the participation of the developing and least developed countries on the decision making process need to be reformed. For instance, Pascal Lamy explains, "the developing countries need a bigger place at the table. We need procedures facilitating consensus, transparency, and efficiency."[125] The informal consultation process is one

---

[121] *Id.*

[122] *Id.* at 106.

[123] *Id.*

[124] WTO, ANNUAL REPORT 2001, *supra* note 104, at 4.

[125] Pascal Lamy, *What Are the Options After Seattle?*, Speech at the European Parliament, Brussels, 25 January 2000.

of the reforms to increase internal transparency. The WTO has been working new progress on intensified consultation process.

In order to improve the external transparency, the WTO must create mechanism to listen to and respond to concerns of the civil society. As explained above, the intervention by the civil society has added an interesting dimension to future rounds in the WTO not only on trade issues, but also on investment issues. If both the failure of the MAI negotiation and the failure of the Seattle Conference are any guide, future works on investment related issues in the WTO will need to take into account the concerns of the civil society. Therefore, the WTO should strength structuring its dialogue with civil society.

The policy on NGO participation in the WTO is specified in Article V (2) of the Agreement on Establishing the World Trade Organization stating that "the General Council may make appropriate arrangements for consultation and cooperation with non-governmental organizations concerned with matters related with trade."[126] In order to implement this article, the WTO General Council approved "Guidelines for Arrangements on Relations with NGOs", stating that whereas NGOs were a "valuable resource" pertaining to international trade negotiations, "it would not be possible for NGOs to be directly involved in the work of the WTO or its meetings."[127] The Guidelines propose exchange of information and informal dialogue between NGOs and the WTO.

---

[126] WTO Agreement, Article V (2).

[127] The WTO, Guidelines for Arrangements on Relations with Non-Governmental Organizations, Geneva, July 1996, WT/L/162.

The WTO's external transparency has improved considerably since 1995. In order to enhance dialogue between the WTO and civil society, the WTO has implemented its NGO Guidelines.[128] There have been some WTO symposiums involving NGOs. For example, in March 1999, the WTO sponsored two symposia on environment and development. After the failure of Seattle Conference, the WTO has tried to improve its external transparency. In November 2000, the General Council discussed external transparency, but there was no decision taken on this issue. However some countries argued that the direct participation of civil society in the WTO was not desirable since it would risk "politicising the operations of the Organization due to sectoral and electoral interests".[129]

Since the adoption of the 1996 Guidelines, the WTO and NGOs relationship has focused on "attendance at Ministerial Conference, participation in issue-specific symposia, and the day to day contact between the WTO Secretariat and NGOs."[130] Furthermore, the WTO has an excellent website on which most official documents are public and has special section for NGOs.

The General Council is discussing new developments on relationship with NGOs. For example, there should be a formal accreditation system for NGOs at the WTO. The representatives of NGOs can serve as official advisors of developed and developing countries. Moreover, governments should initiate dialogue with NGOs in

---

[128] Steve Charnovitz, *Opening the WTO to Non Governmental Interests*, 24 FORDHAM INT'L L. J. 173, 181 (2000).

[129] *Id.* at 195.

[130] WTO, ANNUAL REPORT 2001, *supra* note 104, at 113.

their countries. Members of civil society in developed countries should monitor developed countries' government.

b.   Implementation Problems of Existing Agreements

Many developing and least developed countries are still having implementation problems of existing agreements. Prior to the Seattle Ministerial Conference, some developing countries proposed the extension of the transition period for the implementation of the TRIMs and TRIPs agreements. The vital issue is how to enable developing countries to implement the WTO agreements. The solution for this issue is to provide flexibility based on the circumstances of each developing country. In response to the implementation claims by developing countries, the WTO established the "implementation review mechanism".[131] Further, the WTO is currently working on granting the extension on the transition period for developing countries. It should be noted that without having implemented the WTO agreements, many countries do not want to negotiate the new agreement.

c.   The Content of the Future Agreement

Any agreement including trade and investment issue should take into consideration of the issues raised by the civil society. The issue of foreign investment has broad implications on labour rights, environmental policies. Labor rights and environmental standards are two issues that likely to continue to influence future investment negotiations. Therefore, if the WTO wants to launch a negotiation on

---

[131] *Id.* at 4.

investment issues, these two sensitive issues should be address whether in the negotiation or as a new agreement.

C. The Doha Ministerial Conference: Is it New Era for Multinational Agreement on Investment?

The fourth WTO Ministerial Conference was held in Doha, Qatar from 9 to 14 November 2001.[132] Three declarations adopted by the ministers, are directly or indirectly relevant to investment issues. The three declarations are: The adoption of the Ministerial declaration and two declarations regarding TRIPS and public health and the implementation problems of the WTO agreements. It should be mentioned that the accession of China and Chinese Taipei to the WTO is also one of the outcomes of the Conference. Even though the impact of the Doha Ministerial Conference will become clear in negotiation phase, the outcome of the WTO Ministerial Conference in Doha is satisfactory not only to developed countries, but also to developing countries and civil society groups. The three declarations adopted in this conference address the concerns of the developing countries over the implementation of the existing WTO agreements and the concerns of the civil society groups over the inclusion of the environmental issues.[133]

---

[132] The WTO homepage.

[133] For example, Bob Zoellick points out that the World Wide Fund, one of the leading NGOs on the environmental issues urged to the WTO to negotiate disciplines on fisheries subsidies at this conference that was successfully achieved. USTR Zoellick *Says World Has Chosen Path of Hope, Openness, Development and Growth*, http://www.useu.be (visited 12/4/2001).

The adoption of the three declarations is also welcomed by the developed countries since the members have approved the new round for negotiation of multilateral trade issues. The WTO Director-General Mike Moore spells out that the Doha Ministerial is "an extraordinarily successful meeting ... that will be remembered as a turning point in the history of the WTO and the trading system and in relations between developed and developing countries within that system".[134] In addition, the US Ambassador Bob Zoellick states that "we are now are delighted that we've overcome the stain of Seattle."[135]

Unlike the Seattle Conference, the Doha Ministerial conference produced a Ministerial Declaration for launching new multilateral trade negotiations.[136] The Declaration includes amplification of objectives and timetables for the current negotiations in agriculture, services, and anti dumping and possible negotiations on variety of areas such as, trade and investment, trade and competition, and trade and the environment. Moreover, the declaration establishes a Trade Negotiating Committee for monitoring the working program. According to the declaration, the negotiations will last three years, until 1 January 2005.[137]

It is vital to note that apart from the Ministerial Declaration, the Doha Conference also produced two political declarations concerning TRIPS and public health and the implementation problems of the WTO agreements. The adoption of

---

[134] WTO and the new round of trade talks 14th general meeting of the Pacific Economic Cooperation Council, M2 Presswire, Wednesday, November 28, 2001, 11/28/01 M2PW.

[135] See *supra* note 133.

[136] The World Trade Organization, *Ministerial Declaration*, adopted 14 November 2001, WT/MIN(01)/DEC/1, 20 November 2001.

[137] Paragraph 45 of the Ministerial Declaration.

these two declarations shows that the WTO learnt some lessons from the failure of the Seattle Conference. As mentioned above, the developing countries' main concern and at the same time one of the reasons for the failure of the Seattle Conference is the implementation problems of the WTO agreements such as TRIMs, and ASCM. The declaration on "implementation-related issues and concerns" provides extension of transnational periods for the implementation of the some WTO agreements. For example, paragraph 6.2 of this declaration urges "the council for Trade in Goods to consider positively requests that may be made by least-developed countries under Article 5.3 of the TRIMS Agreement."[138] The declaration on TRIPS and public health provides flexibilities that the agreement grants to governments to deal with health problems.[139] These declarations seem to provide solution for the implementation problems.

Unlike Singapore Ministerial Declaration, the Doha Ministerial Declaration sets the objective of establishing a multilateral agreement on investment. Paragraph 20 of the Doha Declaration states as follows:

> Recognizing the case for a multilateral framework to secure transparent, stable and predictable conditions for long-term cross-border investment, particularly foreign direct investment, that will contribute to the expansion of trade, and the need for enhanced technical assistance and capacity-building in this area as referred to in paragraph 21, we agree that negotiations will take place after the Fifth Session of the Ministerial Conference on the basis of a decision to be taken, by explicit consensus, at that Session on modalities of negotiations.[140]

---

[138] The World Trade Organization, The Decision of 14 November 2001 on Implementation- Related Issues and Concerns, WT/MIN (01)/17, 20 November 2001.

[139] The World Trade Organization, Declaration on the TRIPS agreement and Public Health, adopted on November 14 2001, WT/MIN (01)/DEC 2, 20 November 2001.

[140] The WTO, the Fourth Ministerial Conference, the Ministerial Declaration adopted on 14 November 2001, www.wto.org (visited 12/05/2001).

The Declaration stipulates two-phase negotiation on investment. During the first phase, the work done by the WTO Group on investment to clarify the elements of foreign direct investment should continue. The Declaration mandates the working group to further study following FDI issues: "scope and definition; transparency; non-discrimination; modalities for pre-establishment commitments based on a GATS-type, positive list approach; development provisions; exceptions and balance-of-payments safeguards; consultation and the settlement of disputes between Members."[141] It should be noted that "investors' responsibility" and "investment protection" issues are not specifically mentioned in the declaration. Especially, "the investors' responsibility" issues should be evaluated and included in the negotiation process. In addition, paragraph 21 of the Declaration recognizes the need for further evaluation of the developmental implications of investment issues, and urges the WTO members to provide technical assistance to developing countries in order to grant them competence to negotiate investment issues.[142]

During the second phase, a decision of the negotiation on multilateral agreement on investment at the WTO will be taken at the Fifth session of the Ministerial Conference by an "explicit consensus" among members. The Fifth session of the Ministerial Conference will be held in 2003. India, leading other

---

[141] *Id*. The Ministerial Declaration, Paragraph 22.

[142] Paragraph 21 of the Ministerial Declaration states as follows: "We recognize the needs of developing and least-developed countries for enhanced support for technical assistance and capacity building in this area, including policy analysis and development so that they may better evaluate the implications of closer multilateral cooperation for their development policies and objectives, and human and institutional development. To this end, we shall work in cooperation with other relevant intergovernmental organizations, including UNCTAD, and through appropriate regional and bilateral channels, to provide strengthened and adequately resourced assistance to respond to these needs."

developing countries, was successful to defer the inclusion of the negotiation on multilateral investment agreement till 2003.

It is possible to argue that even though the paragraph 20-22 of the Declaration regarding the relationship between trade and investment does not create a new prospects, it does reiterates the developing countries' point of view. It looks like these paragraphs can cause some interpretation problems among members. Indeed, before the adoption of the Ministerial Declaration, some developing countries (such as India, Tanzania) asked clarification of the paragraphs concerning the relationship between trade and investment. Youssef Hussain Kamal, Qatari Finance, Economy and Trade Minister, and the chairman of the conference made following statement regarding this concern:

> With respect to the reference to an 'explicit consensus' being needed, in these paragraphs, for a decision to be taken at the Fifth Session of the Ministerial Conference, my understanding is that, at that session, a decision would indeed need to be taken by explicit consensus, before negotiations on trade and investment and trade and competition policy, transparency in government procurement, and trade facilitation could proceed. In my view, this would also give each member the right to take a position on modalities that would prevent negotiations from proceeding after the Fifth Session of the Ministerial Conference until that member is prepared to join in an explicit consensus.[143]

The Ministerial declaration and this clarification reflect that the work program agreed in Doha restricts itself to clarifying a various issues regarding FDI. It is still early to predict what will happen at the second stage. That is to say that, we do not know yet as to whether the Doha Conference is new era for multinational agreement on investment or not. Knowing the past history of the WTO trade rounds, the negotiations may take longer than expected. If the working groups do not address the

---

[143] The WTO Homepage regarding Doha Ministerial Conference, *A Historic Moment: "May I take it that this is agreeable?" Gavel. Applause, congratulations*, (visited 12/06/2001).

developing countries' concerns, the negotiations will probably be concluded with failure. Alan Larson, the US official, claims, "the "squishier" language in the Doha Declaration about investment negotiations reflects developing countries' reluctance to participate."[144]

IV. The Future Agenda: Is the WTO an appropriate forum for Multilateral Investment Issues

One may rightly claim that the WTO is an appropriate forum for negotiation of the multilateral investment treaty. The WTO has a long history of active involvement of international trade. As already noted, trade and investment are linked and should therefore be incorporated more heavily into the WTO framework. Indeed, investment-relevant issues are already covered to some extent in WTO agreements such as GATS and TRIMS. In addition, interface between trade and investment has been examined by the WTO Working Group process. Therefore, there is a prospect that future WTO negotiations will include a mandate to have additional multilateral investment rules in 2003.

There are various reasons to support the WTO as a forum for a multilateral investment agreement: The experiences of dealing with trade and investment and the

---

[144] The United States Mission to the European Union, *U.S. Urges Aid to Boost Developing Country Trade Negotiation Capacity*, www.useu.be (visited 12/4/2001).

existing successful models for the negotiation, and the active involvement and respectful treatment of the developing countries.

Firstly, The WTO provides a number of investment-related rules into its existing agreements, such as the TRIMs agreement, and the GATS agreement. For example the GATS model can be utilized as a model for the possible multilateral investment agreement since the progressive liberalization process has been successfully adopted in the GATS agreement.[145] This model is the best option for developing countries because they can decide which sector is available for market access. In order to ensure coherence between these agreements and a possible multilateral investment agreement, the WTO members should consider existing WTO investment-related agreements and focus on issues that are not already within the existing WTO agreements.[146]

Multilateral Investment rules can also be negotiated and signed as a plurilateral agreement within the WTO framework. The Subsidies Code is a good example in which a plurilateral agreement has been subsequently adopted as a WTO agreement during the Uruguay Round.

Secondly, even though the involvement of developing countries in the WTO decision-making process can be problematic as analyzed previously in this chapter, the WTO is still an appropriate forum for possible multilateral investment rules; this is due to the fact that the WTO can take into account the interests of both developed

---

[145] *Id.* at 219.

[146] A.V.Ganesan, *Strategic Options Available To Developing Countries With Regard To A Multilateral Agreement on Investment*, UNCTAD Discussion Papers, No. 134, April 1998, UNCTAD/OSG/DP/134.

and developing countries.[147] Since the WTO agreements contain "special and differential treatment" provisions for developing countries, they can safeguard their economic and social concerns and needs.[148] These provisions include transitional time periods for implementing agreements and technical support. As an example on providing transitional time periods for implementing agreement for developing countries, Article 5.2 of the TRIMs stipulates,

> Each Member shall eliminate all TRIMs which are notified under Article 5.1, within two years of the date of entry into force of the WTO Agreement in the case of a developed country Member, within five years in the case of a developing country Member, and within seven years in the case of a least-developed country Member.[149]

As an example for the technical backstopping, Article XXV/2 of the GATS stipulates,

> Technical assistance to developing countries shall be provided at the multilateral level by the Secretariat and shall be decided upon by the Council for Trade in Services.[150]

In the coming negotiation process, the EC proposed to launch a multilateral framework of rules governing international investment. In order to get support from developing countries and civil society, its agenda takes into account concerns of developing countries and civil society. Nobody knows what will be next, but it looks

---

[147] FIONA C. BEVERIDGE, THE TREATMENT AND TAXATION OF FOREIGN INVESTMENT UNDER INTERNATIONAL LAW TOWARDS INTERNATIONAL DISCIPLINES 219-220 (2000).

[148] According to the Committee on Trade and Development note, "The universe of special and differential treatment consists of 145 provisions spread across the different Multilateral Agreements on Trade in Goods; the General Agreement on Trade in Services; The Agreement on Trade-Related Aspects of Intellectual Property; the Understanding on Rules and Procedures Governing the Settlement of Disputes; and various Ministerial Decisions. Of the 145provisions, 107 were adopted at the conclusion of the Uruguay Round, and 22 apply to least-developed country Members only." The WTO, Committee on Trade and Development, Implementation of Special and Differential Treatment Provisions in WTO Agreement and Decisions, WT/COMTD/W/77, 25 October 2000.

[149] Article 5.2 of the TRIMs Agreement.

[150] Article XXV/2 of the GATS Agreement.

like the following agenda of the EC may be acceptable to the world community, since it reflects both developing and civil societies' concerns.

> We believe that it is in the interest of all countries to create a more stable and transparent climate for FDI worldwide. In our view, the WTO should focus on FDI, leaving aside short-term capital movements.
> Non-Discrimination, transparency and predictability of domestic laws applicable to FDI should be the guiding principles for the investment framework that we envisage to negotiate.
> The admission of investors should be dealt with following a gradual approach; each government should be able to decide which sectors can be opened to foreign investors and which ones cannot, according to transparent, positive and non-discriminatory commitments.
> Each government should also preserve the right to regulate the economic activity within its territory, including in the fields of developments, environment and social conditions,
> The dispute Settlement Mechanism should be that of the WTO. Investor-to-State arbitration does not fit in the WTO framework, and should be left to bilateral agreements.
> Rules on investment protection, for instance in case of expropriation, could also be discussed, if WTO members found it useful. Any such rules, however, must not affect a host country's right to regulate, in a non-discriminatory manner, the behavior of firms in its territory.[151]

---

[151] http://www.europa.eu.int/comm/trade/miti/invest/conswtoag_inv.htm (visited 7/2/2001).

CHAPTER EIGHT. EFFECTIVENESS OF THE MULTILATERAL INVESTMENT GUARANTEE AGENCY

As mentioned before, there is no single multilateral agreement on investment deals with every aspect of the FDI process. However there are multilateral agreements that deal with some aspects of FDI. The agreement on establishing the Multilateral Investment Guarantee Agency (MIGA) is one of the striking multilateral agreements that provide legal security for FDI. First, this study briefly explains MIGA's provisions and activities. Second, it explains the MIGA's involvement in Turkey. Finally it analyzes MIGA's shortcomings and effectiveness.

I. General Knowledge

Foreign investors will face a variety of risks such as currency control, expropriation, refusal to enforce judgment of foreign law, in their investment in developing countries. It is important to understand that no investment is completely free of some sort of risks, but there are many ways to deal with risks. Addressing the risks costs money, but the lower the costs of risks, the greater the increase the foreign investment flows. Insuring an investment project is the most vital way to address the risk that foreign investor may encounter. The Multilateral Investment Guarantee Agency (MIGA) was established by an international convention on 12 May 1988 as one of the World Bank Group's financial institutions to mitigate the political risk, and to provide knowledge for foreign investors.[1] MIGA is formally associated with the World Bank, but financially independent.[2]

---

[1] MIGA was established by the Convention Establishing the Multilateral Investment Guarantee Agency, opened signature October 11, 1985, 24 I.L.M. 1598 (entered into force April 12, 1988), (hereinafter MIGA Convention)

[2] IBRAHIM SHIHATA, TOWARDS A GREATER DEPOLITICIZATION OF INVESTMENT DISPUTES: THE ROLES OF ICSID AND MIGA 20 (1992).

The objective of the MIGA is to encourage the flow of private investments for productive purposes among member countries, and in particular to developing countries.[3] To carry out this objective, MIGA issues guarantees against non-commercial risks for foreign direct investment in member developing countries and provides technical assistance to governments of developing member countries to improve their ability to attract foreign direct investment.[4]

II. MIGA's Guarantee Activities
A. Risk Covered by MIGA Insurance

The MIGA is authorized under the convention to issue guarantees against specified non-commercial risk to foreign investment in developing countries. Under Article 11 (a) of the MIGA convention, the following risks can be guaranteed to eligible investors: Currency transfer restriction, expropriation, breach of contract, war and civil disturbance risk and other non-commercial risks.[5]

---

[3] According to Article 2 of MIGA Convention: "The objective of the Agency shall be encourage the flow of investments for productive purposes among member countries, and in particular to developing countries." Furhermore, Ibrahim Shihata explains MIGA's objective as follows: "It is meant to enhance the mutual understanding and confidence between host governments and foreign investors and to increase information, expertise and skills related to the investment process." *Id.* at 18.

[4] Ibrahim Shihata, *The Multilateral Investment Guarantee Agency*, (Symposium: Current Issues of International Financial Law, Part I International Organizations) 20 INT'L LAW. 485, 489 (1986).

[5] MIGA Convention, *supra* note 1, art 11.

1. **Currency Transfer Risk**

Under Article 11 (a) (i) of the MIGA Convention, the MIGA may offer protection against losses arising from an inability to convert local currency into a freely usable currency or host government restrictions on the transfer outside the host country of either the local currency or the foreign currency into which the local currency was converted.[6] It should be noted that currency transfer risk coverage does not extend to the devaluation of a country's currency.[7]

2. **Expropriation and Similar Measures**

Under Article 11 (a) (ii) of the MIGA convention, the MIGA may offer protection against losses resulting from measures (any legislative action or administrative measures, or omission) by the host government which may eliminate rights to the insured investment.[8] The government measures include expropriation, nationalization and "creeping expropriation". Measures attributable to the host government have been extended and elucidated by the paragraph 1.34 of the Operational Regulations. One may rightly claim that this extension can be considered an appropriate approach for the expropriation issue since there is no precise definition for what constitutes expropriation and similar measures in the convention.[9]

---

[6] *Id.* art 11 (a) (i).

[7] JAMES C. BAKER, FOREIGN DIRECT INVESTMENT IN LESS DEVELOPED COUNTRIES, THE ROLE OF ICSID AND MIGA, 116 (1999).

[8] MIGA Convention, *supra* note 1, art 11 (a) (ii).

[9] Ghassan Ossman, *Legal and Institutional Aspects of the Multilateral Investment Guarantee Agency As the Fifth of The World Bank*, Journal of International Banking Law, 370 (1996)

The same article provides specific exception to the risk of expropriation and similar measures. This article restricts expropriation coverage by excluding "non discriminatory measures of general application which the governments normally take for the purpose of regulating economic activity in their territories."[10] This exception applies only to host government measures that meet all its requirements. The requirements are: a) measures do not discriminate against the investor, b) measures should be taken by governments, and c) measures should be taken for the purpose of regulating economic activities in the host country's territory. The following are the lists as an example of such measures that written in the Commentary on the MIGA convention: "taxation, environmental and labor legislation as well as normal measures for the maintenance of public safety". This provision shows that developing countries' concerns regarding "creeping expropriation" have been taken into account.[11]

3. Breach of Contract Risk

Under Article 11 (a) (iii) of the MIGA convention, MIGA may offer protection against losses from any repudiation or breach by the host government of a contract with the guarantee holder in the following three situations: " a) when the holder of guarantee does not have recourse to a judicial or arbitral forum to determine the claim of repudiation or breach, or (b) a decision by such forum is not rendered within such reasonable period of time as shall be prescribed in the contracts of

---

[10] MIGA Convention, *supra* note 1, art 11 (a) (ii).

[11] Malcolm D. Rowat, *Multilateral Approaches to Improving the Investment Climate of Developing Countries: The Cases of ICSID and MIGA*, 33 HARV. INT'L L. J. 103, 129 (1992).

guarantee pursuant to the Agency's regulations, or (c) such a decision cannot be enforced."[12] Even though this risk coverage is provided in the MIGA convention, MIGA has started to offer this coverage only in 1999.[13]

4. War and Civil Disturbance Risk

Under Article 11 (a) (iv) of the MIGA convention, MIGA may offer protection against losses arising from military action or civil disturbance in the territory of the host country.[14] Examples of the types of action covered are: war, revolution, insurrection, and civil strife. The scope of this risk coverage is subject to the discretionary power of the MIGA.

5. Broad Other Political Risk Coverage

Under Article 11 (b) of the MIGA convention, the investor and the host country may jointly apply the coverage of specific non-commercial risks other than those explained above.[15] The Board of MIGA should approve this request by special majority.

In any event the same article lays down that certain types of risks must not be covered: the risk of devaluation or depreciation of currency and losses arising from any host government action or omission to which the guarantee holder agreed or for which the guarantee holder has been responsible.[16]

---

[12] MIGA Convention, *supra* note 1, art 11 (a) (iii).

[13] MIGA, MIGA REVIEW, at Executive Summary (2000).

[14] *Id.* art 11 (a) (iv).

[15] *Id.* art 11 (b).

[16] *Id.*

B. Eligibility for MIGA Insurance

Prospective investment's eligibility requirements for MIGA insurance contracts are briefly discussed below.

1. Eligible Investment

Article 12 of the MIGA convention sets out the general requirement of eligible investments. According to this article, there are three kinds of investment which are eligible for coverage, namely equity interests, direct investment, and other medium or long term form of investment.[17] One may rightly argue that the convention and operational regulations grant broad discretionary power to the MIGA Board of Directors to define what constitutes investment.[18] It should be noted that MIGA could insure only new investment. New investment contributions associated with privatization, the expansion, modernization or developing of existing investments are also eligible.

Investments may take many forms: equity, shareholder's loans and loan guarantees issued by equity holders, technical assistance and management contracts and franchising and licensing agreements, provided they have terms of at least three years and the investor's remuneration is tied to the project's operating results. This article designates that MIGA is eligible to serve new types of investments.[19]

---

[17] MIGA Convention, *supra* note 1, art 12 (a).

[18] Ossmann, *supra* note 9, at 367.

[19] SHIHITA, *supra* note 2, at 19.

In keeping with MIGA's objective of promoting economic growth and development, investment projects must be financially, economically and environmentally sound and must contribute to the host country needs, such as job creation and technology transfer. The proposed investment projects must meet the four criteria stated Article 12 (d) of the MIGA Convention in order to qualify for a guarantee. Article 12 (d) of the MIGA convention states that "In guaranteeing an investment, the Agency shall satisfy itself as to:

> (i) the economic soundness of the investment and its contribution to the development of the host country;
> (ii) compliance of the investment with the host country's laws and regulations;
> (iii) consistency of the investment with the declared development objectives and priorities of the host country; and
> (iv) the investment conditions in the host country, including the availability of fair and equitable treatment and legal protection for the investment".[20]

One of the main criteria is the investment's potential contribution to the development of the host country. MIGA has assessed the development impact of the proposed investment project through its own assessment, and host governments' statements that the prospective investment is in line with the laws, regulations, objectives and developmental priorities of the country.

2. **Eligible Countries and Investors**

Pursuant to Article 14 of the MIGA convention, MIGA does guarantee investments only made in developing member countries.[21] To be eligible for MIGA insurance coverage under Article 13, an investor must be a national of a member

---

[20] MIGA Convention *supra* note 1, art 12 (d).

[21] MIGA Convention, *supra* note 1, art 14.

country other than the country in which the investment is to be made.[22] However, pursuant to Article 13 (c) host country nationals may be eligible for MIGA insurance coverage, if they transfer the assets to be investment from abroad.[23] The investor can be either natural or juridical person. As regard to the juridical person, Article 13 provides three different factors to comply with the nationality requirement. A corporation is eligible for coverage if it is either incorporated in and has its principal place of business in a member country or if it is majority owned by nationals of member countries.[24] State owned corporations are eligible if they operate on a commercial basis.

It is worthy to note that before the process of underwriting of the insurance contract, the country must approve the application of the guarantee. Article 15 of the MIGA Convention provides that the MIGA "shall not conclude any contract of guarantee before the host government has approved the insurance of the guarantee by the Agency against the risk designated for cover." This is the implementation of the principle of host country's sovereign control over the admission and the treatment of foreign investment into their territories. The host country approval provides security for developing countries. In addition, this reflects the "voluntary character" of the MIGA's activities, since they are available on a voluntary basis.

---

[22] *Id.* art 13.

[23] *Id.* art 13 (b).

[24] *Id.* art 13 (a) (i).

C. **Coinsurance Activities**

The functions of MIGA include providing coinsurance and reinsurance, against non-commercial risks in respect of investments in developing countries.[25] This is an important step for public and private insurance agencies to work closely together in order to supply investment security to foreign investors. The main aim of this function is to persuade private insurance agencies underwriting a risk that they might not have written without MIGA. Furthermore, Gerald T. West rightly claims that collaboration among investment insurers has benefits to the investors.[26] He further spells out the benefits as follows:

a) it potentially increases the amount of investment insurance coverage available for a given project;

b) with the presence of several investment insurers, the "deterrence" benefit of the insurance coverages should be enhanced;
c) the risk reduction benefits should theoretically make some projects acceptable which had previously been on the threshold of rejection because of their risk/reward profile; and
d) reinsurance arrangements, in particular, give the investor greater confidence in the "seamlessness' of their coverage since the insurers must reach agreement on policy language, premiums, claims management, salvage sharing, etc.[27]

MIGA has intensified its efforts to collaborate with other insurers. The Cooperative Underwriting Program (CUP) is one of the coinsurance forms, which MIGA designed to encourage private insurers to provide coverage of investments in developing

---

[25] Paul E. Comeaux, N. Stephan Kinsella. *Reducing Political Risk in Developing Countries: Bilateral Investment Treaties, Stabalization Clauses, and MIGA & OPIC Investment Insurance*, 15 N.Y.L. SCH. J. INT'L & COMP. L. 1, 45 (1994).

[26] Gerald T.West, *Multilateral Investment Guarantee Agency, World bank Group, Investment Insurance: The Quiet Facilitator of Private Telecommunications Projects*, Telecommunications Finance And Investment Forum, February 6-7, 1995, New York.

[27] *Id.*

countries.[28] Under this program, MIGA takes a significant amount of risk, while asking the private sector to reinsure it. MIGA publication, "MIGA: The first Ten Years" elucidates benefits of CUP program as follows:

> For MIGA, his arrangement offers a multiplier effect in the use of its assets in providing coverage. For Private insurers, this arrangement offers the comfort of having MIGA serve as mediator if disputes arise and having MIGA seek remedies if mediation fails (this arrangement also offers the option of protected self-insurance if a project sponsor decides to use a captive insurance entity for the CUP arrangement).[29]

MIGA has issued contracts under MIGA's CUP programs with, for example, ACE, Zurich U.S, and a Llyod's of London.[30] This program is expected to generate additional investment insurance capacity from private insurers in the future.

D. Dispute Settlement Activities

MIGA assists member countries in the settlement of their disputes with investors. MIGA provides legal advise and assistance to parties from member countries that need to solve investment related disputes. It should be noted at the outset that even though MIGA itself is not eligible to be a party to an ICSID process, it could have applied to an arbitration procedure based on ICSID rules, when it is subrogated to a guarantee holder.

Article 56, 57, 58 of the MIGA convention lay down dispute settlement provisions in four different situations:

a) disputes between a member and the Agency concerning interpretation and application of the convention; b) disputes arising under a contract of guarantee or

---

[28] Peter F. Fitzgerald, *Political Risk Insurance Coverage Expands, Practicing Law Institute*, Commercial Law and Practice Course Handbook Series, PLI Order No. A0-003F, 424 March, (2000).

[29] MIGA: THE FIRST TEN YEARS (1998).

[30] Fitzgerald, *supra* note 28, at 424.

reinsurance between the Agency and the other party; c) disputes between the Agency as subrogee of an investor and a member; and d) disputes between the Agency and a member or former member concerning other issues.

With regard to disputes between a member and the Agency, "internal process" is used.[31] That is to say that the MIGA Board of Directors has the authority to settle disputes concerning interpretation and application of the convention. Article 58 of the MIGA convention provides a guarantee holder and the Agency with the right to submit any dispute arising under a contract of guarantee to arbitration. The operational regulations suggests that such guarantee contracts will refer to ICSID arbitration rules. The arbitration award is final and each member country is obliged to recognize the binding nature of such an award. These articles designate that the dispute settlement process of MIGA can provide investment security to foreign investors.

It should be worth to note that MIGA paid its first claim to Enron Java Power Co., on June 16, 2000, pursuant to breach of contract protection for a power project in Indonesia that was deferred due to the Asian financial crises.[32]

III. MIGA's Technical Assistance Activities

As mentioned before, MIGA encourages FDI flows to the developing countries by providing not only guarantee contracts, but also technical assistance activities. Ibrahim Shihata claims that technical assistance activities cannot be deemed as a secondary activity of MIGA since this activities' aim is to promote

---

[31] BAKER, *supra* note 7, at 132.

[32] MIGA, *supra* note 13.

foreign investment in developing countries.[33] The technical assistance program consists of the following activities: a) organizing conferences and seminar concerning with investment and MIGA's role, b) supporting member countries to strength their institutional capacity to attract foreign investment, c) having the Internet homepage (IPA net) for the exchange information on investment issues.

Investment marketing services department (IMS) is the responsibly body of the MIGA for MIGA's technical assistance program.[34] IMS has organized "investment promotion strategy" workshops and symposiums.[35] Furthermore, it has offered executive training programs for public officials and corporate executives in order to discuss legal and economic issues concerning foreign investment.

Technical assistance activities to developing countries have also been provided by other World Bank Group members. Thus, in order to coordinate these activities, MIGA is working closely with not only other Work Bank Group members but also other international organizations, such as UNIDO and UNCTAD to deliver and disseminate information on investment opportunities in developing countries.

---

[33] Ibrahim Shihata explained the MIGA's technical assistance activities as follows: "MIGA is not envisaged simply as another political risk insurer. In addition to its guarantee function, it is mandated to play an important role through a broad array of promotional activities. These include performing research, providing information, offering technical assistance, and providing policy advice to interested member countries. This function should not be considered a secondary activity of MIGA; it constitutes a vital part of its mandate, which, over time, may prove to be the Agency's greatest contribution to an improved investment climate in developing countries." Tracy V. Drake, Reporter, Panel Session, The World Bank and The International Monetary Fund, American Society of International Law Proceedings, April 9-12, 1986, (Ibrahim Shihata, The Multilateral Investment Guarantee Agency), at 23.

[34] MIGA, MIGA: THE FIRST TEN YEARS, *supra* note 29.

[35] According to the MIGA publication, The First Ten Years, "IMS organized four conferences on mining investments in Africa and four tourism conferences between late 1993 and 1997". *Id.*

Recently, MIGA has extended legal technical assistance activities in developing countries. MIGA has advised developing member countries to liberalize their foreign investment instruments. For example it granted assistance to draft new foreign investment regulations in Bangladesh, Fiji, Pakistan and Zambia.[36] Furthermore, it has induced the member countries to sign bilateral and multilateral investment agreements. More importantly, it has offered investment dispute settlement system, mainly mediation, to non-member countries for investment disputes.[37] This activity demonstrates that MIGA's crucial role in foreign investment development has been approved by non-member countries.

IV. MIGA's Activities in Turkey

A. General Knowledge

MIGA has been very active in supporting FDI into Turkey. MIGA plays a central role in financing investments not covered from national or private insurance companies. The justification for Turkey participating in MIGA is that membership not only encourages the FDI inflows in Turkey, but also facilitates investment opportunities for Turkish investors making investment in developing countries. Indeed, Turkey is one of the top ten recipients of MIGA insurance for in and outbound investment.[38]

---

[36] *Id.* at 148.

[37] According to the MIGA Review 2000, MIGA's Legal and Claims Department staff "provided legal advice and guidance to parties from several member countries that sough creative negotiated approaches to the resolution of investment disputes in which they were involved." MIGA, *supra* note 13.

[38] According to the MIGA Publication in 1998, "Turkey, for example occupies a significant place in MIGA's portfolio as both beneficiary and source of foreign direct investment. In 1998, it ranked sixth as a recipient of MIGA-supported foreign direct investment and was one of the top 10 countries originating investments covered by MIGA." MIGA, MIGA: THE FIRST TEN YEARS, *supra* note 29.

"Establishing mobile office" and "working closely with domestic insurance market" are the main activities that have been carried out by MIGA in Turkey. MIGA established a mobile office in Turkey in order to promote its services. The Turkish Mobile office was managed for a two-week period in the offices of the Istanbul Chamber of Industry in October 1998. This program provided MIGA with an excellent opportunity to give presentations concerning MIGA's role in the region to representatives of national and foreign corporations in Turkey.

On October 12 1999, MIGA announced that it had signed a memorandum of understanding (MOU) on cooperation with Turkey's national insurer, Turkish Eximbank. This arrangement is an example of MIGA's ability and willingness to collaborate with other investment insurers. This cooperation's aim is to promote political insurance coverage for Turkish investments in developing countries. Pursuant to this memorandum, MIGA and Turkish Eximbank will try to work closely in the insurance market through coinsurance and reinsurance agreements in order to mitigate political risk insurance. For example, MIGA has issued political risk insurance coverage to Turkish investor for investment in Azerbaijan, Kazakhstan, the Kyrgyz Republic, Romania and Russia.[39]

B.   Example Cases:

MIGA's guarantees benefit FDI in infrastructure, manufacture and banking sectors of Turkey. Following cases are the examples that MIGA bring about investment opportunities for transnational corporations and financial institutions to Turkey.

---

[39] Mimi Mann, *Turkey Enters 2000 on A Positive Note as Reforms Progress*, Middle East Executive Reports, September (1999).

1. **SIEMENS A.G, TURKEY**

MIGA issued a guarantee contract for $40 million to Siemens A.G of Germany for its shareholder loan to its leasing company in Turkey.[40] The political risks covered losses from currency transfer and expropriation of funds. This project created 22 local jobs and approximately fifty percent of the leased products will be manufactured locally. In other words, this investment enabled Siemens to assist the Turkish economy through increased employment and local procurement.

2. **Issues Guarantee for Financial Institutions in Turkey**

MIGA has issued several guarantees to foreign financial institutions to expand financial and banking activities in Turkey. For example, MIGA issued guarantee contracts to three banks, ABN AMRO Bank, N.V, and ING Bank of the Netherlands, and Citibank, N.A of the United States. First, For ABN AMRO Bank, NV, MIGA issued $24 million guarantee covers against the risk of transfer restriction and expropriation of funds. Second, MIGA issued a guarantee of $20 million to expand the ING Bank's banking activities in Istanbul. According to the MIGA press release, the ING Bank tried to increase its activities "in corporate banking, financial institutions banking, treasury securities trading and sales, and capital markets."[41] This project can allow ING Istanbul to provide financing to multinational companies and major local firms. Third, MIGA also issued $15.3 million in coverage for Citibank's shareholder loan to its branch in Istanbul. The political risks covered by MIGA were for losses from currency transfer and expropriation.

---

[40] (visited 05/20/2001) http://www.miga.org/miganews/spr98/spr98.htm#2

[41] (visited 05/20/2001) http://www.iga.org/screens/pubs/miganews/spr_sm99/spr_sm99.htm

One may rightly argue that these projects can provide benefits such as increasing lending authorizations and the diversification of financial services and resources for productive investment in Turkey. On the other hand, the recent economic crisis in Turkey was as a result of the speculations on dollar market by the private banks, mostly foreign banks. Thus, foreign finance institutions can cause economic problems in the host country. In order to find out whether or not promoting foreign financial institutes through issuing guarantees enhances the host countries' economy; there should be evaluation study on this issue. Unfortunately, in Turkey, it is very difficult to find direct database for statistical purpose on the MIGA evaluation, so MIGA should consider reviewing the guarantee activities in financial institutes by itself.

V. Shortcoming of MIGA's Activities: Environmental impact

MIGA's activities have been criticized by environmental NGOs that it lacks environmental standards, and its activities may harm environment. Most NGOs argue that MIGA has issued guarantee contract with transnational corporations in environmentally sensitive sector such as oil, gas, mining and transportation.[42] For example, Friends of Earth claims that MIGA's guarantee contract with the corporation RTZ for the Lihir Gold mine in Papua New Guinea, badly affects environment, since the Lihir gold mine dumps toxic waste into the ocean[43]

---

[42] Friends of Earth, The Multilateral Investment Guarantee Agency, Costing the Environment and the US Taxpayer, <http://www.foe.org/international/worldbank/miga.html> (visited 07/18/2001).

[43] See more information concerning this case, at Berne Declaration, MIGA's Lihir Island Project, <http://www.evb.ch/bd/lihir.htm>, (visited 08/13/2001).

Even though MIGA has not been specifically required by the MIGA Convention to assess the environmental impacts of investment projects under consideration for political risk insurance, the Convention implies that MIGA must assure that the investment projects it supports are consistent with environmental standards. MIGA recognized that "acceptable environmental performance sustainability with respect to natural resource management, and social soundness are critical factors in the "...economic soundness of the investment and its contribution to the development of the host country." ."[44] Furthermore, Chapter 3, Paragraph 3.06 of the MIGA operational Regulations stipulates that "Before issuing a Contract of Guarantee, the Underwriting Authority shall satisfy itself that the investment project is consistent with MIGA's environmental policies and takes into account MIGA's environmental guidelines..."At the beginning, for environmental assessment, MIGA relied exclusively on International Finance Corporations (IFC), a member of Word Bank Group. IFC has reviewed prospective investment projects for MIGA. Later, MIGA recognized the need to expand its environmental assessment capacity to respond to public criticism. Therefore, it drafted and approved its own environmental guideline in line with World Bank Group environmental guidelines.[45] MIGA's own environmental officer is working closely with IFC to evaluate environmental impact of the prospective investment project.

---

[44] <http://www.miga.org/screens/projects/disclose/soc_rev.htm>, (visited 08/22/2001).

[45] According to the Paragraph 3.06 of the Operational Regulations: "MIGA's environmental policies are defined as the following environmental and social policies developed by the IFC: Natural Habitats; Forestry; Indigenous Peoples; Safeguarding Cultural Property in IFC-Financed Projects; Involuntary Resettlement; Pest Management; Safety of Dams; and Projects on International Waterways."

MIGA screens the project application to determine whether its support of the project violate environmental standards stipulated not only MIGA's environmental guidelines but also relevant international standards.[46] Furthermore, all investment projects must comply with local environmental laws and regulations. If the project is not eligible in performance, MIGA may cancel the contract. However, MIGA generally opts to work closely with its client in order to solve the shortcomings.

MIGA should apply reasonable and effective environmental effective standards before issuing any guarantee. In other words, environmental assessment should be considered more carefully in its future activities. MIGA should provide transparency for environmentally sensitive investment projects.

VI. Effectiveness of MIGA

This section elucidates the growth of MIGA's activities, the impact of these activities on host countries' development, the limits of MIGA's effectiveness and finally what should be done to make MIGA more effective.

A. The Growth of MIGA's Activities and Their Impact on Host Countries

MIGA's effectiveness on foreign investment depends on whether it has reached its aim or not. In order to find out its effectiveness, MIGA has analyzed and reviewed its activities in terms of carrying out its developmental objectives, and

---

[46] According to the MIGA Publication: "During the evaluation process, the projects were categorized according to their success in mitigating environmental impacts, using as benchmarks MIGA;s environmental guidelines and policies, as well as the standards of the host country. One of three acceptable ratings, or categorizations, is possible: average, above average, and superior.", GERALD T. WEST & ETHEL I. TARAZONA, INVESTMENT INSUARANCE AND DEVELOPMENT IMPACT, EVALUATING MIGA'S EXPERIENCE, 49 (1998).

establishing its future roles. In order to provide objectivity of the review process and results, MIGA rightly conducted surveys "without identifying MIGA by name".[47] According to the recent review, "MIGA Review 2000", MIGA's activities continue to grow.[48] The utilization of the investment guarantee contract as a political risk management has been increased. According to the MIGA review, approximately 50% of the investor survey respondents agreed that political risk is more of concern today than 5 years ago, while 36% agreed "no change".[49] Thus, MIGA's guarantee activities have been extended.[50] The review demonstrates that MIGA's membership (size), the amount of guarantees (growth) issued each year increased. For example, by the end of June 2000, MIGA had 152 full members. In addition, the amount of new guarantees issued each year increased from 372 million US Dollars to 1.6 billion US Dollars.[51]

The development impact of MIGA's activities in 52 projects is evaluated by the MIGA in 1998. This evaluation concluded that MIGA's projects have had vital developmental effects on developing countries' economies. These developmental benefits can be listed as follows: the creation of jobs, introducing modern technology,

---

[47] MIGA, *supra* note 13, Foreword by Motomichi Ikawa.

[48] This review is conducted in accordance with Article 67 of the MIGA Convention, which states that "the Council shall periodically undertake comprehensive reviews of activities of the Agency as well as the results achieved with a view to introducing any changes required to enhance the Agency's ability to serve its objectives."

[49] MIGA, *supra* note 13.

[50] According to MIGA Review, "The amount new guarantees issued more than tripled from $372 million in fiscal 1994 to $1.3 billion in fiscal 1999, or at annual growth of 28.6 percent. In fiscal 2000, the amount reached $1.6 billion. Gross exposure increased from $1.0 billion to $3.7 billion (and to $4.4 billion in fiscal 2000), or a number of countries benefiting from MIGA's guarantees increased from 26 to 69, notably including 28 IDA-eligible countries."

[51] *Id.*

generating foreign exchange earnings, increasing government revenues and developing capital markets.[52]

MIGA has played significant role in enhancing the flow of FDI. The study completed by MIGA designates that "foreign direct investment facilitated was 21 percent higher than originally anticipated".[53] This study concludes that the MIGA has clearly and broadly carried out its aim of facilitating productive investment in developing countries.[54]

B. The Limits to MIGA's Effectiveness

"Sovereign control over investment", "exclusion of creeping expropriation", and "providing exhaustion of local remedies" provision of the MIGA on the one hand can be considered limit to MIGA's effectiveness, on the other hand can be considered the impetus power to sign the MIGA convention. First, Article 15 of the MIGA Convention provides host government control over MIGA's activities. According to this article, before an investment is guaranteed, the host government must approve MIGA's guarantee contract. This provision may negatively affect the utilization of MIGA activities, if the government does not approve the guarantee contract. On the other hand, this provision can be considered as an impetus power to sign the MIGA Convention. Developing countries, mostly Latin American countries, signed this

---

[52] WEST, *supra* note 46, at 19.

[53] *Id.* 36. The same study spells out that "The amount actually facilitated, about $7.1 billion was 5.4 times the amount of original MIGA coverage ($.1.297 million).

[54] *Id.* 105.

Convention since developing countries demands on sovereign control over the foreign investment issues provided with article 15 of the MIGA Convention.[55]

Second, as already mentioned, Article 11 of the MIGA convention provides specific exception for expropriation risk that may limit the effectiveness of MIGA. This provision " reflects a sensitivity to developing countries that may wish to regulate economic activity on a non-discriminatory basis without being accused of engaging in "creeping" expropriation."[56] This provision on the one hand, may limit the effectiveness of MIGA, since this exception may affect the protection coverage for foreign investors.[57] On the other hand, it can be considered as another impetus power to sign the MIGA Convention, since as we analyzed the failure of MAI in the third chapter, we found out that even developed countries have concerned regarding "creeping expropriation", which is exempted from protection coverage by the MIGA convention.[58]

Third, the 'exhaustion of local remedies" provision is on the one hand an obstacle for foreign investor, since the foreign investor will not be protected until local remedies are exhausted. On the other hand, it is another impetus power to sign the MIGA convention, since many developing countries, especially Latin American

---

[55] Christopher K. Dalrymple, *Politics and Foreign Direct Investment: The Multilateral Investment Guarantee Agency and The Calvo Clause*, 29 CORNELL INT'L L. J. 161, 187 (1996).

[56] Rowat, *supra* note 11, at 129.

[57] Christopher K. Dalrymple spells out the negative effect of this provision as follows: "This incentive (provision) may affect MIGA's ability to effectively protect a foreign investor. MIGA will not provide coverage for expropriations which do not fit within the parameters of Article 11. This may leave the foreign investor uncompensated where a Latin American government can present its expropriation as being "non-discriminatory".", Dalrymple, *supra* note 55, at 187-188.

[58] *Id.* at 188.

countries, have a history for not approving of the international dispute settlement system. Article 11 of the MIGA convention provides breach of contract risk that " a foreign investor will not be covered until he or she exhausts of local remedies or a given remedy is found to be unenforceable".[59]

The MIGA convention can be considered as a model for bilateral, regional, and multilateral agreement on investment. Articles mentioned above grant feasibility and flexibility for most developing countries, which have considered issues of "sovereign control over investment", "exclusion of creeping expropriation", and "providing exhaustion of local remedies" prerequisite to negotiate and to sign any investment agreement. Thus, the MIGA Convention provisions on these issues will be a good example for future agreements on investment.

C-Future Prospects for MIGA's Effectiveness

In order to be more effective, the "MIGA review" concludes that MIGA should follow a "multi-niche strategy" for its future activities. That is to say that MIGA should identify and serve some complementary areas through its guarantee and technical assistant functions.[60] Therefore, MIGA should focus on the following "priority areas":

With respect to its guarantee activities, MIGA should focus on IDA-eligible countries and African countries. Furthermore, it should try to promote investments related to small and medium-sized enterprises, complex infrastructure projects, and investment

---

[59] *Id.* at 188.

[60] According to MIGA Review, this multi-niche strategy program should be "in line with four guiding principles: developmental impact, financial soundness, client orientation, and partnership".

between developing countries. With respect to its technical assistant activities, MIGA should extend its capacity building and Internet-based information dissemination technical services.[61]

The "MIGA Review" elucidates that this multi-niche strategy may create many challenges such as "the risks for Guarantees may be difficult to identify". In order to pursue this strategy, the "MIGA Review" recommended following programs:

1-MIGA should enhance its own main functions as an insurance organizations: "Development of an integrated marketing strategy, enhancement of underwriting and financial risk management, enhancement of claims prevention and resolution, improvement of external communications"

2-MIGA should improve its collaboration with other World Bank Group Members, private insurers, and public agencies.

3-MIGA should develop new products and services in order to meet its client satisfaction. The review points out that international capital markets will be a new area for MIGA in the future.[62] Indeed, MIGA issued its first coverage of capital market issue for Brazilian market.[63]

---

[61] MIGA, *supra* note 13.

[62] MIGA, *supra* note 13.

[63] According to MIGA Corporate Overview, this project "was selected as Structured Finance International's Deal of the Year among securitizations of emerging market assets. MIGA's political risk insurance helped improve the risk profile of the notes, piercing the Brazilian sovereign ceiling and helping the investor secure the financing needed. The Class A Notes received an A2 rating from Moody's and A rating from S&P and Fitch IBCA, significantly above Brazil's rating of B2 (Moody's). MIGA's coverage will facilitate over 230 loans and leases to hospitals and clinics, allowing them to buy much-needed medical equipment.", MIGA, *MIGA Corporation View*, April (2001), <http://www.worldbank.org/html/extdr/pb/miga.htm>, (visited 08/13/2001).

CHAPTER NINE. NATIONAL LAW ON FOREIGN INVESTMENT: FOREIGN INVESTMENT IN TURKEY

As mentioned in the second chapter, host government regulations are the primary sources of law that govern international investment. As Fatouros rightly argues, "the interaction of national laws and international rules is at the center of the legal regulation of FDI."[1] Indeed, this interaction has led many countries to revamp their legal regulations on FDI. Through analyzing Turkish foreign investment policies and regulations as an example of this interaction, this chapter designates developing countries responds to the development of international investment legal framework.

Like many developing countries' governments, the Turkish government realized that foreign investment is an important tool for its economic development. Thus, like many developing countries, Turkey has shifted its foreign investment policies from restrictive policies to liberal policies that seek to attract foreign investment. As a member of OECD and the WTO, and candidate for membership of the EU, Turkey has pursued its foreign investment policies in line with OECD instruments and the WTO agreement on FDI and in accordance with EU regulations. This study first divides the Turkish government's policies on FDI into five periods. Second, the existing law on FDI will be analyzed. Third, the Turkish government's international policies on FDI will be explained. This study argues that the investment environment of Turkey is closely follows the internationally recognized principles.

---

[1] A. A. Fatouros, *Towards an International Agreement on Foreign Direct Investment*, ICSID Review, 192 (1995).

I. The Development of Foreign Investment In Turkey

A. Foreign Direct Investment Policies in Turkey

This section will explain FDI policies in Turkey emphasizing the changes in Turkish economic structure and their affect on FDI policies. The foreign investment movements in Turkey can be separated into five periods.

1. Regulatory Policies

a. The First Period: Unfriendly Environment for FDI

The first period spans the years from 1923-1950. During this period, the country's long historical experience regarding the privileges, particularly "capitulation", given to foreigners under the Ottoman Empire, is accounted for the Turkish people's skepticism and circumspection with respect to foreign investment. It should be noted that capitulation consisted not only in allowing foreign investors to establish private business in Turkey under Turkish law, but also in permitting these foreign investors to operate under the laws of their home countries while doing business in Turkey.[2] During this period, the adverse effects of the capitulations constituted the main reason why Turkey avoided accepting foreign investment in Turkey. One may rightly argue that this policy was drafted under the influence of historical, political and economic factors, and was an inevitable reaction under the conditions of that time.[3] Thus, during this period, there was no attempt to encourage foreign investment.

---

[2] Tugrul Ansay, *Turkey, in* LEGAL ASPECTS OF FOREIGN INVESTMENT (W.G. Friedman, ed., Columbia University International Legal Studies Program 1959).

[3] *Id.* at 52.

In addition, one should examine the Turkish economic situation at this period in order to understand the unfriendly environment for foreign investors. The Turkish economy had been substantially pursuing an inward oriented development strategy, combined with extensive involvement in the public sector till the new economic stabilization program was announced in January 24,1980.[4] In other words, in 1923, as an independent republic, Turkey commenced a model of planned economic development characterized by extensive government regulatory control of public sector undertakings.

As in most developing countries, the state intervened in the economy because Turkey lacked a well-established economic structure for development process.[5] The government was responsible for the direction of specific programs. I contend that at that time etatism was the appropriate policy for Turkish economical development since Turkey was established on the social and economic heritage of the Ottoman Empire.[6]

The Republic at first concentrated on these following issues: promoting private enterprises, distributing land for farmers and migrants, protecting domestic industry and refraining from external borrowing.[7] Further, new laws were enacted and public financial institutions were established. However, these positive economic developments were not enough to achieve the goal for the economic and social development of the new state. So, Turkey pursued a policy of establishing public enterprises called "State Economic Enterprises". It is worth noting that under the etatist policies, the private sector was not

---

[4] TEVFIK F HAS, MEHMET ODEKON, LIBERALIZATION OF THE TURKISH ECONOMY 1 (1998)..

[5] *Id.*

[6] In the 1930s Mustafa Kemal Ataturk, founder of the Republic of Turkey, institutionalized a policy called etatism: government intervention in the economy to achieve rapid industrialization.

[7] *Id.* at 13.

excluded from the national economic structure. The Turkish economic system is based on a combination of the freedom of private enterprise and state intervention proposed at economic development.[8]

This economic policy led Turkey to be unfriendly to foreign investment. One may observe that due to Turkish government's involvement in public sector, public sector is mostly closed investment not only to foreign investors, but also to domestic investors.

b.   The Second Period: Trying to promote and regulate FDI

The second period covers the years from 1950 to 1960. In 1950s, more liberal government policies were formulated in Turkish economy to attract foreign investment. Further, the government promulgated statutory measures for the procurement of foreign investment by means of Statute 5583, put into effect in 1950, and Statute 5821, put into effect in 1951.[9]

During this period there was a favorable policy for foreign investment. In particular, after the elections of 1950, the newly elected government first enacted a new Law No. 5821, in 1951. In order to make foreign investment even more attractive, in 1954 Turkish government invited American specialist Mr.Randall to draft the still extant Law No. 6224, Law for the Encouragement of Foreign Capital.[10] The government had a great expectation for this Law. Law No. 6224 is considered one of the most liberal

---

[8] Hershlag states that: "Even as late 1935, Ataturk defined etatism as a system peculiar to Turkey which has evolved from the principle of private activity of the individual, but places on the state the responsibility for national economy, with consideration of the needs of a great nation and a large economy, and of many other things that have not been done so far.", *Id*. at 5.

[9] *Id*. at 52.

[10] KAZIM OKSAY, GUIDE TO FOREIGN CAPITAL INVESTMENT IN TURKEY (1967).

foreign investment laws in the region perhaps since it was drafted by an American specialist. However, it was ineffective for the foreign investment development in Turkey.[11]

On the other hand, during this period, propaganda tried to show foreign investment to be a means of exploitation of natural resources of Turkish Republic. This propaganda succeeded in discouraging the committee charged with monitoring implication Law No. 6244 from easily approving foreign investment applications. This shows that even though the Turkish government enacted liberal foreign investment law, the public and opposition parties' protest caused implementation problems on this law.

c.   **The Third Period: The proliferation of FDI, but not enough**

The third period covers the years from 1960 to 1980. During this period, and especially after embarking on a planned economy, interest in foreign investment in Turkey increased. According to the data, while the foreign investment entering Turkey from 1951-1960 within the framework of Law No. 6244 was 103.000.000 Turkish Liras (TL), the investment made at the end of the 1961-1966 period reached 409.410.000 TL.[12] However, this was still less than the expected flows of foreign investment.

According to the 1961 Constitution, economic planning became a legal requirement and as a result the State Planning Organization was established.[13] Five-

---

[11] *Id.* at XIV.

[12] *Id.* at XVI.

[13] Library of Congress, Federal Research Division, *A Country Study, Turkey, Chapter 3 the Economy and Development Planing*, http://lcweb2.Loc.gov/frd/cs/trtoc.html (visited 3/3/2001).

Year-Development Plans started to play an important role from 1963 onwards.[14] In other words, this regulatory model designed in the Turkish Constitution by way of periodic five year plans served as the primary basis for economic development.

It should be noted that liberal regulations and development plans are not enough for foreign investment to enter a country. The general economic condition is also another important factor for foreign investor to make investment in the host country. For example, during this period, Turkey had an economic instability, administrative, financial, and statutory limitations, exchange restrictions, market inadequacies, general economic development imbalances, inadequate and inefficient economic and social infrastructures in her economic structure, all of which do not constitute an economic atmosphere attractive to foreign investment.

d. The Fourth Period: The Implementation of a More Open and Flexible Foreign Investment Policy

The fourth period in foreign investment development starts with the year 1980. On January 24, 1980, Turkey announced the new Economic Stabilization Program.[15] The main components of this economic program were reducing government involvement in production activities, implementing a flexible exchange rate policy, liberalizing import regulations, and privatizing State Economic Enterprises, encouraging foreign investment, and deregulating financial markets.[16] In other words, the liberalization process started in

---

[14] *Id.*

[15] DAVID BARCHARD, TURKEY INVESTING IN THE FUTURE, 31 (1990).

[16] *Id.* at 32.

the 1980s. The short-term aims of the program were, to reduce external deficit and inflation and, in the medium term, to increase free market economy and to replace an inward looking strategy with an outward-oriented development strategy.[17]

The Turkish government eliminated most restrictions on FDI, particularly exchange control system in line with its commitments on OECD instruments. The government adopted a Decree No.32 concerning the "Protection of the Value of Turkish Currency" in 1985. According to provisions of this Decree, foreign currencies may be purchased and sold freely.

In order to reduce the bureaucratic process, and to eliminate other obstacles regarding the establishment and treatment of foreign investment, the Foreign Capital Board was established and authority was transferred to this institution. In addition, Turkey created a unique investment model which is called the Built-Operate-Transfer (BOT) so as to encourage foreign investment in major infrastructure projects.[18] In this new method, the Turkish government guarantees to purchase the products or service supply of the investments at a certain price and over a certain period. In order to implement the BOT model, Turkish Parliament enacted a special law entitled Law regarding Engagement in Investments and Services on the BOT Model, on June 13, 1994.[19] Pursuant to Article 2 of the Law, this model is generally being utilized to finance

---

[17] CANAN BALKIR, TURKEY AND THE EUROPEAN COMMUNITY: FOREIGN TRADE AND DIRECT FOREIGN INVESTMENT IN THE 1980s, *in* TURKEY AND EUROPE, 101-105 (Canan Balkir & Allan M. Williams, eds., 1993).

[18] Zeki Kurtcu, The Built-Operate-Transfer Investment Model in Turkey, The New Investment Environment In Turkey, at 26.

[19] Law Regarding Engagement In Investments and Services on the Built-Operate-Transfer Model, Law N0. 3996, Turkish Official Gazette, 13 June 1994.

bridges and tunnels, dams, seaports and airports, telecommunications projects, environmental pollution protection systems, etc.[20]

The changes which have taken place in the legislation on foreign investment since 1980 indicate a clear trend towards an increasingly favorable framework for foreign investment. This reflects the political strategy of Turkey. The effects of these legal reforms on FDI in Turkey, and of the government's attempts to make the administrative procedures and legal regulations governing foreign investment more transparent and less complicated have been significant. In addition, internal political stabilization and the increasing readiness to carry through liberal economic reforms have increased the confidence of foreign investors in the Turkish economy.[21]

Consequently, in the year 1980 alone, the newly created Foreign Investment Department approved foreign investments to a value of US $ 97 million.[22] Pursuant to OECD study, in 1981 almost all the subsidiaries of foreign firms in Turkey applied for approval for capital increases and investment extensions, and in some cases for carrying out new projects.[23] One hundred four foreign corporations received approval for investment to a value of US $338 million.[24] That is to say that in 1981 the total of

---

[20] *Id.* Article 2 of the Law.

[21] YAVUZ YILDIRIM, EFFECTS OF DIRECT INVESTMENT ON ECONOMIC DEVELOPMENT: A STUDY OF THE TURKISH EXPERIENCE, 1980-1995, 44-45 (1996) (Master Thesis, Oklahoma State University) (On file with Oklahoma State University).

[22] *Id.* at 45.

[23] OECD, OECD STUDY 7 (1981).

[24] *Id.* at 7.

approvals for new investment exceeded that of whole of the past, and numbered to three times that of 1980.[25]

e. The Fifth Period: Legal changes on Foreign Investment Law and Privatization Program

The fifth period in foreign investment development starts with the year 1995. Looking at the figures and statistics, the Turkish government realized that foreign direct investors did not prefer to invest in Turkey. Thus, the Turkish government amended the foreign investment Law with new Decree and Communiqué in 1995. With this step, the Turkish government hoped to encourage foreign investors that were wary of the country's unstable economic environment.

Within the context of the new Decree and Communiqué, the provisions regarding permissions on capital transfers to abroad are abrogated.[26] Pursuant to the previous Decree, the General Directorate of Foreign Investment (herein after GDFI) shall give the permission for capital transfer abroad.[27] Another amendment is that according to the former Decree, investments with foreign share capital exceeding US$150 million require the approval of the Council of Ministers. The new Decree amends this provision and without any amount requirement of foreign share capital, all foreign investments are approved by the GDFI. Under the former Decree, in order to increase the capital for existing investment, foreign investors have to get permission from the Undersecreteriat.

---

[25] *Id.* at 7.

[26] Foreign Capital Framework Decree, No.95/6990 dated, June 7, 1995.

[27] Foreign Capital Framework Decree, No.92/2789 dated, March 4, 1992.

According to the new Decree, capital increase can be realized without permission if participant's ratios of foreign partners remain constant. In addition, the condition of approval of license, know-how, and technical agreements are abrogated by the new Decree. Overall, this new Decree annulled primarily provisions of the former decree with respect to capital transfer and capital increase.

According to the statistics provided by the GDFI, as of March 2000, 5,024 foreign firms had invested and were operating in Turkey.[28] Total authorized foreign capital since 1980 was $26.1 billion and actual inflows reached $12.5 billion. EU Countries accounted for about 61 percent of the cumulative foreign investment; OECD countries accounted for 88.5 percent. France and Germany are the top sources of foreign investment, and are followed by the United States and Netherlands.[29]

Turkish government's purpose for its liberal foreign investment policy is to build upon the competitive advantages for foreign investment. The periods show that the Turkish government realized the relationship between its economic development and foreign investment policies and it has focused on implementing a foreign investment law and privatization programs in order to facilitate and promote foreign investment. Turkish government also enacted new laws such as patent law, trademark law, arbitration law and competition law in this period in order to comply with the EU requirements and WTO agreements. Some of these regulations will be analyzed in "international policies" section.

---

[28] See the detail data at http://www.hazine.gov.tr/english

[29] *Id.*

e.1. Privatization Programme

Turkey has launched an ambitious privatization program. The inclusion of foreign investors to a privatization program can enhance the chances of State Enterprises to be transformed into efficient companies since foreign investors increases competition for bid, and they can bring technical expertise.[30] In order to carry out privatization program, the Turkish government should take into consideration domestic and foreign investors concerns. Turkey embarked on privatization program in order to minimize state involvement in the economy and to promote foreign investment in 1984.[31] In 1984, the first regulation regarding privatization, "Law No. 2983, Law to Motivate Savings and to Accelerate Government Investments" was adopted.[32] This law was modified in 1986, by Law No. 3291. These laws had some shortcomings regarding the decision making process of privatization. Pursuant to the law No. 3291, the Council of Ministers were authorized to pass decisions on the privatization of State Owned Enterprises.[33] The Public Participation Administration and the High Planning Council were authorized to decide the transfer of partially state owned companies and subsidiaries to the Public

---

[30] Louis T. Wells & Jr, Alvin G. Wint, *Facilitating Foreign Participation in Privatization*, Foreign Investment Advisory Services Occasional Paper 8, http://www.fias.net/occasional/opp_8.htm (visited 11/12/2001)

[31] The main objectives of the Turkish privatization program are to: minimize state involvement in the economy, provide legal and structural environment for free enterprise to operate, decrease the financing burden of State Economic Enterprises on the national budget, transfer privatization revenues to the major infrastructure projects, expand and deepen the existing capital market by promoting wider share ownership, To provide efficient allocation of resources, enhance competition in the economy

[32] Prof. Dr. Ozer Ertuna, *Constraints of Privatization: The Turkish Case, Public-Private Partnership in the Mena Region Workshop*, Mediterranean Development Forum, September 3-6, 1998, at 15.

[33] *Id.* at 16.

Participation Administration for privatization.[34] The study prepared by Morgan Guaranty Bank concerning the Turkish legal system on privatization concluded that this law did not provide adequate legal frameworks on the implementation problems of privatization with respect to labor, managerial and financial issues.[35]

In order to eliminate the legal and bureaucratic problems and to extend the scope of assets to be privatized, Turkish Parliament enacted a new privatization law on November 23, 1994 with the law No.4046. According to this law, the Privatization High Council is the ultimate decision-making body for privatization and privatization process is being managed by the Privatization Administration under the supervision of the Privatization High Council.[36] Unfortunately, this law did not change anything, apart from renaming the administration.

The Turkish government has begun to privatize state owned economic enterprises through utilizing different methods of privatization such as block sales, sales to strategic investors, transfer of ownership to employees, etc.[37] The Turkish Government has been making block sales to foreign firms since 1986 in cement, iron and steel, appliance, automotive, telecommunication, and airline sectors. Foreign investors can participate in privatization in all cases. Further, they receive national treatment in privatization programs.

There were plenty of legal challenges at the Constitutional Court since the Turkish Constitution did not regulate legal basis for privatization. In order to remove

---

[34] Bircan Bircanoglu Law Firm, *Legal Report on Turkish Investment Law* (2000).

[35] Ertuna, *supra* note 32, at 16.

[36] *Id*. at 16.

[37] *Id*. at 7-8.

legal obstacles to privatization, the Turkish parliament passed a Constitutional amendment to Article 47, on August 13, 1999. The new Article 47 of the Constitution provides for the first time the concept of privatization.[38] This new amendment will be the starting point for removing legal obstacles to privatization. Due to plenty of legal challenges at the Constitutional Court, the privatization process has been slow. I agree with Professor Ozer Ertuna's point of view: the lesson that should be drawn from Turkish privatization case is that it is good to establish well-drafted regulations for legal framework of privatization before starting privatization.[39]

2. Trends in Sectoral Pattern of FDI in Turkey

Whereas the private sectors are always open to investors, the Turkish government restricted foreign and domestic investment in the public sectors. Later, the government also opened the public sectors to investors. The public and the private sectors can be subcategorized as follows: agriculture, mining, manufacturing, and service. It should be noted that some of these subcategories such as mining sectors are some-how restricted to investors.

As we mentioned earlier, along with its development objectives in the early years of the republic, the Turkish government viewed that the government must involve the

---

[38] Article 47 of the Turkish Constitution states that: "...The rules and regulations concerning privatization of the assets and enterprises that are owned by the State, State Economic Enterprises or other public corporations are prescribed by law..."

[39] Prof. Dr. Ozer Ertuna articulates that: "the lack of sufficient attention to the legal framework of privatization has been the most important reasons for limited success in privatization in Turkey. The lessons to be learned is that, it is better to take the time needed to formulate the legal framework before the privatization." *Id.* at 17.

public sectors such as education, health, transportation and energy. Thus, investment in public sector was restricted not only to foreign investors but also to domestic investors.

In order to carry out the development needs of its rapidly growing population, the Turkish government has changed its policies towards opening of the public sectors not only to domestic investors, but also to foreign investors. In particular, since the inauguration of the liberalization program in 1980s, the sectors that are considered public such as transportation, communications, energy, health, and education, are open to private investors.

The government has gradually decreased the public sector involvement in the manufacturing sector in order to reduce its budget deficits.[40] Demands for modern infrastructure and advanced communication systems led the government to change its policies towards the openness of the public sector to foreign investors.[41] In order to carry out this policy, the government has announced new finance projects such as the BOT model, and accelerated the privatization process through the amendments in the Constitution and the enactment of new privatization law.[42] In addition, the government has introduced investment incentives program. These changes will be evaluated in the promotional policies. One may argue that the massive privatization program and the reforms on infrastructure projects have enabled foreign investors to make new

---

[40] Gulten Kazgan, *External Pressures and the New Policy Outlook*, in TURKEY AND EUROPE 90-91 (Canan Balkir & Allan M. Williams eds., 1993).

[41] Ajay Chhiber & Sweder van Wijnbergen, *Public Policy and Private Investment In Turkey*, in REVIVING PRIVATE INVESTMENT IN DEVELOPING COUNTRIES, EMPRICAL STUDIES AND POLIY LESSONS 171-175 (A. Chhibber, M. Dailami & N. Shafik, eds., 1992)

[42] Catherine Pedamon, *How is Convergence Best Achieved in International Project Finance?*, 24 FORDHAM INT'L L. J. 1272, 1284-1285 (2001).

investments in Turkey. Private investment in infrastructure sectors can bring benefit to the Turkish economy.

Foreign investment in Turkey can be grouped into four sectors: agriculture, mining, manufacturing, and service. It should be noted that as Turkey has developed, the relative importance of agriculture has declined, while the service sector has developed stronger. Due to the fact that the government lost its interest in the agricultural sector, private and public investment in this sector were declined.[43] However, Turkey is still an important supplier of agricultural products for Middle East Market. With the Southern Eastern Project, the so-called GAP project, the Turkish government provides incentives in order to promote investment in agricultural sector.

The Turkish government has still played an important role in the mining sector despite the fact that the privatization process of the state enterprises in the mining sector has been introduced. The Turkish government's main objective for the mining sector is to "gain utmost value added from underground riches and to meet raw material and energy requirements safely and economically."[44] Turkey possesses a large amount of mining resources of minerals such as copper, lead, alumina, and ceramic clay.[45] These minerals are mostly used as raw materials for the domestic industry. One may argue that boron is the most valuable mine in Turkey since Turkey possesses two thirds of the boron reserves in the world.[46] The civil society groups rightly criticized the decision of the

---

[43] BARCHARD, *supra* note 15, at 52.

[44] DPT Electronik Sureli Yayinlar, *Profiles of Turkish Public Sector Project for Foreign Funding*, (2000).

[45] Economic Outlook, Mining, ,http://www.igeme.org.tr/english/outlook/mining.htm (visited 11/20/2001)

[46] *Id.*

privatization of boron mines since this mine is considered as one of the important energy supplies in the future.

The competitiveness of the Turkish manufacturing sector, in particular cement, beverages and tobacco, textiles, electrical and electronic equipments, creates an efficient foreign investment environment. Indeed, foreign investors concentrate largely in the manufacturing sector. According to the statistics in 2001, manufacturing accounted with 54.4 % of the foreign investment inflow.[47] Like other sectors, the privatization process and custom union agreement with the European union can be accounted for the reasons of the high interest on this sector by foreign investors.

FDI in the service sector has been growing faster than in other sectors. Tourism is one of the important service sectors that Turkey receives efficient income out of. The Turkish government has a policy that promotes foreign investment in this sector. Indeed, foreign investors have made investment in hotels and airlines businesses that are profitable to them.[48] In addition, the natural, historical and geographical situation of Turkey made her a popular tourist destination. This popularity has also an impetus power for foreign investors to make investment without worrying an economic benefit.[49]

The Turkish government rightly argues that there is a strong demand for infrastructure industry including the energy and telecommunications sectors in Turkey. For example, according to the investment report, "the annual investment requirement is

---

[47] www.treasury.org (visited 12/05/2001).

[48] Peter Buckley & Necla V. Geyikdagi, *Explaining Foreign Direct Investment in Turkey's Tourism Industry*, Transnational Corporations, 100 (1996).

[49] *Id.* at 102.

expected to be 4.5 billion US dollars yearly for power generation until 2010".[50] This demand can be considered as one of the reasons for foreign investor to invest in Turkey since the Turkish government amended its BOTs law and enacted a new "Electricity Market Law" in March 3, 2001, and "Natural Gas Market Law" in May 2, 2001. With enactment of these laws, the Turkish government has pursued following objectives:

> (a) Define a new legal framework for the introduction of competition, monitoring on a new market environment where the private investors will prevail, as the state domination will diminish,
>
> (b) Organization of a new administratively and financially independent Energy Market Regulatory Authority (EMRA) which will undertake monitoring and auditing of both sectors on behalf of public in accordance with the new legal framework and ensuring the formation of Energy Market Regulatory Board which will represent and govern the Energy Market Regulatory Agency,
>
> (c) Liberalization of electricity and gas sectors in harmonization with the EU Electricity and Gas Directives and opening of these sectors to competition. [51]

---

[50] GENERAL DIRECTORATE OF FOREIGN INVESTMENT (GDFI), INVESTING IN TURKEY 1 (2000).

[51] "(d) Unbundling of generation, transmission and, distribution activities in the electricity sector as well as the creation of wholesale and retail sale areas, for the gas sector the separation of import, production, distribution, transmission, storage, wholesale, CNG distribution, transmission, export activities,

(e) Providing non-discriminatory and equal access to all transmission and distribution facilities for all parties state or private as required by EU Electricity and Gas Directivies,

(f) Determining the rights and responsibilities of all real and legal persons to be involved in the gas and electricity market activities,

(g) Decreasing the liabilities of state resulting from investment and operation practices, as well as take or pay obligations in the energy sales agreements and natural gas agreements,

(h) Ensuring that market activities will take place through licensing from EMRA,

(i) Ensuring that all necessary measures are taken to protect the consumers and the environment " The Regulatory Reform In the Electricity and Natural Gas Sector, http://www.treasury.gov.tr/english/ybsweb/energy.htm (visited 11.13.2001).

It can be observed from these objectives that the Turkish government wants to promote a competitive market based on private sector involvement in the gas and electricity sector which are really demanded and needed to be developed.

It should be noted that foreign investment in some sectors requires special government approval in the pre-establishment phrase. For example banking and other financial services require a special permit due to the public trust and fiduciary nature of their activities. Investment in petroleum, mining and insurance sectors are governed by special laws since these sectors, especially petroleum and mining, are related to the natural resources of the country.

3. Promotional Policies

Turkey has offered various programmes in order to improve liberalization standards and promote FDI. In addition, the promotional policies can improve Turkey's economic development and national competitiveness. Turkish promotional policies for foreign investment can be grouped into two categories: investment incentives and free trade law zone.

a. Investment Incentives

a1. The Nature and Importance of Investment Incentives

Turkey provides investment incentives in order to encourage foreign investment in Turkey. As already mentioned, the economic and social development of Turkey has been administered through central planning in principle since 1960. The Turkish government supports investment incentive measures that conform to the developmental plans and annual programs.

The measures used for this purpose are mainly financial aids and tax exemptions. For example, exemption of custom taxes and duties for importation of investment goods or materials used in the manufacturing of export products, exemptions on corporate and value-added taxes, tax rebates and other types of tax incentives are applied for promoting investment.

The purposes of the investment incentive measures are specified in the Decree Concerning State Encouragement to Investments and the Investment Encouragement Fund (Decree No. 98/10755).[52] According to the article of the Decree, the Turkish government encourages and supports investments, which are in line with international commitments. In order to create harmony with the standards and norms adopted by the WTO and European Community, Turkey enacted this decree for investment incentive measures. The main purpose of this decree is to provide support to investments that conform with the development plans and in the sectors and areas, which have given priority in the annual programs. Furthermore, the Turkish government supports and encourages investments that reduce regional imbalances and contain special arrangements that encourage employment. The introduction of modern technologies into the country and the most efficient and effective use of resources are other important objectives to be achieved with these measures.

a2. Organization and Procedure for the Investment Incentives

---

[52] Decree Concerning State Encouragements to Investments and the Investment Encouragement Fund, Decree No: 98/10755, Dated: March 25 1998.

To adopt and carry on measures to encourage investments in Turkey are among the duties of the GDFI, an Undersecretary of Treasury attached to the Prime Ministry. In order to take advantage of incentives, a foreign investor must obtain a special "incentive encouragement certificate". The incentive certificate is a preliminary document containing characteristic values of investment.[53] According to the current incentive regime, in order to issue the Incentive Certificate, the minimum fixed amount of Investment in Priority Development Regions should be 25 Billion Turkish Lira (TL) and for other regions 50 Billion TL.[54] Approval procedures take approximately 3 to 4 weeks. Namely, bureaucratic problems still exist in Turkey.

The way the general incentive regime is applied varies with to location, scale and subject of investments. In terms of the application of general incentives, Turkey is divided into three types of regions:

a) Developed Regions: The city boundaries of Istanbul and Kocaeli; and the municipality boundaries of Ankara, Izmir, Bursa, Adana and Antalya.

b) First Priority Regions: 50 cities determined by the Council of Ministers

c) Normal Regions: The remaining cities[55]

As a general principle, investments made in a developed region cannot be qualified for investment incentives. However, certain investments articulated in Article 5 of the Decree are allowed to benefit from investment incentives.[56] For example,

---

[53] *Id.* Decree, article 4.

[54] *Id.* Decree, article4.

[55] *Id.* Decree, article 3.

[56] *Id.* Decree.

investments to be realized within the framework of the Built-Operate or Build Operate-Transfer Model can benefit from investment incentives measures in developed regions.

Investment incentives are equally available to qualified domestic and foreign investors.[57] The Law No.6224 guarantees non-discriminatory principle.[58] It should be noted that investment incentives are precisely specified in regulations. The amount and availability of incentives depends on the sector, the place and the value of the investment. As mentioned above, Turkey has revised its investment incentive regime to conform to European Union regulations. In particular, article 3 of the decree states that:

> Necessary changes to the related Articles of this Decree, resulting from works in relation to the European Community norms, in order to determine sectors subject to regional and special conditions can be realized by the Under secretariat.[59]

According to this Decree, the possible major incentives for investments are as follows:

a-Exemption from custom duties and fund levies

b-Investment allowance

c-Value Added Tax (VAT) exemption for imported and locally purchased machinery and equipment

d-Exemption from taxes and duties and fees

e-Energy support

f-Credit allocation from the investment encouragement fund

---

[57] GDFI, *supra* note 50, at 6.

[58] *Id.*

[59] *Id.* Decree, Article 3

g-Procurement of land.[60]

b.   **Free Trade Zones in Turkey**

Free Trade Zones are essential investment encouragement measures in Turkey. Free Zones can be defined as special regions within the country that are considered to be outside of the customs border and where the valid regulations related to foreign trade and foreign investment are not applicable, are not partly applicable or in which new regulations are applied. Free Zones Law No. 3218 was enacted on June 6 1985 with the objective of increasing export-oriented investment in Turkey. The law also aims of accelerating the entry of foreign capital and technology, providing inputs to the economy in an economical and orderly manner, and increasing the utilization of foreign trade opportunities and foreign financial instruments.[61]

Pursuant to Article 2 of the Law, the Council of Ministers is empowered to determine the location of the free zones. For example, Mersin and Antalya Free Zones became operational in 1987, Aegean and Istanbul Ataturk Airport free Zones in 1990, Trabzon Free Zone in 1992, the Istanbul-Leather Free Zone in 1995. Furthermore, Free Zone commercial activities have been conducted in Mardin and Eastern Anatolian since October 1995, in Istanbul International Stock Exchange since 1997, in Rize since 1998, Gaziantep since 1999, in Adana Yumurtalik since 1999.[62]

---

[60] *Id.* Decree, Article 2.

[61] Free Trade Zones Law, Law No 3218, Approved 6 June 1985, Issued 15 June 1985, Article 1.

[62] Free Trade Zones, General Information, http://www.foreigntrade.gov.tr (visited 01/19/2001).

In short, the following exemptions and incentives have been offered in Turkish Free Zones:

a- Pursuant to the Article 6 of the Law, Turkish Free Zones are tax-free zones. Income and revenues generated through activities in the zones are exempt from all types of tax including income, and corporate taxes.

b- Pursuant to the Article 12 of the Law, in the Turkish Free Zones, Municipality Law, Foreign Investment and Encouragement Law, and all other articles of law contrary to the provisions of the Free Trade Zones Law are not applicable.[63]

c- Free Zones' earnings and revenues can be transferred to any country, including Turkey, freely without any prior permission and are not subject to any taxes, duties or fees.[64]

d- There is no limitation on the proportion of foreign capital participation in investment within the Free Zones.[65]

e- Pursuant to the Article 6 of the Law, incentives determined by the Council of Ministers may be granted to domestic and foreign real persons and legal entities in Free Zones.[66]

e- Pursuant to the Article 8 of the Law, trade between the free zones and the other regions of Turkey is subject to the foreign trade regime. Namely, transfer of goods from Turkey

---

[63] *Id.* Free Trade Zones Law, Article 12 : In the free trade zones, all provisions of Municipality Law No. 1580 except paragraphs 5,22,25,32 and 47 of Article 15; Passport Law No. 5682; Law No. 5683 for Foreigners Traveling and Residing in Turkey and Law No. 2007 on Professions and Services Allocated for Turkish Citizens including its Annexes and Amendments; Foreign Investment and Encouragement Law No. 6224; Law No. 2677 on the Implementation of Duties and Services of at the Civil Airports, Ports and Border Gates, General Accounting Law No. 1050; Supreme Court of Finance Law No. 832 provisions the State Bidding Law No. 2886 and provisions of other laws contrary to this Law shall not be applicable.

[64] Turkish Economy, State Aid offered in the Turkish Free Zones, (visited 12/9/2000) http://turizm.net/economy/laws_a~2.htm

[65] *Id.*

[66] *Id.* Free Trade Zones Law, Article 6: " During the investment and production stages of their activities, operators and users can be qualified for incentives to be determined by the Council of Ministers."

to the free zones is deemed to be exportation. For trade taking place between the free zones and other countries, neither free zones or the foreign trade regime is applicable because the free zones are deemed to be outside of the custom border of Turkey. [67]

f- Bureaucracy has been minimized during application and operation phases by authorizing only one agency in charge of these procedures.[68]

g- Pursuant to the article 4 of the Law, there are no procedural restrictions regarding price, standards or quality of goods in the Turkish Free Zones.

Turkey has been a member of the World Export Processing Association (WEPZA) since 1991. Moreover, the 17th International conference of Free Zones and Export Processing Zones and the 9th General Assembly were held in Istanbul. Turkish Free Zones, as far as their legislation, infrastructure and volume of trade and investment are concerned, provide a good example of free trade zones in the world.[69] Overall, the geographical location of Turkey provides considerable advantages for the Turkish Free Zones. They are situated near the major Turkish ports on the Mediterranean, Aegean and Black Seas.

II. Legal Basis for Foreign Investment

A. Regulations Regarding Foreign Investment

---

[67] *Id.* Article 8.

[68] Turkish Economy, State Aid offered in the Turkish Free Zones, (visited 12/9/2000) http://turizm.net/economy/laws_a~2.htm

[69] As of the end of 1995 the trade volume of the five operational free zones amounted $1,400 million US in the Mersin Free Zone, $176 million US in the Antalya Free Zone, $704 million US in the Aegean Free Zone, $438 million US in the Istanbul Ataturk Airport Free Zone and $149 million US in the Trabzon Free Zone and $93 million US in the Istanbul-Leather Free Zone and reached $2,900 million US, showing an increase of 51 percent as compared to 1994.

When a foreign investor decides to invest in Turkey, government regulations regarding investment play an important role. Indeed, in order to promote FDI in Turkey, Turkey has devoted considerable resources to the development of its foreign investment law. In this section, therefore, I describe and examine the basic legal framework for foreign investment, specifically giving a brief overview of the Foreign Capital Encouragement Law (herein after Turkish Foreign Investment Law (TFIL) regulating non-petroleum foreign investment in manufacturing and services. Petroleum, mining, insurance, tourism, banking, and leasing sectors are regulated by separate law and different governmental organizations.[70]

The legislation governing foreign investments in Turkey can be summarized as follows:

1-Relevant laws and bilateral and multilateral agreements:

a. Law Concerning the Encouragement of Foreign Capital (NO. 6224 Dated January 18, 1954 as amended by Law No. 4046 dated November 24, 1995 and Law 4105 dated April 27, 1995)

b. Law Concerning the Organizations and Functions of the Undersecretaries of Treasury and the Undersecretaries of Foreign Trade

c. Bilateral and Multilateral Agreements relating to the protection of Investment

2-The relevant Governmental Decrees, Communiqués:

a. Foreign Capital Framework Decree (herein after FCFD) (No. 95/6990 dated June 7, 1995)

---

[70] Petroleum Law No.6326, and No.2808; Law for the Encouragement of Tourism Investment, No. 2634, dated March 15, 1982; Investment in Mining Industry, Law No. 3213, June 1984; Insurance Law, Law No. 3579, June 11,1987; Eric Schneider and Alev Bilgen, *Foreign Investment Laws in the Republic of Turkey: A Model for Reform*, 5 TRANSNAT'L LAW 99 (1992).

b. Decree 32 relating to the Protection of the Value of Turkish Currency (No. 89/1439 dated August 7, 1989 amended)[71]

It should be noted that there are laws such as Corporation Law, Property Law, Administrative Law, Contract Law and Civil Procedure, which are related to foreign investment as well. Although this chapter does not pretend to be exhaustive on all matters, the state of the legal system as it exists in Turkey is explained below.

B. Law No. 6224 Regarding the Encouragement of Foreign Capital (Turkish Foreign Investment Law (TFIL)

Law No 6224 contains 14 articles that define basic legal framework for FDI in Turkey. It is worth noting that Law No. 6224 was considerably modified and liberalized by a 1995 Decree No. 95/6990.

1. Scope and Application

a. **Aim of the Law No. 6224 (herein after TFIL) Regarding the Encouragement of Foreign Capital**

The aim of the TFIL is not specifically stated in the Law.[72] However, the Foreign Investment Framework Decree, which came into force with the Council of Ministers'

---

[71] T.C Basbakanlik Hazine Mustesarligi, YABANCI SERMAYE RAPORU (1993-1995), Yabanci Sermaye Genel Mudurlugu, Ankara, (1996).

[72] Law Concerning The Encouragement of Foreign Capital (Herein after Law), No: 6224, Date: January 18, 1954.

Decree no. 95/6990, determines the purpose of the TFIL, which is to establish the principles of promoting capital coming into Turkey.[73]

b. Definition of Foreign Capital

The definition of foreign investment in the TFIL is based on asset definition and it is also a broad definition. Article 2 of the Law includes the following assets as foreign capital:

a. Capital in cash in the form of convertible foreign currency,

b. Machinery, equipment, tools and similar materials approved by the GDFI,

c. Intellectual property rights such as patent rights and trade marks,

d. Portions of profit converted into investment capital for the purpose of reinvestment.[74]

c. Scope of Law

Article 1 of the TFIL relates to the scope of the investment law. The same article requires the following three conditions that foreign investors' activities must meet:

a. The subject of the investment must contribute to the economic development of Turkey,

b. The foreign investors' activities must be in sectors open to the Turkish private enterprises.

---

[73] Article 1 of the Decree, Foreign Capital Framework Decree (herein after Decree), Decree No: 95/6990, dated on June 7, 1995.

[74] Law Concerning The Encouragement of Foreign Capital (Herein after Law), No: 6224, Date: January 18, 1954

It should be noted that some activities were not allowed to business for private companies such as transportation, telecommunication and production of "distilled sprits". These activities were reserved for government entities. With the privatization program, most of the activities that were operated only by government enterprises were opened to private investors. Thus, in practice, this condition is already outdated since almost every sector is open to private enterprises.

c. Foreign investors cannot acquire a majority shares in companies that are in monopoly in Turkey.[75]

The GDFI grants permission on condition that the business in which the investment will be made is useful for the economic development of the country, is in a field of activity open to Turkish private enterprise, and does not entail any monopoly in Turkey.

d. Right to Private Ownership and Establishment

The foreign investment laws of Turkey provide for free admission of foreign investments. There are no limitations on the amount, the type, or the form of the investment. Under the foreign investment regulations, foreign investors may invest in Turkey in either a hundred percent foreign-owned company, by establishing in or acquiring an existing Turkish company, by establishing branch, liaison offices, or by making a joint venture with local partners.[76] Foreign investors have the right to freely establish and own business enterprises and engage in all forms of industrial, commercial and other fields' activities aimed at the production of good and services. Turkish

---

[75] Article 1, Subject and Scope of the Law.

[76] Scheider, *supra* note 70, at 114.

commercial law does not have discriminatory provisions concerning foreign investors.[77] The only exception is that a foreign investor must get permission from the GDFI before applying to the Ministry of Industry and Commerce.

It should be noted that right to private ownership and establishment is not an absolute right in all sectors. That is to say that foreign investors are subject to restrictions on establishment in certain sectors. For drilling Petroleum, mining, establishment in financial services, including banking and insurance are the sectors that require special permission from the Turkish government. Moreover, the equity participation ratio of foreign shareholders is limited to 20 percent in broadcasting, and 49 percent in aviation and maritime transportation.

e. **Permit requirement for foreign investment**

The TFIL requires for the entry of all FDI get an authorization from the GDFI. In other words, foreign investment in Turkey is within the scope of the authority of the Under secretariat for the Treasury (Herein after UT), GDFI. All foreign investment applications pass through this governmental body and are subject to its approval. With the new decree screening decisions became centralized. Before 1980, several ministries of government used to approve foreign investors' applications. Therefore, potential foreign investors were effectively discouraged in their attempts by having to deal with heavy bureaucratic process. The UT has the power to screen foreign investments. However, in practice, screening mechanisms are routine and non-discriminatory. On the other hand, one may argue that foreign investors are not accorded national treatment in

---

[77] Deloitte & Touche, *Turkey*, 27 (1999).

pre-establishment stage since domestic investors' proposals are not usually screened.[78]

Article 3 of the FCFD states the general principles regarding granting of a permit for foreign capital. For example, real and legal persons' resident abroad must bring a minimum of 50.000 US Dollars per person to establish corporations, to become partners in companies or to open branch offices.[79]

f.   Employment of foreign personnel

Article 7 of the TFIL permits the foreign investor to employ foreign personnel.[80]

---

[78] Country Commercial Guides, *FY 1999: Turkey*, <http://www.state.gov> (visited 12/10/2000)

[79] Article 3 of the Foreign Capital Framework Decree provides:

a) The applications of real and legal persons resident abroad about investing in Turkey, engaging in commercial activities, participating in partnerships, opening branch offices and establishing liaison offices are examined within the Legislation in effect by Undersecretariat.

b) Undersecretariat is empowered to make amendments relating to issuance of permits for new investments and participation, capacity increase, liquidation and mergers, alterations in participation ratio for existing firms with foreign capital and also to make amendments on duration, quantity, export undertaking, field of activity, value and proportion of share.

c) Real and legal persons resident abroad must bring a minimum 50.000 USA Dollars per person to establish corporations, become partners in existing companies and opening branch offices. In the case of that the number of foreign shareholders is above one, the participation amounts of foreign partners in total capital can be arranged freely.

d) Capital increase can be done without taking any permission if the participation ratios of foreign partners do not change. After making capital increase, the application is done to Undersecretariat for only registration.

e) Real and legal persons resident abroad can buy or sell the shares of existing companies in Turkey in accordance with the principles defined by Undersecretariat.

f) Undersecretariat can endorse a transfer guarantee on shares or temporary receipts, which are registered in the name of foreign partners.

g) License, know-how, technical assistance and management agreements concluded by Turkish public and private sector enterprises with real and/or legal persons resident abroad shall put into effect after registering these agreements to Undersecretariat.

h) Establishments with foreign capital can assure every type of foreign credits freely. Foreign Capital Framework Decree, Official Gazette Date: July 23, 1995 No: 22352, Decree No: 95/6990 dated on June 7, 1995. T.C Basbakanlik Hazine Mustesarligi, Yabanci Sermaye Raporu (1993-1995), Yabanci Sermaye Genel Mudurlugu, Ankara, 1996, at 32.

[80] Article 7 of the Law.

Pursuant to the "Law on Professions and Services Allocated for Turkish Citizens", Law No 2007, there are some limitations on job categories for foreigners. For example, according to the law, only Turkish citizens can work as peddler, musician, photographer, barber, broker, waiter and waitress, etc. However, Foreign investment law (Law No 6244) clearly states that the Law No 2007 does not apply to foreign investors investing pursuant to the TFIL. That is to say that, foreign investment law provides unrestricted opportunities for foreigners to work in Turkey.

2. **Non-Discrimination Principle (National Treatment Principle)**

Upon the authorization and admission of FDI, the TFIL grants the foreign investor certain rights, including national treatment. According to Turkish foreign investment regulations, foreign investors receive full national treatment once they establish investment in Turkey. Article 10 of the TFIL states that all rights, exemptions and privileges granted for domestic investment and investors shall be equally applicable to foreign investment and foreign investors engaged in the same field of business.[81] This principle is explicitly reiterated under Article 7 of the Foreign Capital Decree under the heading "Equality Principle". Article 7 of the Decree states, "With taking necessary permission within the scope of Law No. 6224, the firms and branch offices established according to Turkish Commercial Code and registered to Turkish Trade Registry are considered as Turkish firms and branch offices."[82]

---

[81] Article 10, Equal Treatment For Domestic and Foreign Capital, states that: "All rights, exemptions, privileges and facilities recognized for domestic capital and enterprises shall be equally applicable to foreign capital and foreign enterprises engaged in comparable fields of business." Id. Law.

[82] *Id.* Decree.

3.   **Investment Protection Obligations**

a.   **Transfer of Funds**

The TFIL guarantees the free transfers of profits, fees and royalties, and repatriation of capital.[83] The foreign investors may repatriate FDI in a freely usable currency. In addition, Article 5 of the Decree (FCFD) states:

> The transfers of reinvestment of profits, dividends, proceeds of sale and liquidation, compensation payments, payments under license, technical assistance agreements, repayments of foreign credit principal and interest, corresponding to the shares in foreign capital, within the framework of this Decree, is unrestricted.[84]

The only restriction is that the right of transfer is subject to the payment of taxes.[85] This indicates the commitment of Turkey to respect and guarantee one of the most essential interests of foreign investors.

b.   **Expropriation and Compensation**

---

[83] *Id.* Law, article 4 and 5.

[84] *Id.* Decree, article 5.

[85] *Id.* Law, article 4, and article 8 of the Communique Concerning the Decree on the Framework for Foreign Investment, Date June 27, 1996.

Turkish Foreign Investment Law unfortunately does not have specific provisions regarding expropriation and compensation. However, Article 46 of the Turkish Constitution provides that:

> The State and public corporations shall be entitled, where the public interest requires it, to expropriate privately owned real estate wholly or in part or impose administrative servitude on it in accordance with the principles and procedures prescribed by law, provided that compensation is paid in advance. The method and procedure for calculating compensation for expropriation shall be prescribed by law. In determining the compensation, the law shall take into account tax declarations, current value established by official assessment at the time of expropriation, unit prices and construction costs for real estate, and other objective criteria. The procedure for taxing and difference between the sum due in compensation and the value declared in the tax declaration shall be prescribed by law. Compensation shall be paid in cash and in advance.[86]

The TFIL should specify how compensation is to be determined in expropriation cases. Expropriation Law No. 2942 is applied for expropriation and compensation situation. Turkish authorities should amend the Law No 6224 and insert the provision with respect to expropriation and compensation in order to provide transparency for this issue.

4.   Performance Requirements

No special performance requirements are imposed as a condition for establishing, maintaining or expanding an investment.[87] The Turkish government does not impose any conditions on the permission to invest, including specific percentage of local content for

---

[86] Article 46 of the Turkish Constitution.

[87] Turkey 1999, *Country Commercial Guide- (FY-1999)*, (visited 12/10/00) http://www.state.gov/www/about_state/business/com_guides/1999/europe/turkey99_07.html

goods or services, employment of host country nationals, or local financing.[88] There are no requirements that the foreign investor should transfer technology on certain terms. Foreign investors do not need to purchase from local sources or export a certain percentage of output. Both foreign and domestic investors are subject to the same requirements. There are however, some requirements for access to tax and investment incentives.

5. Dispute Settlement Process: New Development in International Arbitration on Concession Agreements

The TFIL does not provide for a dispute settlement process regarding international investment disputes. This does not mean that foreign investors cannot resort to international investment dispute settlement process regarding their investments in Turkey. Turkey has a signatory of some international agreements on arbitration. For example, Turkey signed the Washington Convention on the Settlement of Investment Disputes (ICSID), dated 1965, in 1988.[89] It is worth noting that even though the specific requirements for resort to international arbitration vary somewhat, most BITs to which Turkey is party provide for a dispute settlement process for international investment disputes.

Turkey is also a signatory to the 1961 European Convention on International Commercial Arbitration.[90] Furthermore, Turkey is a signatory to the 1958 New York

---

[88] *Id.*

[89] Turkish Official Gazette 6.12.1988 / 19830.

[90] Turkish Official Gazette 23.9.1991 / 21000.

Convention on the Enforcement of Foreign Arbitral Awards.[91] Turkey implemented the New York Convention and European convention by the International Private Law and Civil Procedures (Law No. 2675).[92] This Law has provisions enacted from those conventions. Indeed, the general principles of foreign arbitral awards are regulated by the Law No. 2675.[93]

This Law does not provide any definition of the foreign arbitral award. Pursuant to decisions of the Turkish Courts and the views of scholars, an arbitral award rendered according to the procedural law of a foreign state shall be deemed to be a foreign arbitral award.[94] The nationalities of the parties or the arbitrators and the place of arbitration do not have any effect on the designation of an arbitral award as foreign.

Prior to the amendment on certain articles of Turkish Constitution, the arbitration related to administrative disputes was problematic in Turkish Investment Law. Thus, this study specifically explains what the problems regarding concession agreements were, and what the amendments are. International arbitration on concession has been debated for years. Foreign investors consider the international arbitration a prerequisite for making investment in infrastructure areas in Turkey. They lobbied for the amendment of the Constitution.

One of the most important problems of the concession agreement was that before the Constitutional amendments, pursuant to the Article 155 of the Constitution of Turkey

---

[91] Turkish Official Gazette 25.9.1991 / 21002.

[92] Law No 2675, Turkish Official Gazette, 22.5.1982 / 17701.

[93] *Id.*

[94] Serdar Bezen, Recent Developments in International Commercial Arbitration in Turkey, Mealey's International Arbitration Reports, March (2001).

provided that the agreements in the nature of "administrative concession agreements" were subject to the review of the High Administrative Court (Danistay). That is to say that Danistay had exclusive jurisdiction on concession agreements. Ironically, the Turkish Constitution did not define the concession agreements. The definition and scope of concession have been characterized through the decisions of the Constitution Court and High Administrative Court. Pursuant to the Constitution Court decision, Concession agreement was defined, "agreement made by the administration with a legal person who is a joint stock company for institution and operation of a public service for long term, against a fee to be profits and losses to belong to the partner investor".[95] In other words, agreements which transfer the right to render public services, including BOT, TOR, and TPP, are concession agreements and they are subject to the scrutiny of the Danistay.

Another problem occurred when the Turkish government decided to modify the BOTs Law, No 3996, in order to increase foreign investment flows. The government amended the legislation providing that concession agreement is governed by private law. This amendment was challenged by the Turkish Constitutional Court. In the Decision No. 1995/23, the Turkish Constitutional Court proclaimed Article 5 of Law No. 3996 "Regarding the Rendering of Certain Services pursuant to the Build/Operate and Transfer Model" ("BOT Law") unconstitutional.[96] The BOT Law attempted to remove BOT arrangements from the category of administrative agreements simply by definition.

---

[95] Bircanoglu & Bircanoglu Law Office, *Doing Business in Turkey*, <http://www.doingbusinessinturkey.com/articles/arbit.html>, (visited 9/12/2000).

[96] Decision dated June 28, 1995, published March 20, 1996 Official Gazette, No. 22586, Case No. 1994/71, Decree No. 1995/23.

Pursuant to the Article 5 of Law No. 3996 energy investment contracts (e.g., concession contracts) would be governed by private law.

The Constitutional Court declared Article 5 of Law No. 3996 unconstitutional in the Decision No. 1995/23. The Constitutional Court annulled the wording "…that does not constitute a concession" and the provision "... this contract is subject to private law provisions of Article 5 of law No. 3996."[97] In other words, pursuant to this decision, such contracts constitute concessions and they are subject to administrative law provisions.[98] Thus, administrative contracts for public services have to be scrutinized by the Council of State (Danistay).

Foreign investors worried about the jurisdiction of the Danistay to examine a concession agreement since the examination was a very lengthy and bureaucratic open-ended procedure. The Constitutional Court annulment ruling did not forbid the arbitration clauses to be inserted in administrative contracts, however the problems arose with the negative attitude of the Danistay for not accepting the arbitration in concession agreements. The Constitutional Court Decision has discouraged foreign investors from making new investment. In order to solve this uncertainty completely, Turkish Parliament passed the Amendment of Article 47, 125 and 155 of the Turkish Constitution in 13 August 1999.

It should be noted that even prior to the Constitutional amendments and despite the 1995 Constitutional Court Decision, some foreign investors could access international arbitration for administrative agreement disputes through the BITs concluded between

---

[97] Ahmet Kenan Tanrikulu, *International Commercial Arbitration*, YASED, Insight YASED, December 1999, Volume 1, Issue 3.

[98] *Id.*

Turkey and many countries.[99] As explained above, many BITs signed by Turkey provide for arbitration under the ICSID Convention. The Turkish Constitution acknowledges and provides that international law in the form of ratified treaties has priority over Turkish Constitutional law and domestic law. In particular, Article 90 of the Turkish Constitution stipulates, "International agreements duly put into effect carry the force of law".[100] Furthermore, the Constitutional Court cannot review the constitutionality of the international treaties.[101] That is to say, international treaties have supremacy over domestic law. On the other hand, the Turkish Constitution has some provisions such as article 125 and 155 conflict with the statues of international treaties.[102] Therefore, it was necessary to resolve the conflict between the international agreements on investment and domestic law.[103]

---

[99] Bezen, *supra* note 94.

[100] Ratification of International Treaties is governed by Article 90 of the Turkish Constitution. This Article States that: "The ratification of treaties concluded with foreign states and international organizations on behalf of the Republic of Turkey, shall be subject to adoption by the Turkish Grand National Assembly by a law approving the ratification. Agreements regulating economic, commercial and technical relations, and covering a period of no more than one year, may be put into effect through promulgation, provided they to not entail any financial commitment by the State, and provided they do not infringe upon the status of individuals or upon the property rights of Turkish citizens abroad. In such cases, these agreements must be brought to the knowledge of the Turkish Grand National Assembly within two months of their promulgation. Agreements in connection with the implementation of an international treaty, and economic, commercial, technical, or administrative agreements which are concluded depending on an authorization given by law shall not require approval by the Turkish Grand National Assembly. However, agreements concluded under the provision of this paragraph and affecting the economic, or commercial relations and private rights of individuals shall not be put into effect unless promulgated. Agreements resulting in amendments to Turkish laws shall be subject to the provisions of the first paragraph. International agreements duly put into effect carry the force of law. ..."

[101] Article 90 of the Turkish Constitution states that: "...No appeal to the Constitutional Court can be made with regard to these agreements, on the ground that they are unconstitutional."

[102] PROF. DR. ERGIN NOMER, DOC. DR. NURAY EKSI. DOC. DR. GUNSELI GELGEL, MILLETLERARASI TAHKIM (INTERNATIONAL ARBITRATION) 88 (2000).

[103] *Id.* at 88.

The arrangements for resolving this conflict have already been made. Three articles of Turkish Constitution were amended by the Turkish Parliament through "The Act Concerning Amendments on Certain Articles of the Constitution of Republic of Turkey", Law No. 4446, on 13 August 1999. It is worth examining these three amended articles of the Turkish Constitution.

Article 125 of the Turkish Constitution provides general principles for judicial review of most administrative acts of the Government.[104] The Constitutional amendment of Article 125 inserts two new sentences thereafter which have the effect of removing concession agreements from the exclusive jurisdiction of the Turkish administrative courts. The new Article 125 precisely allows for both domestic and international arbitration in disputes with respect to concessions and contracts for public service.[105] As specified under the Article 125, international arbitration is only available in disputes involving a foreign element. In other words, Article 125 of the Turkish Constitution now allows concession agreements to be subject to international arbitration where disputes regarding such agreements have "a foreign element."[106]

Article 155 of the Turkish Constitution describes the duties, and powers of the Council of State or Danistay.[107] Before the August 1999 constitutional amendment was

---

[104] Bezen, *supra* note 94.

[105] *Id*.

[106] Gurcan Law office, *Turkish BOT Law*, www.gurcanlaw.com/under5.htm (visited 12/10/00).

[107] Article 155 of the Turkish Constitution states that: " The Council of State is the last instance for reviewing decisions and judgments given by administrative courts and which are not referred by law to other administrative courts. It Shall also be the first and last instance for dealing with specific cases prescribed by law. The Council of State shall try administrative cases, give its opinions on draft legislation submitted by the Prime Minister and the Council of Ministers and the conditions and contracts under which concessions are granted within two months, examine draft regulations, settle administrative disputes and discharge other duties as prescribed by law. Three-fourths of the members of the Council of State shall be appointed by the Supreme Council of Judges and Public Prosecutors from among the first category

approved, Article 155 of the Constitution provided that the agreements in the nature of concession agreements were subject to the review of the Danistay without any time limit.

The amendment changed Danistay's role on concession agreements. The amendment provided that Danistay would give its opinion on concession agreements and contracts regarding public service within two months.[108] Namely, Article 155 confines the review of concession agreements by the Danistay to a non-binding opinion to be rendered within two months.

Article 47 of the Turkish Constitution is amended and entitled "Nationalization and Privatization". Prior to the amendment, Article 47 of the Turkish Constitution did not provide the ground for privatization. It was only provided the ground for nationalization. Thus, it was entitled "Nationalization"[109] The amendment of Article 47 of the Turkish Constitution provides constitutional basis for privatization. The new Article 47 provides that the principles and procedures of the privatization of state-owned

---

administrative judges and public prosecutors, or those considered to be of this profession; and the remaining one-fourth of the members by the President of the Republic from among officials meeting the requirements designated by law. The president, chief public prosecutor, deputy president, and heads of division of the Council of State shall be elected by the Plenary Assembly of the Council of State from among its own members for a term of four years by secret ballot and by an absolute majority of the total number of members. They may be reelected at the end of their term of office. The organization, the functioning, the qualifications and procedures of election of the president, the chief public prosecutor, the deputy presidents and the heads of division and the members of the Council of State, shall be regulated by law in accordance with the principles of specific nature of the administrative jurisdiction, and of the independence of the Courts and the security of tenure of judges."

[108] Article 155 of the Turkish Constitution states that "...give its opinions on draft legislation submitted by the Prime Minister and the Council of Ministers and the conditions and contracts under which concessions are granted within two months ."

[109] Turkish Constitution Article 47 states that: "Nationalization and Privatization Private enterprises performing public service may be nationalized when this is required by the exigencies of public interest. Nationalization shall be carried out on the basis of real value. The methods and procedures for calculating real value shall be prescribed by law."

business, state economic enterprises and other public legal entities are governed by statute.[110] Furthermore, the amendment of the Article states that:

"Which of the investments or services that are carried out bye the State, State Economic Enterprises or other public corporations may be performed by or delegated to real or corporate body through private law contracts are prescribed by law."[111] Article 47 states that the requirements and the procedures for privatization of public investments and services are regulated by statute and the privatization of such investments and services governed by private law.

The amendment of Articles 47, 125, and 155 and designates the intent of the Turkish Parliament to comprehensively eliminate the legal barriers to foreign investment in the infrastructure sector set up by the Constitutional Court decision. The Constitutional amendment would allow for international arbitration in concession agreements to some foreign investors who did not have it before through BITs. For other investors who have the right to international recourse through BITs, the Constitutional changes may provide flexibility, transparency and certainty in selecting dispute resolution provisions in concession agreements.

The Constitutional Court holds that judiciary, not the legislature, had the power to decide what constitutes public service arrangements. The Amendment of Article 47 grants the parliament a constitutional basis for deciding what contracts are governed by

---

[110] Turkish Constitution Article 47 states that : "...The rules and regulations concerning privatization of the assets and enterprises that are owned by the State, State Economic Enterprises or other public corporations are prescribed by law. ."

[111] *Id.*

private law.[112] That is to say, under amended Article 47, it is possible for the legislature to enact a new law stipulated that a legal entity or real person to perform public services in accordance with agreement governed by private law.[113]

The amendments of Article 125 and 155 are the outcomes of the Constitutional Court Decisions.[114] At the end of amended Article 125 of the Turkish Constitution specified that disputes arising from concession agreements related to public services could be subject to international arbitration. Under amended Article 155/2, the Danistay's power with regard to concession agreements related to public services has been abrogated.

By all means, these constitutional amendments gave rise further amendments and enactment of new legislations in Turkish Law. Indeed, the following laws were enacted by the government: Law No 4501, which provides Arbitration rules and procedures, and Law No 4492, which amends the Law of Council of State, the Law No 4493 is related to BOT law.[115] Under amended article 5 of the BOT Law, "Contracts to be signed by the capital investment company or the foreign company and the Agency determined by the High Planning Council are subject to provisions of private law".[116]

Law No 4501, with respect to "Principles to be applied in case of recourse to arbitration in disputes arising out of concession agreements and contracts", was enacted

---

[112] H.Elizabeth Kroeger, Timothy J. Kautz, Ercan Acikel, *Turkey Revisited: Developments in Energy Project; Arbitration in the Content of Bilateral Investment Treaties and ICSID*, Mealey's International Arbitration Reports, September (1999).

[113] *Id.*

[114] *Id.*

[115] Law No. 4493, Date 12.20.1999, Turkish Official Gazette, 22.12.1999/23914.

[116] *Id.*

in January 21, 2000 so as to determine the principles for the application of international arbitration in concession agreements.[117] Prior to the enactment of this Law, one may argue that the amendment of Article 125 creates new problems since the phrase "foreign element" was not defined in Article 125. Indeed, there was no legal definition of the "foreign element" in Turkish law. However, Law No.4501 precisely defines "foreign element" in order to solve the problem. Under the Article 2/c, foreign element is defined as; "Having at least one foreign shareholder in the company according to the regulations regarding the encouragement of foreign investment or requirement of foreign capital, credit or guarantee for the implementation of the agreement."[118]

Article 5 of the Law No 4501 provides that the recognition and enforcement of the arbitral awards will be proceeded by the civil courts of Turkey. The court of Cassation (Yargitay) is the authority for the appeal of the arbitral awards. One may argue, "The provision regarding appeal of the arbitral awards should be construed, as the local arbitral awards should be subject to the appeal of Yargitay."[119]

These substantive changes in the Constitution and the legal enactments indicate that international investment dispute settlement process, especially international arbitration is encouraged, particularly for the settlement of investment disputes regarding concession agreements. These changes will give more confidence to foreign investors to enter into Turkish market. Turkish government is expected this situation as well. Turkey's Energy Minister Cumhur Ersumer states that the new law would retroactively

---

[117] Law No. 4501, Date 1. 21.2000, Turkish Official Gazette, 22.1.2000.

[118] *Id.*

[119] Doing Business in Turkey, <http://www.doingbusinessinturkey.com/articles/arbit.htm>, (visited 9/12/2000).

apply to 46 contracts already signed worth $7 billion. Ersumer suggested that the law would also clear the way for the future tendering of an additional 89 contracts worth $15 billion.[120]

6. Concluding Remarks on Foreign Investment Law

The TFIL can be considered liberal. One can observe that the TFIL is based on the principle of national treatment. Almost all sectors which are open to Turkish investors are also open to foreign investors. In addition, Turkish law provides the free transfer of payments in connection with investment. With the amendments of Decree, Turkey has simplified its screening and approval process. Turkish laws do not provide "local content requirement". However, foreign investors can voluntarily negotiate agreement with their joint venture partners to include "local content requirement" which is consistent with the TRIMs Agreement.[121]

The Turkish Law has permission process which can be utilized by the government in a way that impedes FDI. Indeed, most foreign investors have complained about the permission process since it takes time and creates red-tape problems. In order to solve the bureaucratic problems, the Turkish government should clarify and simplify the permission process. Moreover, the changes in the Constitution and new laws on international arbitration and privatization may create legal security and market access for foreign investor particularly in investment in public sector.

---

[120] Mimi Mann, *Turkey Enters 2000 on a positive Note as Reform Progress*, Middle East Executive Reports (1999).

[121] WTO, TRADE POLICY REVIEW BODY, REVIEW OF TURKEY, PRESS/TPRB/84, 13 October 1998, http://www.wto.org/new/tprb84.htm (visited 3/12/1999)

III. International Policies: Bilateral and Multilateral Agreements Relating to the Protection of Investment in Turkey

As mentioned before, since 1980 Turkey has enacted significant number of laws and initiatives designed to improve the foreign direct investment environment. With the enactment of the new laws and decrees, Turkey has implemented the international agreements that it previously ratified. Thus, the legal framework for foreign investment is compatible with the international legal system.

There are two important factors that contribute to interaction between international law and Turkish domestic law regarding foreign investment: The long and successful history of the Turkish legal system's modernization, and Turkish Constitutions' provision regarding international treaty law. One may claim that Turkey's gradual and successful reforms and experiences with regard to codifying her legal system according to various foreign laws shows Turkey's commitment to willingly comply with the international rules on foreign investment. Since the promulgation of the Turkish Republic in 1923, secular laws and institutions have been adopted from different national European laws. For example, the Swiss Civil Code, the Code of Obligations, and the Code of Civil procedure were adopted by the Turkish Parliament with small modifications as the Turkish Civil Code and Turkish Code of Obligations. In addition, the Turkish Commercial Code of 1957 was drafted under the influence of the German and Swiss Commercial Codes. [122]

With the "westernization" and the "modernization" of the Turkish legal system, Turkey rightly chooses to form an integral part of the global economy through

---

[122] Vakur Versan, *The Kemalist Reform of Turkish Law and Its Impact of Turkey*, in ATATURK AND THE MODERNIZATION OF TURKEY (Jacob Landau ed., West view Press, 1984).

participating in most of the international organizations' activities and signing international agreements. In order to show the efficacy of international law's incorporation into Turkish legal framework, it is worthwhile to reemphasize that according to the Article 90 of the Turkish Constitution, international agreements preempt inconsistent domestic laws. Namely, international treaties made under the procedure stipulated in the Article 90, are the "supreme law of the land."

The following main agreements concerning FDI concluded by Turkey will be analyzed below:

1. Turkey has signed many bilateral investment treaties with developed and developing countries;
2. Turkey has signed three essential international agreements on arbitration;
3. As a member of the OECD, Turkey has been following OECD's policies on FDI;
4. As a member of the WTO, Turkey signed and ratified the WTO agreements related to investment;
5. As a candidate to the European Union, Turkey has adopted many regulations concerning FDI in line with the EU policies;
6. As a signature of the MIGA, Turkey has approved various MIGA projects (see MIGA's activities in Turkey at Chapter 8.).

Apart from signing international investment instruments, Turkey is closely working with international organizations. Turkey has recently entered into a technical cooperation project with the UNCTAD, the UNDP, the OECD and the World Bank Group, the purpose, among others, being to amend the existing legal framework of foreign investment. The main reason for this technical cooperation is to eliminate Turkish administrative barriers to foreign investment.[123] As a recent example of the implementation of international organizations' work into Turkish legal system, the Turkish Government adopted a decree establishing the organizational framework to implement Foreign Investment Advisory Service (the World Bank Group)'s reports on administrative barriers. [124]

A. Bilateral Investment Treaties

Turkey commenced to negotiate BITs with a view to encourage and promote foreign investment in Turkey. The main goal of this policy was to provide fair, predictable and transparent non-discrimination principles for foreign investment. The purpose of Turkey to sign BITs has changed over time as its role as home and host state evolves. Thus, the most important objective of signing BITs is not only to attract foreign investment in the interest of its development, but also to protect Turkish investors' investment abroad.[125]

Since 1985, Turkey has been negotiating and signing agreements for reciprocal promotion and protection of investments with various countries. As of October 2000, Turkey has signed bilateral investment protection and promotion agreements with 65 countries. Forty-three of these agreements are now in force with countries such as the

---

[123] Melek Us, *Removing Administrative Barriers to FDI: Particular Case of Turkey*, OECD Global International Investment, New Horizons and Policy Challenges for Foreign Direct Investment in the 21st Century, Mexico City, 26-27 November (2001).

[124] FIAS Projects, Turkey, http://www.fias.net/data/mena.html (visited 05/24/2002).

[125] WTO, *Communication From Turkey, Turkey's Experience With Bilateral Investment Treaties*, 18 September 1998, WT/WGTI/W/51.

United States, Germany, Belgium, China, Estonia, Bangladesh, Switzerland, Holland, Denmark, Japan, the United Kingdom, Tunisia, South Korea.[126]

While analyzing the BITs in Chapter 3, I already provide some example provisions of BITs concluded by Turkey. The most BITs concluded by Turkey confer national and most-favored treatment including unrestricted transfer of profits, dividends and royalties, compensation for expropriation, exemptions from performance standards, and impartial international arbitration of investment disputes.[127] The Bilateral Investment Treaties' (BIT) progress is considerably dynamic. Although each successive agreement with a new country may include some new provisions, compared to Turkish foreign investment law (TFIL), most BITS concluded by Turkey often reflect and are consistent with provisions of the TFIL. As analyzed in this chapter, TFIL provides investment security through its national treatment provisions and free transfer of funds provisions, which are in harmony with most BITs concluded by Turkey.

As noted in Chapter 3, there is a lack of detailed information on the relationship between the growth of FDI inflows to Turkey and the conclusion of BITs. According to the working paper submitted to the WTO, BITs have had no remarkable effect on the development of FDI inflows to Turkey.[128]

---

[126] See the list of countries with which Turkey has signed an agreement on the protection and promotion of investments at the Appendix 6, GDFI, *supra* note 50, at 55.

[127] WTO, *supra* note 121.

[128] *Id*. This paper states that: " Concerning efficiency of protection standards brought by BITs, there is very little practical experience to make an evaluation of the use of BITs. However, it is observed that BITs provisions for dispute settlement induce settlement through negotiations and thus prevent disputes from maturing. The picture to emerge from the analysis of Turkey's experience with BITs reveals that BITs do not automatically produce an increase in FDI inflows. However, these agreements are important as an imperative for including foreign firms at least to consider undertaking investments in a given country."

B. **International Agreements on Arbitration**

As mentioned before, Turkey is signatory of main international agreements on arbitration such as the ICSID, the 1961 European Convention on International Commercial Arbitration, and the 1958 New York Convention on the Enforcement of Foreign Arbitral Law.[129] These three agreements were signed and ratified by the Turkish Parliament in 1980s, which is the period of the liberalization of the Turkish economy.

As regards ICSID Convention, Turkey made two reservations. Firstly, Under the Article 25/4 of the Convention, Turkey notified the ICSID Centre that Turkey would not consider submitting disputes regarding the real property rights to the Centre.[130] Secondly, Turkey, pursuant to Article 64 of the Convention, excluded the role of International Court of Justice on the interpretation and application of the ICSID agreement.[131] The reservation spells out that "With respect to Article 64 of the Convention, the Government of Turkey is of the opinion that the disputes which may arise from the interpretation and application of the Convention can be solved through meaningful negotiations between the parties to the dispute, without the need of having recourse to third party settlement."[132]

---

[129] Bezen, *supra* note 94.

[130] The text of Turkish Notifications states, "I also have the honour to hereby notify, pursuant to Article 25 (4) of the "Convention on the Settlement of Investment Disputes Between States and Nationals of Other States" concerning classes of disputes considered suitable or unsuitable for submission to the jurisdiction of the Centre that only the disputes arising directly out of investment activites which have obtained necessary permission, in conformity with the relevant legislation of the Republic of Turkey on foreign capital, and that have effectively started shall be subject to the jurisdiction of the Centre. However, the disputes, related to the property and real rights upon the real estates are totally under the jurisdiction of the Turkish courts and therefore shall not be submitted to jurisdiction of the Center."
http://www.worldbank.org/icsid/pubs/icsid-8/icsid-8-d.htm (visited 05/25/2002)

[131] Bezen, *supra* note 94.

[132] http://www.asser.nl/ica/wash_sign.htm#1 (visited 05/25/2002)

As a member of the UNECE, Turkey participated in the negotiated of the 1961 European Convention on International Commercial Arbitration. As Serdar Bezen rightly asserts, "The Convention was the first legislation with regard to international commercial arbitration in Turkish Law. Therefore, the convention contributed to the emergence of a number of new legislation on this matter."[133] On ratifying the 1958 New York Convention, like many developing countries, Turkey also made a "reciprocity reservation" and "commercial reservations".[134]

C. Relationship Between International Organizations and Turkey With Respect To Foreign Investment

1. The World Trade Organization (WTO)

Turkey is a member of the WTO. Turkey undertakes obligations as a developing country under various WTO agreements that deal with international investment such as TRIMs which prohibits practices that impede investment.[135] Through its strict state-to-state dispute settlement process, the WTO has compelled member states to amend their regulations in accordance with the WTO agreements. Turkey's accession was the culmination of series legislative reforms to improve the investment environment. Indeed as noted in section 5 of this chapter, Turkey has amended its foreign investment law by governmental decree. According to the 1998 WTO Press Release, "Turkey has faced no

---

[133] Bezen, *supra* note 94.

[134] http://www.asser.nl/ica/nyca-eng.htm#IT14 (visited 05/25/2002).

[135] WTO, *Turkey's Trade Agreement With the EU Leads to Improved Business Environment For All Foreign Investors and Traders*, PRESS/TPR/83, 7 October 1998, http://www.wto.org/new/tprb83.htm (visited 3/12/1999).

difficulty to harmonize its legislation with the new rules set forth in the Trade Related Investment Measures (TRIMs) Agreement." [136]

It is essential to note that Turkey lodged exemptions to the scope of the Most-Favoured Nation Treatment provision under the General Agreement on Trade and Services (GATS) with respect to protect its bilateral investment policies.[137] GATS Article II provides that each Member is required to "accord immediately and unconditionally to services and service suppliers of any other Member treatment no less favourable than that it accords to like services and service suppliers of any other Member." Article II/2 permits lodging exceptions to this principle. Turkey has lodged exemptions to GATS Article II for all sectors in terms of extending full national treatment for the investments of the nationals or companies of enumerated countries such as Germany, United States, Bangladesh and China. The reason for lodging these exceptions is to create favorable conditions for greater economic cooperation between Turkey and enumerated countries and to encourage investments by nationals and companies of one country in the territory of the other countries.[138]

2. The Organization for Economic Co-Operation and Development (OECD)

As analyzed in the Chapter 4, in order to promote the liberalization of international investment, the OECD establishes and enforces legal disciplines and undertakes analytical work with respect to foreign investment and its relationship to other

---

[136] *Id.*

[137] OECD, *Working Party of the Trade Committee, Trade and Investment Interface*, Paris, 11-12 September 1996, TD/TC/WP (96) 32, at 9.

[138] See other listed countries, *Id.* at 17.

policy disciplines such as labor relations, sustainable development, trade, taxation and competition policies. After Turkey became a member of the OECD, in 1961, Turkish economic policies progressively changed from state economy to market economy. Specifically, foreign investment policies changed according to the OECD legal instruments.

As analyzed in Chapter 4, the OECD has issued many legal instruments regarding foreign investment, such as OECD codes of Liberalization, Declaration and Decisions on International Investment and Multinational Enterprises. The OECD Codes (Code of Liberalization of Capital Movements and the Code of Liberalization of Current invisible Operations) provide a framework of notification, examination and consultations on the liberalization. As mentioned in Chapter 4, the Codes are a legally binding instrument and the main purpose of the Codes is that residents of different Member States be as free to transact business with each other as are residents of a single country. In order to reach this objective, the OECD Codes stipulate that Member States undertake a process of progressive liberalization, allowing reasonable scope for countries in different circumstances, mainly economic circumstances they face.[139]

Article 2 and 7 of the OECD Codes provide exception and derogation clauses for the process of progressive liberalization. Article 7 states that: "a. if its economic and financial situation justifies such a course, a member need not to take whole of the measures of liberalization provided for in Article 2(a)."[140] Turkey derogated to the OECD Codes in accordance with Article 7 till 1986 since its economic and financial

---

[139] Article 1, 2, 7 of the OECD Codes.

[140] *Id*. Article 7 of the OECD Codes, (visited 2/3/3000) www.oecd.org/daf/investment/legal_instruments/clcmart.htm

situation were not in good condition.[141] After withdrawing its general derogation to the OECD Codes, capital movement and invisible transactions have been liberalized to a great extent in Turkey.

In cohering to the OECD Codes, Turkey undertakes in particular the following obligations:

a. To notify the Organization of any existing measures affecting capital movements;

b. To apply any measures without discrimination among OECD Members;

c. To liberalize all the operations specified on the liberalization lists of the Codes, except with respect to items against which reservations are lodged;

d. Not to introduce any new restrictions which would not be covered by reservations.[142]

Turkey lodged reservations in accordance with the Article 2 of the OECD Codes. If we analyze Turkey's reservations to the OECD Codes, we can find out that Turkey did not make many reservations to the Code of Liberalization of Current Invisible Operations.[143] Maritime freights, inland waterway freights, road transport, insurance, are some of the sectors about which Turkey lodged reservations.[144] However, this does not

---

[141] RAMAZAN ULUDAG, TURKIYEDE YABANCI SERMAYE UYGULAMASI, (FOREIGN INVESTMENT PRACTICE IN TURKEY) 215 (1991).

[142] OECD, The Experience of the OECD with the Code of Liberalization of Capital Movements, (visited 2/3/2000) < http://www.oecd.org/daf/investment/legal_instruments/oecdexp.htm>, at 2.

[143] ULUDAG, *supra* note 141, at 216.

[144] OECD, *Turkey: Reservations to the Code of Liberalization of Current Invisible Operations*, (Visited 12/28/2000) <htpp://www.oecd.org/daf/investment/country/turkey.htm>

mean that all these sectors' transactions by foreign investors are prohibited. Further, most reservations are limited reservations. For example, the reservation on the Road transport applies only to the enumerated operations.[145]

On the other hand, Turkey made reservations mostly for securities market issues to the Code of Liberalization of Capital Movements.[146] With respect to direct investment, Turkey also lodges reservations. For instance, Article 1 of the operations covered by the OECD Capital Movements Code states that:

Investment for the purpose of establishing lasting economic relations with an undertaking such as, in particular, investments which give the possibility of exercising an effective influence on the management thereof:

A. In the Country concerned by non-residents by means of:

1. Creation or extension of a wholly owned enterprise, subsidiary or branch, acquisition of full ownership of an existing enterprises;

2. Participation in a new or existing enterprises;

3. A loan of five years or longer....[147].

Turkey lodged a reservation to this article. The reservation states that:

The reservation applies

---

[145] Article C/3 "Road transport: passengers, and freights, including chartering. Remark: The reservation applies to the following operations: a) for passengers; -transit,-picking up or setting down on an international journey, transport within the country: b) for freights: -transit, -delivery on an international journey; -collection on an international journey, -return cargo where collection is authorized, -return cargo where delivery is authorized, -transport within the country." OECD, Code of Liberalization of Current Invisible Operations, May 2001, at 93.

[146] See detail reservations from OECD, *Turkey: Reservations to the Code of Liberalization of Capital Movements*, (visited 12/28/2000) http://www.oecd.org/daf/investment/country/turkey.htm

[147] *Id*. OECD, The OECD Code of Liberalization of Capital Movements, (visited 2/3/2000) http://www.oecd.org/daf/investment/legal_instruments/clcmoper.htm

i) investment in the mining sector, except through a company to be established in Turkey;

ii) investment in exploration and exploitation of petroleum by enterprises controlled or owned by foreign states, unless an authorization is granted;

iii) investment in refining, transportation through pipelines and storage of petroleum, unless an authorization is granted;

iv) investment in all sectors, if the value of the investment is less than US $50, 000.[148]

Furthermore, Turkey has reservations on operations in real estate. Turkey has also notified following reciprocity provision, listed in Annex E to the Capital Movements Code: " Foreign investment in banking and financial services sector other than insurance may be subject to a reciprocity requirement."[149]

Apart from reservations to the OECD Codes, Turkey substantially eliminated restriction on foreign investment in line with the OECD Codes. The establishment of modern exchange and the stock and securities market, the liberalization of capital movements, and the reform of the banking sector are the results of international obligations regarding the OECD Codes. As mentioned earlier in this chapter, Turkey adopts a new approach to promote foreign investment. The following legal reforms can be deemed as the results of the Turkey's commitment to the OECD legal instruments. The Department of Foreign Investment was created so as to strengthen the program in

---

[148] OECD, *Turkey: Reservations to the Code of Liberalization of Capital Movements*, (visited 12/28/2000) http://www.oecd.org/daf/investment/country/turkey.htm

[149] *Id.*

addition to lessening the bureaucratic transactions. All restrictions on foreign currency movements were repealed with Decree No.32 concerning the "Protection of the Value of Turkish Currency" in 1985. In addition, Turkish Laws guaranteed that profits, fees, royalties, dividends, and capital can be transferred freely.

As noted Chapter 4, the Declaration on Foreign Investment and Multinational Enterprises (The Declaration) was adopted in June 1976. In March 1981, Turkey acceded to the 1976 OECD Declaration and Decisions. Unlike the OECD Codes, the Declaration is not a legally binding instrument. However, member states are willing to implement the Declaration. Turkey has since established a National Contact Point under government authority to deal with all matters regarding the Guidelines, as is the case for all member countries. In addition, Turkey lodged exceptions to the National Treatment Instrument for Mining, Banking, Insurance, Air-transport, Maritime transport, Real estate/ Retail trade and Education sectors.[150] For example, in the insurance sector, reciprocity conditions apply in Turkey. Further, for real estate, foreign-controlled enterprises are prohibited from engaging in real estate trading, except for acquisitions related to their permitted operations.[151]

The OECD Convention on Combating Bribery of Foreign Public Officials in International Business Transactions entered into force on February 15, 1999. The signatory countries have committed themselves to amend applicable laws to specifically provide that foreign, as well as domestic, bribes are illegal and not tax deductible. Turkey is a signatory to this convention. Furthermore, the Turkish Grand Nation

---

[150] OECD, *Turkey: Exceptions reported under the National Treatment Instrument*, (visited 12/28/2000) http://www.oecd.org/daf/investment/country/turkey.htm

[151] *Id.*

Assembly approved the legislation for the ratification of the convention on, February 1, 2000 and the ratification bill entered into force on February 6, 2000.[152] Turkey deposited its instrument of ratification to the OECD Secretary General on July 26, 2000.[153] In addition, the draft bill on the implementation of the convention, which was approved by the Ministry of Justice and the Prime Minister, was submitted to Parliament on November 3, 2000.[154]

Turkey participated in the OECD's negotiations on a multilateral agreement on investment (MAI), which combined disciplines in three areas of FDI rule making: investment protection, investment liberalization and dispute settlement. At the outset of the negotiations, the Turkish public was so engaged with internal political developments that there was no substantial debate over the MAI.[155] However, in the later stages of the negotiations, the Turkish public criticized the MAI negotiations as a new capitulation. Turkish governments argued that signing the MAI would be helpful for the foreign investment flow and the economic development of Turkey.

Like all of the other OECD Countries, Turkey notified exemptions for the MAI. Most of the reservations that were filed had already been lodged as a reservation to the OECD Investment Instruments. For example, air transportation, maritime transportation, retail trade, real estate, mining, petroleum are the sectors that Turkey lodged reservations

---

[152] OECD, *Steps Taken and Planned Future Actions by each Participating Country to Ratify and Implement the Convention of Combating Bribery of Foreign Public Officials in International Business Transactions*, (visited 1/17/2001) www.oecd.org/daf/nocorruption/annex 2.htm

[153] *Id.*

[154] *Id.*

[155] Haldun Armagan, *A Free Trade Too Far? Turkish Technocrats Champion MAI*, August, 1997 (visited 8/25/1998), http://www.worldpaper.com/Aug97/armagan.html

to the OECD Investment Instruments.[156] However, as Tony Clark observed, Turkey made reservation with respect to the investor-state dispute settlement process by reserving certain laws that will nullify the MAI's substantive rules and the purpose of the treaty.[157]

3. Turkey-European Community (EC) Relationship

The history of the relationship between Turkey and the European Community has been a heavyhearted story. Turkey applied for the first time for association with the European Economic Community (EEC) on July 31, 1959. An agreement establishing an association between the EEC and Turkey, so called Ankara Agreement, was signed on

---

[156] Turkey made following reservations to the MAI: "1-Law No. 6224, Dispute Resolution does not cover pre-establishment phase of investment, 2-Law 6224, Minimum US 50 000 required for foreign investment; authorization needed for all foreign investment (mainly statistical purpose), 3-All sectors-Dispute Resolution : once established , foreign investments are considered Turkish companies under administrative law and so cannot use investor to state dispute resolution, 4-Medical; only Turkish citizen can be doctors, nurses, pharmacists, vets, opticians, 5-Law no.2007; only Turkish citizens can be peddlers, brokers, musicians, photographers, typesetters, etc., 6-Land Registration Act (Law NO 2644) , restrictions on foreign land ownership not needed for business activities, 7. Air transport- domestic flights- Turkish companies only, 8. Maritime transport- cabotage act 815- national flag only for Turkish controlled companies, 9. Retail trade- no foreign investors except hyper markets, 10. Real estate- no foreign investment in real estate trading; foreign acquisition of land outside municipal boundaries is restricted, 11. Fishing/ fish processing- fishing Law No. 1380- Foreign investment allowed in fish processing but not fishing, 12. Mining- foreign investment in mining only through locally incorporated companies, 13. Petroleum- Petroleum Law No. 6326- marketing/selling- no restrictions; exploration/exploitation- no foreign state companies; pipeline/ refining- need government approval, must establish Turkish branch or company, 14. Broadcasting Law No. 3984- each foreign investor limited to investment in one broadcasting company (up to 20% ownership), 15. Port services/ privatization- Turkish only, 16. Banking- Act 3182- approval required for establishment and opening of first branch, 17. Financial services- approval required to operate in financial advisory industry, 18. Foreign non banking securities companies can't establish branches, 19. Mutual funds- must have Turkish subsidiary to offer mutual funds, 20. Portfolio agents- require authorization, 21. Financial leasing companies- foreign owned get less favorable treatment than domestic with regard to paid in capital, 22. Branch manager of foreign insurance company must live in Turkey, 23. Insurance-limited to consultancy/ risk management in auxiliary insurance functions, 24. No branches of foreign non bank intermediary institutions, 25Reciprocity for foreign investment in banking and financial services.", Tony Clarke, *The Multilateral Agreement on Investment, The Council of Canadians*, (visited 1/15/1999) http://www.canadians.org/reservations.html

[157] *Id.* Tony Clarke, *The Multilateral Agreement on Investment, The Council of Canadians*, (visited 1/15/1999) http://www.canadians.org/reservations.html

September 12, 1963, and entered into force on December 1, 1964. Turkey applied for membership in the European Community on April 14, 1987. The Commission citing both economic and political reasons rejected the application on December 18, 1989. However, the Commission recognized that the European Community should pursue its cooperation with Turkey, given the country's general opening towards Europe. During the last European Union Submit held in Helsinki on December 10, 1999, Turkey was finally recognized as a formal candidate for full membership. Ironically, Turkey is the European Community's longest standing associate, and for the past 38 years, Turkey has participated practically all of the activities in international bodies involved in European integration. A detailed examination of the relationship between the EC and Turkey falls outside of the scope of this dissertation.

It is worth noting that in spite of Turkey's not having been accepted as a member of the EC, Turkey has continued to improve her legal and economic reform in line with EC laws and policies. With respect to free movement of capital between the EC and Turkey, there were many provisions set out in Article 20, 50, 51 and 52 of the Ankara Agreement and the Additional Protocol. The aims of the Agreement are to encourage capital movements between EEC countries and Turkey, and to encourage the investment of those countries in Turkey. According to the Article 51 of the Agreement, favorable conditions for foreign investments by EEC countries in Turkey will be provided if these investments contribute to Turkish development. Even though there are no obligatory rules and no enforcement mechanism concerning liberalization of capital movements under the Association, Turkey has progressively liberalized her legal and economic instruments with respect to foreign investment.[158] Indeed, the Ankara Agreement and the Additional Protocol do not impose any obligations upon Turkey; they simply intend the encouragement of the type of foreign capital investment that affects economic development positively.

The "Commission Regular Report on Turkey's Progress Towards Accession" explicitly points out Turkish liberalization process of foreign investment instruments in the following: "Owing to its obligations under the OECD Codes of Capital Movements, Turkey's regime is substantially liberal in some areas. However, to comply the acquis, liberalization must be extended to all transactions and authorization procedures must be abolished."[159] The EU report recommends to Turkey lift the restrictions which are still in place on certain sectors such as mining, transportation, banking and real estate so as to assure the free movement of capital between the EC and Turkey.[160]

The Customs Union Agreement between the European Union and Turkey came into force on January 1, 1996, thereby creating the closest economical and political relationship between the EU and any non-member country. Under the Custom Union Agreement, Turkey is obligated to eliminate its tariffs and levies on imports of manufactured products from the EU. By all means, a custom union requires not just abolition of tariffs and quotas between the EU and Turkey, but a common trade policy. Thus, Turkey is obliged to change the common custom tariff on MFN basis on imports from third countries. Full adoption of EC trade policy is postponed for five years.

---

[158] European Union, Regular Report from the Commission on Progress towards Accession, Turkey, November 4, 1998.

[159] European Union, Turkey 2000, Regular Report, From the Commission on Turkey' Progress Towards, Accession, 8 November (2000).

[160] Id.

Moreover, under the Agreement, Turkey must adopt the EC's tariff preferences and negotiate preferential agreements with third states over this five-year period. The main features of custom union concerning foreign investment are:

1- The adoption by Turkey of legislation in the field of intellectual property protection to guarantee a level of protection equivalent to that in the EC.

2- Agreed competition rules and the alignment by Turkey of its legislation in this area with that of the EC.

The EU Customs Union Agreement has positive effects. With respect to foreign investment, it can be argued that the establishment of Custom Union with the EU will encourage FDI in Turkey.[161] Successful conclusion of this agreement will reduce the risk of investing in Turkey since the new legal framework for the intellectual property rights and the Competition rules will establish transparent and predictable legal environment for foreign investors.[162] In addition, third country investors may want to take advantage of new export opportunities with other EC member countries.

a.   **Intellectual Property Rights**

Turkey unfortunately for years has lacked adequate, effective, and contemporary laws concerning intellectual property rights. However, there has been significant progress on the legislative front in early 1995. This was impelled mainly by Turkey's

---

[161] Glenn W. Harrison, Thomas F. Rutherford, David G. Tarr, *Economic Implications for Turkey of a Custom Union with the European Union,* The World Bank, Policy Research Working Paper 1599, 4 (1998).

[162] On the other hand, Pursuant to the OECD Economic Survey: "FDI inflows in 1996 were a relatively modest $10 billion, little changed from 1995, despite expectations of stronger inflows following the Customs Union. However, there was a sharp pick-up in foreign capital permits issued at the end of 1996, and measures are being considered to expedite the entry of foreign capital through waiving minimum capital requirements and by extending domestic incentives to FDI related to modernization".

desire to enter into a customs union with the European Union on January 1, 1996. Article 31 of the Decision of the Association Council No 1/95, dated March 6, 1995 stipulated that Turkey must ensure adequate and effective protection and enforcement of intellectual property rights.[163]

The agreement with the EU requires to Turkey meet EU standards for IP protection, which are essentially the same as standards agreed to in the Uruguay round. Turkey is a member of the World Trade Organization and a party to the Trade related aspects of intellectual property (TRIPS) Agreement.[164] Turkey is also a member of the World Intellectual Property Organization (WIPO). As a member of WIPO, Turkey guarantees nationals of other member states the same protection of intellectual property rights as Turkish nationals. In addition, Turkey became a party to a number of International conventions in 1995, including the Patent Cooperation Treaty, Nice, Vienna, and Strasbourg Agreements, and Stockholm Act of the Paris Convention so as to align its legislation with the EC rules.[165]

---

[163] Article 31 of the Decision. Decision No. 1/95 of the EC-Turkey Association Council of 22 December 1995 on implementing the final phase of custom union (96/142/EC), Official Journal No. L 035, 13/02/1996, P. 001-0047

[164] The TRIPS Agreement has entered into force in all member states in January 1, 1995. As it is well known that the developed countries had 1 year transition period for adoption of national legislation making them being compatible to TRIPS Agreement. As a Developing Country, Turkey had 5 years for transition the provisions of TRIPS to her national legislation. However, Turkey has adopted its national intellectual property rights legislation in June 1995.

[165] Following Agreements are adhered by Turkey: Law No. 4117 on adoption to the Paris Act (1971) related to Bern Convention (Turkish Official Gazette, July 12, 1995), Law No. 4116 on adoption to Rome Convention (1961), (Turkish Official Gazette, July 12, 1995), Decree No. 95/7094 on adoption to Nice Agreement, Law No. 4115 on adoption to Patent Cooperation Treaty (1970, including amendments), Decree No. 95/7094 on adoption to Vienna Agreement on figurative elements of Trademarks, (Turkish Official Gazette, No.22373, August 13, 1995), Decree No. 5093 on adoption of Stockholm Text of the Paris Agreement on the Protection of Industrial Property.

Turkey has rapidly and successfully modified and harmonized its regulations concerning intellectual property rights in order to assure the implementation of the Custom Union. In 1995, Turkish Parliament issued the new regulations, including new patent, trademark, industrial design and geographic signs laws, and amendments to the copyright law.[166]

This new legislation, while offering improvements, does not fully answer a number of key developed countries concerns, e.g., with protection for pre-existing works, sanctions against violators, or pharmaceuticals protection.[167] Over the past several years, Turkey has largely improved protection of intellectual property rights. However, there is still a need to pursue this process on the basis of considering the own requirements of a developing country.[168] It is necessary to create a coherent IPR enforcement system in Turkey so as to combat piracy. Due to Turkey's inadequate enforcement mechanism for protection of intellectual property rights, the United States has still listed Turkey on the "priority watch list" of countries, which fail to protect American firms' intellectual property rights, as stipulated under the Special 301 provisions of the 1988 US Trade Act.

---

[166] Following Legislation enacted by Turkey for the adoption of the intellectual property rights: Law No; 544 Dated June 24, 1994 for Establishment and Functions of Turkish Patent Institute, Decree No. 95/551 on the Protection of Patent Rights (Turkish Official Gazette No. 22326, dated June 27, 1995), Decree No. 556 on the Protection of Trademarks (Turkish Official Gazette No. 22326, dated June 27, 1995), Decree No 554 on the Protection of Industrial Designs (Turkish Official Gazette No. 22326, dated June 27, 1995), Decree No. 555 on the Protection of Geographical Indicators (Turkish Official Gazette No. 22326, dated June 27, 1995), Law No. 4128 on the Arrangement of Penalty Provisions Related to Industrial Property Rights, Law No 4110 amending Several Provisions of the Law No. 5848 on Intellectual and Artistic Work, (Turkish Official Gazette No. 22311, dated June 27, 1995)

[167] Ergun Ozsunay, *The New Turkish Trademark Law*, 19 FORDHAM INT'L L. J. 1542 (1996).

[168] The United States Trade Commission Special 301 Report states that : "Remaining work needs to be done to enhance Turkey's copyright regime to include copyright protection for pre-existing works and sound recordings and ex parte and injunctive relief, and to include deterrent penalties and jail terms. Passage of amendments to the copyright law to address these concerns is anticipated in the near future, and we urge expeditious legislative action. With respect to enforcement, efforts have increased to curb copyright piracy, but remain ineffective.".

There is no doubt that Turkey will continue to harmonize its intellectual property law not only to keep pace with developments in the world community, but also to create better environment for foreign investment.

b.   Competition Law

Under the Turkish Constitution drafted in 1982, the protection of free competition is a constitutional responsibility for the State. Indeed, Article 167 of the Turkish Constitution states that a State must take all necessary measures to provide and improve the proper functioning of the markets for goods and services, capital credits and money. Further a State must prevent the formation, in practice or by agreement, of monopolies and cartels in the markets.[169] Even though the Turkish Constitution has a basis for the adoption of the Competition Law, there was no sufficient attempt to adopt the Competition Law till 1990s.[170]

The introduction of Competition Law is the result of the international obligations regarding the Custom Union Decision with EC. For example, Article 39 of the Decision of the Association Council No 1/95, dated on March 6, 1995 states that: "with a view to achieving the economic integration sought by the Customs Union, Turkey shall ensure that its legislation in the field of competition rules is made compatible with that of the

---

[169] Article 167 of Turkish Constitution states that: " The State shall take measures to ensure and promote the sound, orderly functioning of the money, credit, capital, goods and services markets; and shall prevent the formation, in practice or by agreement, of monopolies and cartels in the markets. In order to regulate foreign trade for the benefit of the economy of the country, the Council of Ministers may be empowered by law to introduce or lift additional financial impositions on imports, exports and other foreign transactions in addition to tax and similar impositions.

[170] DOC.DR. BILGIN TIRYAKIOGLU, REKABET HUKUKUNDAN DOGAN KANUNLAR IHLITAFI, (Conflicts of Law in Competition Law), 15 (1997).

European Community..."[171] Furthermore, the articles 32,33 and 41 of the same Decision provide competition rules to be applied for the proper functioning of the Custom Union.[172] Turkey is obliged not only to adopt a law prohibiting anti-competitive practices of companies under the conditions laid down in Article 85 and 86 of the EC Treaty, but also to effectively implement the competition rules and principles of the EC.[173]

Accordingly, Turkey Parliament passed the Law No. 4054 on Protection of Competition on 7th December 1994, and this Law entered into force as of 13 December 1994 following the publication on the Official Gazette.[174] The Act is largely based on the main principles of the EC antitrust rules. The objective set out in the Law is to: "establish a system ensuring the necessary regulation, supervision and prevention of abuse of dominant position by undertakings and agreements, decision and concerted practices which have as their object or effect the prevention, restriction or distortion of competition".[175] Thus, the Law prohibits the agreements, decisions and concerned practices between undertakings which have as their object or effect the prevention, restriction or distortion of competition, the abuse of dominant position and unlawful mergers and acquisitions.

---

[171] Decision No. 1/95 of the EC-Turkey Association Council of 22 December 1995 on implementing the final phase of custom union (96/142/EC), Official Journal No. L 035, 13/02/1996, P. 001-0047.

[172] *Id.*

[173] TIRYAKIOGLU, *supra* note 170, at 16. Turkey has accepted the effectiveness of the case-law constituted by the Institutions of the EC pursuant to the article 39(2)(a) of the Decision of the Association Council No. 1/95. Thus the cases of EC Court of Justice have been adopted to the national legislation.

[174] The Law on the Protection of Competition Law No: 4054, dated 7.12.1994 Turkish Official Gazette No. 22140, dated 13.12.1994.

[175] *Id.* The Law on the Protection of Competition Law No: 4054, dated 7.12.1994 Turkish Official Gazette No. 22140, dated 13.12.1994.

Unfortunately, although the Law was enacted in 1994, it was not applied until 1997. This is due to the fact that the Council of Ministers never appointed the members of the Competition Board, which is the decision making body of the Competition Administration, and responsible for the application of this law. [176] The Competition Board was established to enforce the Law on February 27, 1997.[177] Pursuant to the Article 20 of the Law, the Competition Administration has a legal personality and administrative and financial independence.[178]

Overall, Turkey has successfully adopted the Competition Law in line with EC rules.[179] EC Regular report on Turkey states that: "The application of antitrust provisions appears satisfactory with a considerable number of cases having been dealt with from the start of the operation of the Competition Authority."[180] The same report spells out that further amendment is necessary in terms of the EC's new policies on block exemptions for vertical restraints and on block exemptions for horizontal cooperation agreements.[181]

VI. Concluding Remarks on Turkish Foreign Investment Policies

Turkey has already established a liberalized national regimen to govern FDI. Encouragement of foreign investment is among the primary objectives of the Turkish

---

[176] Prof. Arif Esin, *The Impact of Competition Law on Foreign Direct Investment*, Insight Yased. (1999).

[177] Law. No. 97/9090 on Appointment of the Competition Board, Turkish Official Gazette, Dated 27 February 1997.

[178] *Id.* Law No. 22140, In addition, Article 20 states that: "... The Administration shall perform its duties independently. No body, authority, person or institution may order or instruct to influence the final decisions of the Administration. ..."

[179] See an overview of the activities of the Competition Authority, OECD Report, Turkey 1999, http://www.oecd.org//daf/clp/Annual_reports/1999-00/turkey.pdf

[180] *Id.* European Union, Turkey 2000, *Regular Report, From the Commission on Turkey' Progress Towards, Accession*, 8 November 2000.

[181] *Id.*

government's policy. Accordingly, Turkey has a liberal investment regime in which foreign investments receive national treatment. Almost all areas open to the Turkish private sectors are also open to foreign participation and investment. In addition, the size and growth of the market, and the progressive industrialization as well as the favorable export possibilities towards Eurasia, Eastern Europe and the Near East represent the main market advantages of Turkey.[182] It is worth mentioning that after the collapse of the Soviet Union, Turkey has rightly changed her strategy to improve economic and trade relations in the Eurasian market. This market includes Central Asia, the Caucasus, and the countries of the Black Sea.[183] Turkey has historic, cultural and linguistic ties with most of the countries in these regions. Turkey does not only seek to improve relations in trade but also actually encourages foreign investors to make investment in Turkey.

International rules become effective and significant when they are able to translate into appropriate and compatible legal frameworks within Turkey. It is evident that countries have started taking steps toward making their national rules complementary to internationally agreed rules. Turkey is convinced of the importance of foreign investment and the need for transparent and fair rules for investors and investments. Turkey's legal development on FDI issues is one of the examples from this transition period for the reconstructing of its legal framework through adopting international rules on FDI.

Indeed, this chapter concludes that Turkey is taking continuous steps towards updating and harmonizing its foreign investment legislation with its commitments under

---

[182] Bircanoglu & Bircanoglu, *supra* note 34.

[183] *Id.*

the OECD instrument, the WTO Agreements, and the EC rules. With such legal developments, particularly in international arbitration, competition, and intellectual property laws, Turkey offers an open and secure environment for foreign investors.

It should be noted that there is still a weak flow of foreign investment into Turkey. Some of the shortcomings for promoting foreign investments are: political instability, economic instability, lack of adequate law enforcement, limited privatization, corruption, and inefficient bureaucratic process.[184] For example, the debates on the privatization process of the telecommunication sector, and the corruption investigations especially on private bank sectors, prevented foreign investors from investing in Turkey. In addition, unfortunately Turkish economy has substantial fundamental problems including hyperinflation, high interest rates, large budget deficits and strongly depreciating currency.[185] One of the biggest economic problems Turkey has is the high inflation rate, which needs to be knocked down. Moreover, even though the Turkish government has pursued open foreign investment policies in energy sectors, administrative courts and the Constitutional court ruling have delayed many energy projects. However, it is good to observe that the new amendments at the Turkish Constitution can help address this problem. These deficiencies must be overcome so as to attract the FDI, and eventually complete the Turkish government's program on economic liberalization.

---

[184] YASED submitted report called "Foreign Investors' Outlook Towards the investment Environment in Turkey: Problems and Suggestions" to the Deputy Minister Husamettin Ozkan in December 20, 2000. <http:// www.yased.org.tr/en/reports/annuals_00.htm> (visited 10/21/2001).

[185] Helmut Ziegelschmidt, *OECD Observer*, Turkey, June 1, (1994).

On the basis of the foregoing, the Turkish Foreign Investment Law (TFIL) needs further modification or redrafting since it does not provide specifically for the following issues: fair and equitable treatment, expropriation, and dispute settlement procedure. One of the problems regarding transparency of the TFIL is that after modifying it by Decrees, Turkish authorities did not clearly mention these amendments in the Law. Thus, it is really hard to understand some amendments. Therefore, Turkey should revise its TFIL in order to stimulate foreign investment. The new law should be drafted both to provide foreign investors with the basic guarantees necessary to promote FDI and to avoid unclear provisions that might otherwise impede FDI.

Indeed, in order to further liberalize the TFIL and to stimulate foreign investment and to overcome the deficiencies that were identified by foreign investors, in consultation with a YASED, the Turkish government drafted a new law, which is still being scrutinized by the Turkish parliament.[186] However, there has been no indication by the Turkish parliament regarding when this draft will be approved. It is good to observe that the non-governmental organization YASED was involved in the formulation of this draft.

The draft law was designed to avoid unclear provisions or provisions that might impede FDI. If the draft law is approved by the Turkish parliament in the form in which it has been drafted, the new law might solve the problems that foreign investors face. One of the most important changes in the law is to eliminate "permission process" in which the Treasury Under secretariat has discretionary power to screen the investment.

---

[186] YABANCI SERMAYE KANUN TASARISI, (Draft Law on Foreign Investment),Number, 1/774, Date, 06/11/2000, Turkish Parliament, www.tbmm.gov.tr/develop/owa/tasari_teklif_ss.ilgili_komisyonlar?kanunlar_sira_no, (visited 11/8/2001), YASED Foreign Investors Association, ANNUAL REPORT 2000, at 3. http://www.yased.org.tr/en/reports/annual_00.htm (visited 10/21/2001).

[187] The draft law stipulates "registration process" only for tax information. With the amendments of the permission process, the draft law also amends Article 1 of the law that requires conditions such as "the investors' activities must be in a field of activity open to Turkish private sector and they do not consist of monopoly in Turkey." This amendment clarifies the current legal situation of these requirements due to the fact that the Turkish government enacted competition law that governs the monopoly and other competition issues, and with the privatization process almost every sector is open to private sector.

Unlike the TFIL, the draft stipulates that the foreign investors must inform their investment activities to the Under secretariat.[188] Pursuant to Article 6 of the Draft, the Turkish government has ability to observe transnational corporations' behavior. As we analyzed in the Chapter 5 and 6, developing countries and NGOs rightly demand a "balanced approach" for the negotiation of multilateral investment treaties. That is to say that the agreement should grant rights and duties for foreign investors. The draft is based on a "balanced approach". In addition, it is possible to argue that the Turkish government included this provision into the draft in order to comply with the OECD Declaration on Foreign Investment and Multinational Enterprises.

The draft includes a provision that confirms the Turkish government's point of view towards international law. Article 3 of the draft states, "The special provisions contained in international treaties and laws are guaranteed by law."[189] In addition, unlike the TFIL, the draft is designated in a very clear and specific language. For example, the

---

[187] *Id.* YASED, ANNUAL REPORT (2000).

[188] Article 6 of the Draft states: Foreign firm falling under the scope of this Law are required to provide the Undersecretariat with information regarding their operations within the framework of the procedures and principles laid down by the Council of Ministers." English version of the draft was send from YASED via email.

[189] *Id.* Art.3 of the Draft Law on Foreign Investment.

purpose of the draft is explained in one sentence: "This Law governs the principles relating to the framing of foreign investment policies and the operations of foreign investors in Turkey for the purpose of increasing foreign investment."[190]

The draft also altered the existing provision regarding the determination of the "value of capital". According to the present law, the assessment is made by experts to be appointed by the Undersecretariat. However, the draft grants assessment authority to officials appointed under the regulation of home states, or international assessing firms.[191]

---

[190] *Id.* Article 1 of the Draft Law on Foreign Investment

[191] *Id.* Article 2 of the Draft states, "… The value of capital apart from cash shall be determined within the framework of the provisions of Turkish Commercial Law. If, however, stocks of companies incorporated in foreign countries are put down as capital, they shall be assessed either by officials authorized to make such assessments under the legislation of the country of origin, or by experts to be appointed by the courts of the country of origin, or by international assessing firms."

CHAPTER TEN. CONCLUSION

The international foreign investment law consists of various national and international instruments. The existing international legal framework includes customary international law, bilateral investment treaties, international organizations' activities, and multilateral agreements. This study concludes that there is an interaction between national and international rules on FDI. Most countries amend their investment policies and laws in response to changes and developments in international investment law. If there will be a multilateral agreement on investment, this interaction will be completed. In addition, the investment rules will be more transparent.

Customary International law and national laws on FDI are still the prominent sources of international foreign investment law. Even though customary international law is the most problematic area of international law, it recognizes the fundamental principle of international foreign investment law that the host countries have the right to regulate admission of foreign investment. Most countries have special laws govern foreign investment in order to promote their economic development through granting investment protection rights and incentives to foreign investors. Most countries' laws align with the development on international investment law.

As a case study, this thesis analyzed the Turkish foreign investment regimen. Changes in national and global economic conditions have led the Turkish government to change its policies on FDI. Since 1980s, the Turkish government has made gradual and great progress in developing laws to promote and facilitate foreign investment. The Turkish government attributes considerable importance to foreign investment for its economic development. Indeed, Turkey is taking continuous steps towards updating and harmonizing its relevant regulations in accordance with the OECD instruments, the EU regulations on FDI, and the WTO agreements.

Most governments also seek to improve the legal framework for FDI at the bilateral, regional and international level. Bilateral investment treaties (BITs) have played an important role in the development of international foreign investment law. Although, like other legal scholars, I contend that BITs constitute *lex specialis*, establishing treaty rights and obligations for the parties, they do have impact on two issues in international law: the subject matter of international law, and the protection of shareholder's right. For example, as analyzed in the Barcelona Traction case, with out any agreement, the shareholders do not have the right to have resource claim against violation of their investment protection. In addition, BITs can induce countries to revamp their laws.

The international organizations such as the UN, the OECD, the regional organizations (such as the EU, the ASEAN), and the WTO play an essential role in developing international rules on FDI through legally binding or non- binding instruments. In addition, the international organizations provide technical and logistic help to their members to enact and to amend foreign investment laws in line with the new developments, and to host bilateral investment negotiations.

Most of the legal instruments negotiated or adopted by international organizations can be considered "soft law", non-binding rules. This does not mean that soft law rules do not have an impact on international foreign investment law. Many countries can adopt the guidelines, the model laws, and the declarations in their legal system. For example,

Turkey adopted the UNCITRAL Arbitration Model Law and the OECD Guidelines for Multinational Enterprises.

There is no comprehensive multilateral agreement on investment. However, there are multilateral agreements that are some how related to foreign investment. The WTO agreements cover some aspects of investment such as the TRIMS, and the GATS agreement. In addition, MIGA Convention provides insurance for political risk which promotes legal security for investors. These agreements can be utilized as examples for future negotiations on investment. For example, the MIGA's provisions on "exclusion of creeping expropriation", and "providing exhaustion of local remedies", can be considered as an impetus for the future agreement since these provisions grant feasibility and flexibility for most developing countries.

This study analyzed the MAI draft treaty and the WTO conference in Seattle in terms of their failure. There are lessons to be learned from the MAI negotiations, and the failure of the WTO conference in Seattle both in relation to substance and the procedure for future negotiations on FDI.

RECOMMENDATIONS

The followings are the recommendations for a possible negotiation on multilateral agreement on investment:

With respect to procedure of negotiation process:

- International organizations should closely work together in any future negotiations on FDI. In particular, the work done by other international organizations should be taken into account. For example, the UNCTAD's work on the development perspective of foreign investment should be taken into account by the working group.

- Pre-establishment phrase of negotiations should be well organized.
- The negotiation process should be democratic and transparent. Internal transparency and external transparency should be provided through involving more national delegates, and civil society groups. The number of participants in the negotiations on behalf of the negotiating countries should be increased in a way that participants can work in coherence with government and at the same time let public and especially opposition parties know the negotiation process. There should be a mechanism in order to exchange information among civil society groups and representatives of government.
- Developing countries should participate actively in the negotiation process. In order to provide their active involvement, the international organizations such as UNCTAD should continue technically and financially help them.
- NGOs attendance for the negotiation process should be well designed. NGOs should have some sort of legal status and they should participate in negotiations at least as an "advisor" status. Their selection in the negotiation process should depend on whether they have code of conduct or not. There should be a mechanism for their registration, as seems to have been the case with the World Bank Group and the WTO.
- The regional commissions should play a leading role in organizing the negotiation process of the multinational investment treaty since they fortify the negotiation capacities of developing countries in the areas of FDI. The regional commissions can provide "technical backstopping" for developing countries, supporting such

countries' participation in negotiations of the multilateral agreement on investment. In addition, they can bring regional perspectives to global problems.

With respect to substantive and procedural issues on Agreement:
- "Gradual liberalization" and "bottom up" approaches should be accepted in the negotiation process. GATS should be utilized as a model for this approach because the progressive liberalization process has been successfully adopted in the GATS agreement. This model is the best option for developing countries because they can opt which sector is available for market access.
- A balanced approach should be the basis on any international investment agreement. The agreement should provide a balance between investor's rights and responsibilities. The agreement should regulate the control of transnational corporations' activities such as competition, the protection of environment, corrupt practices, and money laundering in order to contribute to achieving balanced approach. In order to do that, the agreement should take into account the draft UN Code of Conduct on Transnational Corporations, and the OECD Guidelines.
- The debated issues such as "environmental protection", and "labour rights" should be included in future agreement in a way that addressing the concerns of both developing and developed countries.
- The future agreement should be consistent with existing investment arrangements, particularly with WTO agreements related to FDI and the MIGA.
- The future agreement should provide investment protection through expropriation, and transfer fund provisions. The failure of the MAI shows that the "regulatory

taking" issue in expropriation provision should not be included in the future agreement.

- The future agreement should not prevent host countries from utilizing investment policies to promote their economic policy aims such as new job creation, export promotion, and technology transfer.

- As was analyzed in Chapter 5 and 6, one of the disagreements on substantive issues on the MAI was "the exception provisions". This shows that even developed countries cannot agree on exception issues. Thus, the future agreement should provide flexibility. Future agreement should provide rights to lodge exemptions in order to promote economic development. In addition, transitional period should be considered for developing countries.

- The future agreement should include dispute settlement procedures through providing a state-state and investor-state dispute settlement process.

BIBLIOGRAPHY

Abbott, Kenneth W., The Many Faces of International Legalization, American Society of International Law Proceedings, April 1-4, (1998).

Adair, Anthony, A Code of Conduct For NGOs- A Necessary Reform, October 1999, http://www.iea.org.uk/wpapers/NGO.htm, (visited 10/25/2001).

Adair, David R, Investors' Rights: The Evolutionary Process of Investment Treaties, Tulsa Journal of Comparative and International Law, 216 (1999).

Ahnlid, Anders, Special Topics, The Multilateral Agreement on Investment, State of Play as of February (1997).

Ahnlid, Anders, Performance Requirements and Investment Incentives, The Multilateral Agreement on Investment, State of Play in April (1997).

Aksen, Gerald R., Legal Principles and Practices Relating to Private Foreign Investment, Reporter, Matthew P. Jaffe, Amreican Society of International law Proceedings, April 14-16, (1983).

Ajay C, & Sweder van Wijnbergen, Public Policy and Private Investment In Turkey, (REVIVING PRIVATE INVESTMENT IN DEVELOPING COUNTRIES, Empirical Studies and Policy lessons, edited by A. Chhibber, M. Dailami and N. Shafik, 1992).

Ansay, Tugrul, Turkey, In legal Aspects of Foreign Investment, (Edited by W.G. Friedman, assisted by R.C Pugh), Columbia University International Legal Studies Program, (1959).

Asante, S.K.B, International law and Foreign Investment: A Reappraisal, International and Comparative law Quarterly, Vol.37, (1988).

ASEAN, Handbook of Investment Agreements in ASEAN, it can be found in ASEAN Homepage. http://www.aseansec.org (Visited 10/16/2001).

Baker, James C., FOREIGN DIRECT INVESTMENT IN LESS DEVELOPED COUNTRIES, THE ROLE OF ICSID AND MIGA, (1999).

Balkir, Canan, Turkey and the European Community: Foreign Trade and Direct Foreign Investment in the 1980s, in TURKEY AND EUROPE, (Canan Balkir & Allan M. Williams, eds., 1993).

Barchard, David, TURKEY INVESTING IN THE FUTURE, A Euromoney Publication, (1990).

Baumgartner, Chris, The Demise of the Multilateral Agreement on Investment, 1998 COLO J. INT'L ENVTL. L. & POL'Y. 40 , 44 (1998).

Bercero, Garcio, Functioning of the WTO System: Elements for Possible Institutional Reform, International Trade Law & Regulation, 105, (2000).

Bergman, Bergman Mark S., Bilateral Investment Protection Treaties: An Examination of the Evolution and Significance of the U.S. Prototype Treaty, 16 N. Y.U. J. INT'L L&POL. 1 (1983).

Beveridge, Fiona C., The Treatment and Taxation of Foreign Investment under International Law Towards International Disciplines, (2000).

Bezen, Serdar, Recent Developments in International Commercial Arbitration in Turkey, Mealey's International Reports, (2001).

Bircan Bircanoglu, Legal Report on Turkish Investment Law, (2000).

Bjorklund, Andrea K., Contract Without Privity: Sovereign Offer and Investor Acceptance, Chicago Journal of International Law, Spring (2001).

Blomstrom, Magnus & Ari Kokko, How Foreign Investment Affects Host Countries, The World Bank, Policy Research Working Paper, March (1997).

Bolivar, Omar Enrique Garcia, Issues for International Law of Foreign Investment, (http://www.geocities.com/CapitolHill/3421/fiart.htm) (visited by 3/1/1999).

Boswell, Nancy Zucker, , An Emerging Consensus on Controlling Corruption, 18 University of Pennsylvania Journal of International Economic Law. 1165 (1997).

Brewer, Thomas L. and Stephen Young, The MULTILATERAL INVESTMENT SYSTEM AND MULTINATIONAL ENTERPRISES, (1998).

Brewer, Thomas L. Brewer, International Investment Dispute Settlement Procedures: The Evolving Regime for Foreign Direct Investment, 26 LAW & POL'Y INT'L BUS. 633, (1995).

Buckley, Peter, & Necla V. Geyikdagi, Explaining Foreign Direct Investment in Turkey's Tourism Industry, Transnational Corporations, Vol. 5, NO. 3 (December 1996).

Burt, Eric. M., Developing Countries and the Framework for Negotiations on Foreign Direct Investment in the World Trade Organization, 12 AM. U. J. INT'L L. & POL'Y. 1015 (1997).

Camponovo, Christopher N., Dispute Settlement and the OECD Multilateral Agreement on Investment, UCLA Journal of International Law and Foreign Affairs, Spring (1996).

Canner, Stephen J., The Multilateral Agreement on Investment, 31 CORNELL INT'L L. J. 657 (1998).

Charnovitz, Steve, Two Centuries of Participation: NGOs and International Governance, 18 MICH. J. INT'L L. 183. (1997).

Charnovitz, Steve, Opening the WTO to Non Governmental Interests, 24 FORDHAM INT'L L. J. 173, (2000).

Charolles, Valerie, National Treatment, Most Favoured Nation Treatment and Transparency, OECD, Multilateral Agreement on Investment, State of Play as of February (1997).

Chhiber, Ajay & Sweder van Wijnbergen, Public Policy and Private Investment In Turkey, in REVIVING PRIVATE INVESTMENT IN DEVELOPING COUNTRIES, EMPRICAL STUDIES AND POLIY LESSONS 171-175 (A. Chhibber, M. Dailami & N. Shafik, eds. 1992).

Chinkin, C.M. The Challenge of Soft Law: Development and Change in International Law, 38 Int'l & Comp. L.Q. 850 (1989).

Christy III, Paul Bryan, Negotiating Investment in the GATT: A Call For Functionalism, 12 MICH. J. INT'L L. 743, (1991).

Civello, Paul, The TRIMS Agreement: A Failed Attempt At Investment Liberalization, 8 MINN. J. GLOBAL TRADE. 97, 103, (1999).

Comeaux, Paul E., N. Stephan Kinsella,. Reducing Political Risk in Developing Countries: Bilateral Investment Treaties, Stabalization Clauses, and MIGA & OPIC Investment Insurance, 15 N.Y.L. SCH. J. INT'L & COMP. L.1 , 45 (1994).

Craik, A. Neil, Recalcitrant Reality and Chosen Ideals: the Public Function of Dispute Settlement in International Environmental Law, 10 GEO. INT'L ENVTL. L. REV 551, 573 (1998).

Crane, William, Corporations Swallowing Nations: The OECD and The Multilateral Agreement on Investment, 9 COLO. J. INT'L ENVTL. L & POL'Y. 429, 458 (1998).

Crock, John R., Applicable Law in International Arbitration: The Iran-U.S. Claims Tribunal Experience, The American Journal International Law, April 1989, V. 83.

Dalrymple, Christopher K., Politics and Foreign Direct Investment: The Multilateral Investment Guarantee Agency and The Calvo Clause, 29 CORNELL INT'L L. J. 161 (1996).

Damrosch, Lori Fisler, Scholars in the Construction and Critique of International Law, American Society of International Law Proceedings, April (2000).

Dattu, Riyaz, A Journey From Havana To Paris: The Fifty- Year Quest For The Elusive Multilateral Agreement on Investment, 24 FORDHAM INT'L L. J.275 (2000).

Degan, V.D. , SOURCES OF INTERNATIONAL LAW, (1997).

Dell, Sidney, THE UNITED NATIONS AND INTERNATIONAL BUSINESS, (1990).

Deloitte & Touche, Turkey, (1999).

Dhooge, Lucien J., The North American Free Trade Agreement And The Environment: The Lessons of Metalclad Corporation v. United Mexican States, 10 MINN. J. GLOBAL TRADE. 209 (2001).

Dolzer, Rudolf & Margrete Stevens, Bilateral Investment Treaties, ICSID, (1995).

Don, R.Y., PROTECTION OF FOREIGN INVESTMENT UNDER INTERNATIONAL LAW, (1979).

DPT, Electronik Sureli Yayinlar, Profiles of Turkish Public Sector Project for Foreign Funding, (2000).

Drake, Tracy V., Reporter, Panel Session, The World Bank and The International Monetary Fund, American Society of International Law Proceedings, April 9-12, (1989).

Duca, Patrick Del & Detlev F. Vagts reviewed Luigi Migliorino, GLI Accordi Internazionali Sugli Investment, American Journal of International Law, January (1991).

Dupuy, Pierre Marie, Soft Law and The international Law of the Environment, 12 MICH. J. INT'L L 420, 428 (1991).

Edwards, Robert H., Jr.& Simon N. Lester, Towards a More Comprehensive World trade Organization Agreement on Trade Related Investment Measures, 33 STAN. J. INT'L L. 169, 195 (1997).

Eizenstat, Stuart, Under Secretary for Economic, Business and Agricultural Affairs, and Jeffrey Lang, Deputy U.S. Trade Representative, Remarks following the OECD meeting on MAI, Paris, France, February 17, 1998. http://www.state.gov/www/policy_remarks/1998/980217_eizen_mai.html (visited 11/22/00)

Elliot, et al Larry., French Scupper " Charter for Multinationals"; Investment Pact in Tatters, Guardian (London), (October 15, 1998).

Ertuna, Prof. Dr. Ozer, Constraints of Privatization: The Turkish Case, Public-Private Partnership in the Mena Region Workshop, Mediterranean Development Forum, (September 3-6, 1998).

Esin, Arif, The Impact of Competition Law on Foreign Direct Investment, Insight Yased, (1999).

Euro-Focus, The Center for Strategic and International Studies, Hello Jospin! Bye Bye EMU? Volume 2 Number 3 June 9, (1997).

European Union, Turkey 2000, Regular Report, From the Commission on Turkey' Progress Towards, Accession, (8 November 2000).

European Union, Regular Report from the Commission on Progress Towards Accession, Turkey, (November 4, 1998).

Fatourus, A.A., Towards an international Agreement on Foreign Direct Investment in Towards Multilateral Investment Rules, OECD Documents, (1996).

Fatouros, A.A., Towards an International Agreement on Foreign Direct Investment?, ICSID Review, v.10, Number 2, Fall (1995).

Fitzgerald, Peter F., Political Risk Insurance Coverage Expands, Practicing Law Institute, Commercial Law and Practice Course Handbook Series, PLI Order No. A0-003F, March, (2000).

Folsom, Ralph H., Michael W. Gordon, International Business Transactions, West Publishing, (1995).

Folsom, Ralph H., Michael Walace Gordon, John A. Spanogle, Jr., INTERNATIONAL TRADE AND INVESTMENT, West Nutshell Series, (1996).

Gamble, John King, & Charlotte Ku, International Law-New Actors and New Technologies: Center Stage For NGOS?, 31 LAW & POL'Y INT'L BUS. 221 (2000).

Ganguly, Samrat, The Investor-State Dispute Mechanism (ISDM) and a Sovereign's Power to Public Health, 38 COLUM. J. TRANSNAT'L L 113, 129 (1999).

Gantz, David A. Failed Efforts to Initiate the "Millennium Round" in Seattle: Lessons for Future Global Trade Negotiations, 17 Arizona Journal of International and Comparative Law 349 (2000).

Geiger, Rainer, Towards Multilateral Agreement on Investment, 31 CORNELL INT'L L. J. 467 (1998).

General Directorate of Foreign Investment, INVESTING IN TURKEY, (2000).

Genesan, A. V., Strategic Options Available to Developing Countries with Regard to a Multilateral Agreement on Investment, UNCTAD Discussion Papers, UNCTAD/OSG/DP/134, (April 1998).

Gold, Joseph, Strengthening The Soft International Law of Exchange Arrangements, American Journal of International Law, July (1983).

Graham, Edward M., Regulatory Takings, Supernational Treatment, And the Multilateral Agreement on Investment: Issues Raised By Nongovernmental Organizations, 31 CORNELL INT'L L. J. 599 (1998).

Grau, Michael, Temporary Stay and Work of Investors and Key Personnel, The Multilateral Agreement on Investment, State of Play in (April 1997).

Green, L.C., The Raw Materials of International Law, INT'L & COMP. L. Q., (1980).

Gunawardana, Asoka de Z., The Inception And Growth of Bilateral Investment Promotion and Protection Treaties, in Gennady Pitch, The Development and Expansion of Bilateral Investment Treaties, American Society of International law Proceedings, (April 1-4, 1992).

Guzman, Andrew T., Why LDCS Sign Treaties That Hurt Them: Explaining the Popularity of Bilateral Investment Treaties, 38 VA. J. INT'L. L. 639, 659 (1998).

Guzman, Andrew, Explaining The Popularity of Bilateral Investment Treaties: Why LDCS Sign Treaties That Hurt Them, 26 August 1997, (visited October 6 1999) (http://www.law.harvard.edu/Programs/JeanMonnet/papers/97/97-12-VII.html)

Haffouz, Amel, Institutional Framework for Civil Society Cooperation with UNCTAD and Suggestions for its Further Evolution, in UNCTAD-CIVIL SOCIETY DIALOGUE, 47 (UNCTAD, ed., 2002).

Hamrock, Kurt J., The Elsi Case: Toward An International Definition of 'Arbitrary" Conduct, 27 TEX. INT'L L. J. 837 (1992).

Handl, Gunther F., A Hard Look at Soft Law, American Society of International Law Proceedings, April 20-23, (1998).

Harrison, Glenn W., Thomas F. Rutherford, David G. Tarr, Economic Implications for Turkey of a Custom Union with the European Union, The World Bank, Policy Research Working Paper 1599, (May 1998).

Hart, Michael, A Multilateral Agreement on Foreign Direct Investment-Why Now?, This paper was originally prepared as a chapter for a forthcoming C.D Howe Institute Study on Investment edited by Daniel Schawanen and Pierre Sauve. (1996).

Has, Tevfik F., Mehmet Odekon, Liberalization and the Turkish Economy, (1988).

Henderson, David, The MAI Affair, A Story and its Lessons, (1999).

Heper, Metin, Islam and Democracy in Turkey: Toward Reconciliation? The Middle East Journal, Volume 51, No. 1, at 33 Winter (1997).

Hillier, Timothy, PRINCIPLES OF PUBLIC INTERNATIONAL LAW, (1999).

Hill, Tony, UNCTAD and NGOs: An Evolving Cooperation, in UNCTAD-CIVIL SOCIETY DIALOGUE, 55-56 (UNCTAD ed., 2002).

Houtte, Hans van, Changed Circumstances and Pacta Sunt Servanda, Transnational Rules in International Commercial Arbitration, ICC, (1993).

Huey, Wendy, International Litigation: United States and Italy FCN Treaty and I.C.J. Jurisdiction over Disputes- United States v Italy, 1989 I.C.J. 15 (1989), 32 HARV. INT'L L. J. 236 (1991).

Jackson, John H., William J. Davey, Alan O. Sykes, Jr., LEGAL PROBLEMS OF INTERNATIONAL ECONOMIC RELATIONS, CASES, MATERIALS AND TEXT, Third Edition, (1996).

Janis ,Mark W., AN INTRODUCTION TO INTERNATIONAL LAW, (1993).

Janis, Mark J, John E. Noyes, International Law Cases and Commentary, (1997).

Jarreau, J. Steven, Interpreting the General Agreement on Trade in Services and the WTO Instruments Relevant to the International Trade of Financial Services: The Lawyer's Perspective, 25 N. C. J. INT'L L. & COM. REG.1, 54-55 (1999).

Johnson, Chris Alan, Protectionism Toward Transplants and obligations under GATT, FCN Treaty and OECD Instruments; Trojan Horse or Engine For Growth?, Transnational Law and Contemporary Problems, Spring (1994).

Joint NGO Statement on the MAI, NGO/ OECD Consultation on the MAI, Paris: 27 October, 1997, In DISMANTLING DEMOCRACY, (edited by Andrew Jackson and Matthew Sanger), (1998).

Juillard, Patrick, MAI: A European View, 31 CORNELL INT'L L. J. 477, 478 (1998).

Karl,Joachim, Investment Protection, The Multilateral Agreement of Investment, State of Play as of February 1997, OECD.

Kazgan, Gulten, External Pressures and the New Policy Outlook, (TURKEY AND EUROPE, edited by Canan Balkir and Allan M. Williams, 1993).

Kell, George & John Gerard Ruggie, *Global Markets and Social Legitimacy: The Case for the "Global Compact"*, Transnational Corporations, 103, (1999).

Kendall, Sue, France Pulls Out of International Investment Talks, Agence France Presse, October 14, 1998, Paris.

Khalil, Muhammed I., Treatment of Foreign Investment in BIT, ICSID Review, Foreign Investment Law Journal, 339-359 (1992).

Khor, Martin, the MAI and Developing Countries, at Dismantling Democracy, edited by Andrew Jackson and Matthew Sanger, (1999).

King, Betty, The UN Global Compact: Responsibility For Human Rights, Labor Relations, And the Environment in Developing Nations, 34 CORNELL INT'L L. J. 481, (2001).

Kishoiyian, Bernard, The Utility of Bilateral Investment Treaties in the Formulation of Customary International law, 14 NW. J. INT'L L. & BUS, 327, 335-336 (1994).

Komurcu, Mehmet & Yusuf Caliskan, "Yolsuzluk Problemine Karsi Uluslararasi Toplumun Tepkileri ve Ortak Bir Hukuki Duzenleme Olusturma Cabalari, (Global Efforts to Curb Corruption and Towards Multilateral Rules on Combating Corruption)", Turkiye Barolar Birligi Dergisi (Journal of Turkish Bar Association), (2000).

Koulen, Mark, the WTO Framework: From TRIMs to Treaty?, Transatlantic and global Economic Integration: The Role of Investment, Report of The European Institute's Seventh Annual Transatlantic Seminar on Trade and Investment, November 17-18, 1997, Washington, DC.

Kroeger, H. Elizabeth, Timothy J. Kautz, Ercan Acikel, Turkey Revisited: Developments in Energy Project; Arbitration in the Content of Bilateral Investment Treaties and ICSID, Mealey's International Arbitration Reports, September (1999).

Kubiatowski, Stephen A., The Case of Elettronica Sicula S.P.A: Toward Greater Protection of Shareholders' Rights in Foreign Investments, 29 COLUM. J. TRANSNAT'L. J. 215, 222-223 (1991).

Lamy, Pascal, What Are the Options After Seattle?, Speech at the European Parliament, Brussels, 25 January (2000).

Lang, Jeffrey, Keynote Address, Symposium, The International Regulation of Foreign Direct Investment: Obstacles & Evolution, 31 CORNELL INT'L L. J. 455 (1998).

Lauterpacht, Elihu, International Law and private Foreign Investment, Indiana Journal of Global Legal Studies, Spring (1997).

Lehmann, Alexander, Liberalizing Investment Policies, Prospects After the Uruguay Round, Royal Institute of International Affairs, (1995).

Ley, Robert, The Scope of the MAI, Multilateral Agreement on Investment, State of Play in April (1997).

Maclean, Robert M., The Lessons of Seattle and the Need for WTO Institutional Reform, International Trade Law & Regulation, (2000).

Maharajan, Vidaya Dhar, PUBLIC INTERNATIONAL LAW, (1972).

Mann, F.A., British Treaties For the Promotion and Protection of Investment, 52 Brit. Y. B. Int'l L. 241 (1981).

Mann, Mimi, Turkey Enters 2000 on A Positive Note as Reforms Progress, Middle East Executive Reports, September (1999).

May, Elizabeth, Fighting the MAI, in Dismantling Democracy, edited by Andrew Jackson and Matthew Sanger, (1998).

Mercredi, Ovide The MAI and The First Nations, in Dismantling Democracy, edited by Andrew Jackson and Matthew Sanger, (1998).

MIGA, MIGA REVIEW (2000).

MIGA, MIGA: THE FIRST TEN YEARS, (1998).

MIGA Homepage.

Morgan, Robin, Treatment and Protection of Investors and Investments, OECD, Multilateral Agreement on Investment, State of Play in April (1997).

Mosk, Richard M, Book Review, VAND. J. TRANSNAT'L L, V.24, at 587-590 (1991).

Mubey, Nick, International Investment Agreements and their Implications for Arab countries, WWF Presentation to the UNCTAD/League of Arab States Regional Symposium, May (1999).

Muchlinski, Peter T., The Rise and Fall of the Multilateral Agreement on Investment: Where Now?, 34 INT'L LAW. 1033 (2000).

Muchlinski, Peter T., Attempts to Extend the Accountability of Transnational Corporations: The Role of UNCTAD, in LIABILITY OF MULTINATIONAL

CORPORATIONS UNDER INTERNATIONAL LAW 99-100 (Menno T. Kamminga & Saman Zia Zarifi eds., 2000).

Murphy, Ewell E., Jr, The Lessons of Seattle: Learning From the Failed Third WTO Ministerial Conference, 13 TRANSNAT'L LAW. 273 , 286 (2001).

Murphy, Sean D., The Elsi Case: An Investment Dispute at the International Court of Justice, 16 YALE J. INT'L L. 391, (1991).

Mustill, M., The New Lex Mercatoria: The First Twenty-five years', Arbitration International, (1988).

Mutharika, A. Peter, Creating an Attractive Investment Climate in the Common Market for Eastern and Southern Africa (COMESA) Region, Foreign Investment law Journal, ICSID Review, (1997).

Newman, Parley W., Jr.,*Regionalism in Developing Areas: United Nations Regional Economic Commissions and Their Relations With Regional Organizations*, in REGIONALISM AND THE UNITED NATIONS (Berhanykun Andemicael ed., 1979).

Nomer, Ergin, Nuray Eksi, and Gunseli Gelgel, Milletlerarasi Tahkim (International Arbitration), (2000).

Nowrot, Karsten, Legal Consequences of Globalization: The Status of Non-Governmental Organizations Under International Law, 6 Indiana Journal of Global Legal Studies 579 (1999).

OECD Policy Brief, No. 2, (1997).

OECD Homepage .

OECD, Declaration by the Governments of OECD Member Countries and Decisions of the OECD Council on International Investment and Multinational Enterprises.

OECD Report on the MAI, OECD/GD (95)65, (1995).

OECD, The MAI Negotiating Text, as of 24 April (1998).

Oksay, Kazim, Guide to Foreign Capital Investment in Turkey, (1967).

Oppenheim, INTERNATIONAL LAW, (1992).

Oppenheim's International Law, Ninth edition, Volume I Peace, (Edited by Sir Robert Jennings, and Sir Arthur Watts). (1991).

Ossman, Ghassan, Legal and Institutional Aspects of the Multilateral Investment Guarantee Agency As the Fifth of The World Bank, Journal of International Banking Law, (1996).

Oxfam GB Update on the MAI (Multilateral Agreement on Investment), December 1998, <http://www.oxfam.org.uk> (visited 1/15/1999).

Ozsunay, Ergun, The New Turkish Trademark Law, Fordham International Law Journal, April, (1996).

Pedamon, Catherine, How is Convergence Best Achieved in International Project Finance?, 24 FORDHAM INT'L L. J. 1272, (2001).

Poret, Pierre, The Experience of the OECD with the Code of Liberalization of Capital Movements, OECD, Paper presented in May 1998 at in IMF Seminar on Current legal Issues Affecting Central Banks.

Ricupero, Rubens, opening remarks at the Regional Symposium for Asia on " International Investment Arrangements and their Implications for Developing Countries", held in New Delhi in July (1998).

Rivera, Luis E. Rodriguez, Is The Human Right to Environment Recognized under International Law? It Depends on the Source, 12 COLO. J. INT'L ENVTL. L &POL'Y 1, (2001).

Robin, Patricia M., The BIT won't Bite: The American Bilateral Investment Treaty program, 33 AM. U.L. Rev. 931, 938-39 (1984).

Robertson, David, The Role of Foreign Investors in Developing Countries, OECD Conference on the Role of International Investment in Development, Corporate Responsibilities and the OECD Guidelines for Multinational Enterprises, Paris, 20-21 September (1999).

Roffe, Pedro, Inter-regional Advisor, UNCTAD, Opening Speech, at the Regional Symposium Arab Countries: The Government of Egypt, the United Nations Conference on Trade and Development and the Inter Arab Investment Guarantee Corporation with the Participation of the League of Arab States: International Investment Agreements and Their Implications for Arab Countries, 17-18 May (1999).

Rowat, Malcolm D., Multilateral Approaches to Improving the Investment Climate of Developing Countries: The Cases of ICSID and MIGA, 33 HARV. INT'L L. J. 103, 129 (1992).

Rugman, Alan M., Towards and investment agenda for APEC, Transnational Corporations, Volume 6, Number 2, August (1997).

Schachter, Oscar, Compensation for Expropriation, 78 AM. J. Int'l L 121. (1984)

Schekulin, Manfred, Scope of the MAI, Definition of Investor and Investments, OECD, The Multilateral Agreement on Investment, State of Play as of February (1997).

Schlegelmilch, Rupert, International Rules on Foreign Direct Investment: A New Challenge For the World Trade Organization, International Trade Law & Regulation, (1996).

Schlegelmilch, Rupert, WTO, Why Still Not Multilateral Rules for Foreign Direct Investment, International Trade Law & Regulation, (2000).

Schneider, Eric Alev Bilgen, Foreign Investment laws in the Republic of Turkey: A Model for Reform, Transnational Lawyer, Spring, (1992).

Scholz, Wesley, International Regulation of Foreign Direct Investment, Symposium, 31 CORNELL INT'L L. J 485, 486 (1998)

Schwarzenberger, George, Foreign Investments and International Law, (1969).

Schwebel, Stephen, The Story of the U.N's Declaration on Permanent Sovereignty Over Natural Resources, 49 A.B.A.J., (1963).

Sciarra, Vanessa P., The World Trade Organization: Services, Investment, and Dispute Resolution, 32 INT'L LAW. 923 (1998).

Selinger, Marc, Nations Drop Efforts on Global Investment Deal, Washington Times, December 5, (1998).

Shaw, M.N., INTERNATIONAL LAW, Second Edition, (1986).

Shenkin, Todd, Trade Related Investment Measures in Bilateral Investment Treaties and The GATT: Moving Toward a Multilateral Investment Treaty, 55 U. PITT. L.REV. 541, 571 (1994).

Shihata, Ibrahim, Towards a Greater Depoliticization of Investment Disputes: The Roles of ICSID and MIGA, (1992).

Shihata, Ibrahim, The Multilateral Investment Guarantee Agency, (Symposium: Current Issues of International Financial Law, Part I International Organizations, 20 International Lawyer, 485 (1986).

Silva, Madalena Oliveira, Privatization and Monopolies, Multilateral Agreement on Investment, State of Play in April 1997, OECD.

Simmonds, Kenneth R., LEGAL PROBLEMS of MULTINATIONAL CORPORATIONS, (1977).

Siqueiros, Jose Luis, Bilateral Treaties on the Reciprocal Protection of Foreign Investment, 24 CAL. W. INT'L L. J.255, 258 (1994).

Sornarajah, M., THE INTERNATIONAL LAW ON FOREIGN INVESTMENT, Cambridge University Press, (1994).

Spiro ,Peter J., New Global Potentates: Non-Governmental Organizations and the "Unregulated" Marketplace, 18 CARDOZO L. REV. 957, 962 (1996).

Steiner, Henry J, & Detlev F. Vagts & Harold Hongju Koh, TRANSNATIONAL LEGAL PROBLEMS, (1994).

Stephan III Paul B., & Don Walllace, Jr. & Julie A. Roin, Documents For International Business and Economics, (1996).

Summers, Clyde, The Battle in Seattle: Free Trade, Labor Rights, and Societal Values, 22 University of Pennsylvania Journal of International Economic Law, 61 (2001).

Swearchuk, Michelle, The MAI and The Environment, in DISMANTLING DEMOCRACY, edited by Andrew Jackson and Matthew Sanger (1998).

Tanrikulu, Ahmet Kenan, International Commercial Arbitration, YASED, Insight YASED, December 1999, Volume 1, Issue 3.

T.C Basbakanlik Hazine Mustesarligi, Yabanci Sermaye Raporu (1993-1995), Yabanci Sermaye Genel Mudurlugu, Ankara, (1996).

Tieleman, Katia, The Failure of The Multilateral Agreement on Investment (MAI) and The Absence of a Global Public Policy Network, UN Vision Project on Global Public Policy Networks.

Tinker, Catherine, Is a United Nations Convention the Most Appropriate Means to Pursue the Goal of Biological Diversity? Responsibility For Biological Diversity Conservation Under International Law, 28 VAND. J. TRANSNAT'L L. 777 (1995).

Tiryakioglu, Bilgin, Rekabet Hukukundan Dogan Kanunlar Ihtilafi, (Conflicts of Law in Competition Law), Ankara, (1997).

Trachtman, Joel P., Foreign Investment, Regulation and Expropriation: A Debtor's Jubilee?, in Mulan Ashwin, Capitalism in Transition: The Role of International law, American Society of International law Proceedings, April 5-8, (1995).

Uludag, Ramazan, Turkiye'de Yabanci Sermaye Uygulamasi, (Foreign Investment Practice in Turkey), (1991).

United Nations Conference on Trade and Development, The TRIPS AGREEMENT and DEVELOPING COUNTRIES, United Nations, (1998).

United Nations Conference on Trade and Development, Bilateral Investment Treaties and their relevance to a possible multilateral framework on investment: issues and questions, TD/B/COM.2/EM.1/2, 21 March (1997).

UNCTC Current Studies, THE UNITED NATIONS CODE OF CONDUCT ON TRANSNATIONAL CORPORATIONS, (1988).

UNCTAD Home Page, www.unctad.org.

UNCTAD, World Investment Report 1995, United Nations, (1995).

UNCTAD, Trade and Development Board Commission cn Investment, Technology and Related Financial Issues, Expert Meeting on Existing Agreements on Investment and Their Development Dimensions, Geneva, 28-30 May 1997, Bilateral Investment Treaties and their relevance to a possible multilateral framework on investment: issues and questions, TD/B/COM.2/EM.1/2, 21 March (1997).

UNCTAD, Trade and Development Board Commission on Investment, Technology and Related Financial Issues, Report of the Commission on Investment, Technology and Related Financial Issues on its third Session, held at the Palais des Nations, Geneva, from 14 to 18 September 1998, TD/B/45/9, Td/B/COM.2/15, 26 October (1998).

UNCTAD Trade and Development Board Commission on Investment, Technology and Related Financial Issues, Expert Meeting on International Investment Agreements, Geneva, 24-26 March 1999, TD/B/COM.2/Em.5.L.1).

UNCTAD, TRENDS IN INTERNATIONAL INVESTMENT AGREEMENTS: AN OVERVIEW, (1999).

UNCTAD, BILATERAL INVESTMENT TREATIES IN THE MID-1990S, (1998).

UNCTAD, LESSONS FROM THE MAI, (1999).

UNCTAD, SCOPE AND DEFINITION, (1999).

UNCTAD, MOST FAVOURED NATION TREATMENT, (1998).

Vallianatos, Mark, De-Fanging the MAI, 31 CORNELL INT'L L.J. 713 (1998).

Vandevelde, Kenneth J., Sustainable Liberalism and the International Investment Regime, 19 MICH. J. INT'L L. 373 (1998).

Vandevelde, Kenneth J., Investment Liberalization and Economic Development: The Role of Bilateral Investment Treaties, 36 COLUM. J. TRANSNAT'L L. 501 (1998).

Vandevelde, Kenneth J., The BIT Program: A Fifteen-Year Appraisal, The Development and Expansion of Bilateral Investment Treaties, American Society of International Law Proceedings, April 1-4, (1992).

Vandevelde, Kenneth J., in Toward an Effective International Investment Regime, (Maurits Lugard, ed., American Society of International Law Proceedings, April 9-12, 1997).

Versan, Vakur, The Kemalist Reform of Turkish Law and Its Impact of Turkey, in ATATURK AND THE MODERNIZATION OF TURKEY (Jacob Landau ed., West view Press, 1984).

Veytia, Hernany, The requirement of Justice and Equity in Contracts, TUL. L. REV, V. 69, 1191 (1995).

Viscasillas, Dr. Maria Del Piar Perales, UNITROIT Principles of International Commercial Contract: Sphere of Application and General Provisions, Arizona Journal International and Comparative Law, Fall (1996).

Vocke, Matthias, Investment Implications of Selected WTO Agreements and the Proposed Multilateral Agreement on Investment, International Monetary Fund, IMF Working Paper, 1997, WP/97/60.

YASED, ANNUAL REPORT (2000).

Yildirim, Yavuz, Effects of Direct Investment on Economic Development: A Study of the Turkish Experience, 1980-1995, (1996), (Master Thesis, Oklahoma State University).

Wallace, Don, Jr, David B. Bailey, Don Wallace, Jr & David B. Bailey, The Inevitability of National Treatment of Foreign Direct Investment With Increasingly Few and Narrow Exceptions, 31 CORNELL INT'L L. J. 615 (1998)

WALLACE, REBECCA M.M., INTERNATIONAL LAW, (1997).

Watrin, Christian, Europe's "New" Third Way, Heritage Lectures, No.634, May 11, (1999).

Watson, Geoffrey R., The OECD Convention on Bribery, March 1998, ASIL, Insight.

Wei, Shang- Jin, How Taxing is Corruption on International Investor?, May 1997, National Bureau of Economic Research, NBER Working Paper.

Wells, Louis T., Jr, & Alvin G. Wint, Facilitating Foreign Participation in Privatization, Foreign Investment Advisory Services Occasional Paper 8, http://www.fias.net/occasional/opp_8.htm (visited 11/12/2001).

West, Gerald T, Multilateral Investment Guarantee Agency, World bank Group, Investment Insurance: The Quiet Facilitator of Private Telecommunications Projects, Telecommunications Finance And Investment Forum, February 6-7, 1995, New York.

West, Gerald T., Ethel I. Tarazona, INVESTMENT INSUARANCE AND DEVELOPMENT IMPACT, EVALUATING MIGA'S EXPERIENCE, (1998).

Westberg, John A., International Transaction and Claims involving Government Parties Case Law of Iran- USA Tribunal Claim, (1998).

Wickham, John, Toward A Green Multilateral Investment Framework: NAFTA and The Search for Models,12 GEO. INT'L ENVTL. L. REV 617, 618 (2000).

Wiesner, Eduardo A., ANCOM: A new Attitude Toward Foreign Investment?, 24 U. MIAMI INTER-AM. L. REV. 435, 444 (1993).

Witherall ,William H., The OECD Multilateral Agreement on Investment, Transnational Corporations, Vol.4, no.2, (1995).

Witherell, William H, Towards an International Set of Rules for Investment, OECD Documents, Towards Multilateral Investment Rules, (1996).

World Bank, HANDBOOK ON GOOD PRACTICES FOR LAWS RELATING TO NON_GOVERNMENTAL ORGANIZATIONS (Discussion Draft) Prepared for the World Bank by The International Center for Not for Profit Law on May (1997).

World Bank, The World Bank Operational Manual, Good Practices, Involving Nongovernmental Organizations in Bank Supported Activities. GP 14.70, February (2000).

World Trade Organization, TRADING INTO THE FUTURE, (1998).

World Trade Organization, REPORT (1998) OF THE WORKING GROUP ON THE RELATIONSHIP BETWEEN TRADE AND INVESTMENT TO THE GENERAL COUNCIL, WT/WGTI/2.

World Trade Organization, ANNUAL REPORT 2001, 23 May (2001).

World Trade Organization, PREPARATIONS FOR THE 1999 MINISTERIAL CONFERENCE, Proposal Regarding the Agreement on Trade-Related Investment Measures, Communication from the European Communities, 9 July 1999, WT/GC/W/245, Communication from Japan, 6 July 1999, WT/GC/W/239.

WTO, TRADE POLICY REVIEW BODY, REVIEW OF TURKEY, PRESS/TPRB/84, 13 October 1998, http://www.wto.org/new/tprb84.htm (visited 3/12/1999).

WTO, Communication From Turkey, Turkey's Experience With Bilateral Investment Treaties, 18 September 1998, WT/WGTI/W/51.

WTO Communication From Turkey, Working Group on the Relationship between Trade and Investment, WT/WGTI/W/51, 18 September 1998 (98-3573).

WTO, Working Group on Relationship between Trade and Investment, Report of the Expert Meeting on Existing Regional and Multinational Investment Agreements and Their Development Dimension, WT/WGTI/W/46, 29 July (1998).

Zacher, Mark W., The United Nations and Global Commerce, United Nations, New York, (1999).

Ziegelschmidt, Helmut, OECD Observer, Turkey, June 1, 1994.

www.ingramcontent.com/pod-product-compliance
Lightning Source LLC
Chambersburg PA
CBHW081756300426
44116CB00014B/2141